THE NAVAL BLOCKADE
1914—1918

The Naval Blockade
1914—1918

By
Lieut. Louis Guichard
French Navy; attached to the Historical Section
of the French Ministry of Marine;
Doctor of Law

Translated and Edited by
Christopher R. Turner

LONDON
PHILIP ALLAN & CO., LTD.
QUALITY HOUSE, GREAT RUSSELL STREET W.C.1
MDCCCCXXX

*Made and Printed in Great Britain by
The Camelot Press Limited,
London and Southampton.*

FOREWORD

THIS work has been written with the aid of documents in the possession of the historical section of the French Navy. The opinions expressed by the author, however, are entirely his own, and the Ministry of Marine must not necessarily be considered as identifying itself with them in any way.

TRANSLATOR'S FOREWORD

THE thanks of the translator are due to the Librarians of the Admiralty and of the Foreign Office, the Sub-Librarian and Officials of the Library of the House of Commons, Mr. J. Kewley, Chief Chemist of the " Shell " group, Mr. David Nutt, Sir Robert Johnson, K.B.E., and, above all, to Dr. C. J. Lamb, of Cambridge University, for the assistance they have kindly rendered him, which has much facilitated his task.

CONTENTS

	PAGE
FOREWORD	v
TRANSLATOR'S FOREWORD . .	vi
PREFACE	1

PART I
THE CONDUCT OF THE ECONOMIC NAVAL WAR

CHAPTER
I. FROM THE DECLARATION OF WAR TO THE ORIGINAL DECLARATION OF SUBMARINE WAR: 2ND AUGUST 1914 TO 4TH FEBRUARY 1915

The Position of the Mercantile Marine of the Central Empires at the Commencement of the War	9
The Importance of Maritime Trade for Germany	10
Various Solutions of the Problem of encircling Germany economically, afforded by International Law on the 2nd August 1914 . .	12
Declaration of Paris, 18th April 1856 . .	14
Declaration of London, 26th February 1909 .	16
Fate of the Declaration of London . .	19
Intervention of the United States and First Steps taken by the Allied Governments. Decree of 25th August 1914. Order in Council of 20th August 1914	21
Protest of the United States against the Order in Council of the 20th August 1914 . .	25
The Allies' Reply to the United States. The Order in Council of 30th October 1914 (Decree of the 6th November 1914) is substituted for the Order in Council of 20th August 1914.	25

CONTENTS

	PAGE
Disputes between the Allies and the United States with regard to the Order in Council of the 30th October 1914.	26
Development of the Right of Search during the latter Months of 1914.	28
Controversies between the Allies and the United States on the Subject of the Exercise of the Right of Search.	34
The Organisations in charge of the Blockade from August 1914 to February 1915	38
Early Negotiations with the Neutrals	40
Results Attained by the Allies by the Beginning of 1915	43

CHAPTER

II. From the First to the Second Declaration of Submarine War: February 1915 to February 1917

The first German Declaration of Submarine War.	46
Counter-Measures of the Allies: Order in Council of 11th March 1915. (Decree of 13th March 1915)	47
Controversy between the Entente and the United States on the Subject of the Order in Council of 11th March, 1915.	49
Extension of the Lists of Contraband	55
Inadequate Results of the Decree of 6th November 1914, and of the 13th March 1915	57
First Appearance of the Quota	59
Protests of the United States against the Quota System	62
The Machinery of the Blockade in 1915 and 1916	63
Attempts to Organise the Blockade on an inter-Allied basis	72
Abandonment of the Declaration of London (7th July 1916).	75

CONTENTS

	PAGE
General Survey of the Negotiations with Neutrals during 1915 and 1916	80
Survey of the Results of the Blockade at the End of 1916	83
Germany's Reasons for Declaring Unrestricted Submarine Warfare	85
The Position of Allied Tonnage at the End of 1916	86
Organisation of the Merchant Fleets in Great Britain and France from 1914 to 1916	89
Allied Pressure upon Neutral Shipping	93
Germany's Calculations	99

CHAPTER
III. FROM THE SECOND DECLARATION OF SUBMARINE WAR TO THE END OF THE WAR: FEBRUARY 1917 TO NOVEMBER 1918

Declaration of Unrestricted Submarine Warfare and Entry of the United States into the War	101
New Aspect of the Blockade subsequently to the Entry of the United States into the War	102
General Embargo of 9th July 1917	105
Development of the Organisations which directed the Blockade in London and Paris between the beginning of 1917 and the End of the War	109
The Allies achieve Unity of Direction of the Blockade	113
The Economic Effects of the Submarine War and their alleviation	115
Joint Organisation by the Allies of Maritime Transport	117
Pressure upon Neutral Navigation. Order in Council of the 16th February 1917	119
Survey of the Negotiations between the Allies and Neutrals on the Subject of Tonnage	
Final Attempts on the Part of Germany to interfere with the Economic Policy of the Allies	123

ix

CONTENTS

	PAGE
Preparation of a General Scheme for provisioning the Allies during the Year 1918–19 .	129
The Results of the Blockade in 1918 .	131

PART II
HOW THE ECONOMIC NAVAL WAR AFFECTED THE NEUTRALS

CHAPTER
I. THE THREE SCANDINAVIAN COUNTRIES . . . 137

SWEDEN

Political and Economic Situation in Sweden in 1914 .	139
Negotiations between Sweden and the Allies (November 1914 — February 1917) .	141
Swedish Tonnage (1917–18) .	145
The Question of Swedish Iron Ore .	148
Final Discussions between Sweden and the Allies .	150

NORWAY

Political and Economic Situation in Norway in 1914 .	152
The Rationing of Norway .	154
Norway and Unrestricted Submarine Warfare .	155
Events which Led to the Conclusion of the Agreement of the 30th April 1918 .	157

DENMARK

Economic and Political Situation in Denmark in 1914 .	161
The Rationing of Danish Imports .	163
Denmark and Unrestricted Submarine Warfare .	167
Negotiations between Denmark and the Allies in 1917 .	168
Negotiations between Denmark and the United States in 1918 .	169
The Agreement of 18th September 1918 .	173

CONTENTS

CHAPTER   PAGE

II. THE NETHERLANDS

Economic Situation in the Netherlands in 1914	177
First Attempts to control Dutch Imports	178
Creation of the N.O.T.	179
The Rationing of Holland	182
Purchase by the Allies of the Agricultural Produce of Holland	185
Consignments of the Dutch Government	188
Holland and Unrestricted Submarine Warfare	190
Dutch Negotiations with the Belligerents	192
Exercise of the Right of Angary with Regard to the Dutch Merchant Fleet	196
Discussions between Germany and Holland in 1918	197
The Affair of the Dutch Convoy	200
Resumption of Discussions with the Allies (October 1918)	205

III. SWITZERLAND

Economic Situation in Switzerland Prior to the War	208
The Franco-Swiss Agreement of March 1914	209
Formation of the S.S.S.	211
Initial Difficulties of the S.S.S.	214
Reforms in the Organisation of the S.S.S.	216
Difficulties Caused by the Question of Compensation Goods	219
Revision of the Swiss Quotas	222
The German-Swiss Agreement of 5th May 1917	225
The Swiss-American Agreement of 5th December 1917	226
Further Franco-Swiss Agreements	227
Final Negotiations between Switzerland and the Belligerents	229
Effect of the Blockade upon the Economic Life of Switzerland	231

CONTENTS

CHAPTER
IV. SPAIN   **PAGE**

The Economic Situation in Spain Prior to the War 236
The Economic Situation in Spain During the War 238
Economic Negotiations between Spain and the Allies 241
Negotiations with regard to the Utilisation of Spanish Tonnage by the Allies . . . 243
Requisition of the Spanish Merchant Fleet . 244
The Question of Safe Conducts . . . 248
Spain Takes Possession of German Shipping in order to Make Good her Losses at Sea . . 251

PART III
GERMANY

INTRODUCTION 259
I. VARIATIONS IN THE BALANCE OF TRADE 261
II. INDUSTRY
   1. The Cotton Problem 266
   2. The Copper Problem 270
   3. The Problem of Metals in General . . 274
   4. The Problem of Oils and Fats . . . 278
   5. The Rubber Problem 281
   6. The Leather Problem 283

III. FOOD   285
   The Situation on the 11th November 1918 . 299

IV. LESSONS OF THE BLOCKADE   307
    BIBLIOGRAPHY 313
    INDEX 315

PREFACE

THE story of the economic blockade in its relation to the war at sea would be a comparatively simple one to tell if it were confined solely to the action taken by the Allied cruising squadrons with regard to hostile and neutral merchant shipping : we should merely have to set forth the instructions given by the Allied Governments to their cruisers and see how the economic life of Germany was affected in consequence. The story becomes necessarily more involved owing to the part played by factors other than the purely naval one in the economic encirclement of the Central Empires.

The command of the sea was, of course, a condition antecedent thereto. But the command of the sea, however efficacious it might be in putting a stop to trade under a hostile flag, was subject, with regard to neutral maritime trade, to the restrictions imposed by the recognised principles of international law. It was the application of these principles which prevented the Allies from putting a stop to the provisioning of the Central Empires under neutral flags save at great expenditure both of time and money.

By the end of 1914 the Allies had already been compelled to supplement the work of their navies by diplomatic action in the neutral capitals, and since they were unable to stop altogether the supplies which were arriving by sea at neutral ports adjacent to Germany they tried to prevent these goods, when landed, being sent on to the Central Empires. They even attempted, as diplomatic negotiations proceeded, to divert the output of these neutral states from the German market, either by purchasing it in part or by threatening to put a stop to the importation of the raw material essential to its manufacture.

None of these negotiations would in themselves have proved unduly complicated if the hands of the Allies had not been tied with regard to neutrals by considerations dictated by their own interests. During the first two years of the war the neutral states of Europe were continually applying to the United States for further supplies, and the United States, whose industrial co-operation was essential to them, was the very country which the Allies had the most weighty reasons for not offending.

The Allied Powers on the other hand were obliged to be careful how they behaved to the European neutral states which supplied them with certain products; Great Britain was accustomed to Dutch butter and Danish hams; France kept a large proportion of her powder factories going by means of the produce of Norway.

Last of all, for reasons connected with finance, the Allies, and Great Britain in particular, were very reluctant to lose the custom of these European neutrals whom they were trying at the same

PREFACE

time to ration; and anxiety as to their balance of trade, by which the rate of exchange of the pound and, consequently, of the franc was maintained, caused them at times to tolerate consignments of merchandise being sent by their own traders to neutrals, in spite of some uncertainty as to its ultimate destination.

In this way the economic encirclement of the Central Empires, which at the outset was carried on solely by naval means, developed into an undertaking of a diplomatic, economic and financial character.

Suddenly, owing to an unexpected inversion of the rôles in 1917, naval considerations once more became of paramount importance for the Allies. Up to that point it had been taken for granted that Germany would not react against the encirclement by which she was threatened, whereas she did react with the utmost vigour and made this menace the excuse for the submarine war which she began as early as 1915, with some restrictions at first as regards neutrals, but subsequently, from February 1917 onwards, without any restraint as soon as she was convinced that victory lay that way. This brings us to the turning point of the blockade, the day upon which the United States entered the war.

Thenceforward the market of the United States was practically closed to the European neutral states, and as the Allied and Associated Powers, moreover, controlled nearly all the other markets of the world, the economic encirclement of the

THE NAVAL BLOCKADE

Central Empires was brought about almost automatically.

The main anxiety of the neutral European states was no longer concerned with the reprovisioning of Germany but of themselves, and that of the Allies was no longer to ration neutral states but to receive in their own ports the raw material and foodstuffs indispensable for the conduct of the war.

Thenceforth the word which recurred most frequently in the negotiations between Allies and neutrals was that of ' tonnage,' as the Allies were only willing to revictual the neutrals in so far as the latter were willing to lend their merchant fleets to make good the losses sustained in submarine warfare.

The diverse character and complex nature of the subjects included under the heading commonly used of " Economic blockade of the Central Empires " will therefore be apparent. It is the aim of this work to present them in a synthetic form.

I have divided this synthesis into three parts :

The first deals with the conduct by the Allied Powers of the economic war at sea ;

The second deals with the effect of this war upon the economic life of the neutral Powers and with the negotiations which ensued between the neutrals and the Allies ;

The third deals with the effects of the measures taken by the Allies upon the economic life of the Central Empires.

PREFACE

The scheme of the second and third parts is simple and logical in character; I have tried to explain the effects of the blockade from 1914 to 1918, country by country, upon Sweden, Norway, Denmark, Holland, Switzerland and Spain; then to study the economic situation of Germany during hostilities, with separate reference to the various goods she stood in need of.

The first part, "The conduct of the naval economic war by the Allied Powers," is divided into three chapters, the length of which depends upon the degree of intensity of submarine warfare, the truth being that the submarine and the naval economic war were closely connected, as action and reaction followed one upon another.

Commander Laurens has already established this synchronism in his very clear synthesis entitled *Submarine War and the Blockade*. In this work I would present to my readers the reverse side of the subject treated by Commander Laurens—it will be noticed that where I subordinate he emphasises, and *vice versa*. He has laid stress above all upon the importance of the submarine war, whereas I have sought to throw light upon the economic blockade.

The first chapter of Part I deals with the period comprised between the declaration of war and the original declaration of submarine war (2nd February 1915).

The second treats of the period between the first and second declaration of submarine war (2nd February 1915–4th February 1917).

THE NAVAL BLOCKADE

The third treats of the period between the second declaration and the end of the war.

I would observe, by the way, that if February 1915 and February 1917 (and I might have added February 1916 and February 1918 if this division in point of time had not seemed to me to apply rather to the submarine than to the economic war) demarcate the principal periods into which the first part of my book is divided, this is not due to mere chance. The month of February played an important part in naval warfare; it was at that time that the various Admiralties made their most important decisions because they were in possession by that date of the economic results of the previous year and were almost in a position to make an economic forecast for the year ensuing.

I would observe, in conclusion, that this treatise makes no pretension of reviewing every one of the problems created by the economic encirclement of the Central Empires, but rather to indicate in a concise manner the relative position to be assigned to each important question in the structure as a whole.

PART I

THE CONDUCT OF THE ECONOMIC NAVAL WAR

CHAPTER I

FROM THE DECLARATION OF WAR TO THE ORIGINAL DECLARATION OF SUBMARINE WAR: 2ND AUGUST 1914—4TH FEBRUARY 1915

The Position of the Mercantile Marine of the Central Empires at the Commencement of the War

THE entry of Great Britain into the war on the 4th of August 1914 gave the Allies the command of the sea. The Central Empires, however, in their belief that the war would last but a very short time, did not even await that date to retain their merchant shipping in their ports or to give orders to those ships which could not reach home waters to take refuge in neutral ports.

The German mercantile marine amounted to 5,200,000 tons, that of Austria to 1,000,000 tons.

The combined tonnage of the two fleets, 6,200,000 tons, amounted to 14.7% of the total tonnage of the mercantile marines of the world. The Allies owned 24,000,000 tons or 58%, and the neutrals 13,000,000 tons or 27.3% of that total.

From the 28th July 1914 onwards 623 German and 101 Austrian steamers took refuge in neutral waters, thereby entailing upon the Central Empires a loss of 2,875,000 tons of shipping. On the other hand the Allied cruisers captured 405,000 tons of enemy shipping in the course of the last five months of 1914. Lastly, the following tonnage was detained in Allied waters: at Antwerp 165,000 tons, in British ports 390,000 tons, in French ports 25,000 tons, and about 100,000 tons in Russian ports.

If we add to these figures the 80,000 tons of enemy shipping that had sought refuge in the Suez Canal it will be seen that at the end of 1914 the Central Empires had only 2,160,000 tons of shipping available in their home waters out of the 6,200,000 tons which belonged to them. Moreover, even this residue dared not put to sea and could only be utilised for coastal traffic or for trade with Dutch ports and the Scandinavian ports in the Baltic.

The international maritime trade of the Central Empires, whether sailing under the German or Austrian flags, had practically come to an end by August 1914.

The Importance of Maritime Trade for Germany

Now this international maritime trade played a paramount part in the economic life of Germany. An examination of the commercial balance sheet of Germany for 1913 shows that her imports exceeded her exports by £100,000,000 in respect of foodstuffs, and by £172,000,000 in respect of the raw material necessary for her industry.

The exports of finished goods, which exceeded the imports by £248,000,000, more or less re-established the equilibrium. Germany could not do without maritime trade if she was to be supplied afresh with foodstuffs and raw material.

German agriculture is notoriously dependent upon fertilisers, three of which, potash, phosphates and nitrogen, are essential to it. Her deposits at Salzig supplied her with unlimited quantities of potash, but she imported 50% of her phosphatic fertilisers from the United States and Northern Africa, and Chili sent her more than half her nitrogenous fertilisers in the form of nitrates.

With regard to corn Germany imported $1\frac{1}{2}$ million tons of wheat from the United States because she had extended at home the cultivation of rye, for which her soil was better suited; but as she exported 2 million tons of the latter her situation as regards corn stuffs used in bread making was not unfavourable.

As against this she consumed 6 million tons of barley and only produced 3 million tons, the balance coming from Russia. Russia also supplied one-fifth of her requirements in fodder.

Lastly Germany produced, on an average, 40 million tons of potatoes, which were sufficient for her needs. She imported, however, a small quantity of meat.

If her imports of raw material are examined the advantages to her of a mercantile marine become even more obvious. The United States sent her nearly all her cotton, three-fifths of her copper, and three-quarters of her mineral oils. The Argentine supplied her with wool and hides, and British India with textile plants and oleaginous grain. Germany also imported by sea indiarubber, manganese, tin, and all the rare metals essential to her industry.

Of this commerce overseas, 60% was carried on under the German flag and the remainder in foreign bottoms.

As her flag had disappeared from the surface of the seas it was obvious that Germany would endeavour to reprovision herself afresh under a neutral flag, either by means of neutral shipping proceeding directly to German ports or of goods discharged by neutral ships in either Dutch or Scandinavian ports to be subsequently conveyed to Germany by rail or coastal shipping. The Allies sought to put a stop to this neutral traffic in order to surround the Central Empires with an economic fence. We shall see what sort of a solution of the question was afforded by international law.

Various Solutions of the Problem of encircling Germany economically, afforded by International Law on the 2nd August 1914

Neutral ships are permitted by international law to continue to trade freely with belligerents: they must however submit to the right of search

AUGUST 1914—FEBRUARY 1915

and may be brought before a prize court in the following cases :

    (1) If they offer resistance to search,
    (2) If they carry contraband,
    (3) If they render aid to the enemy,
    (4) If they attempt to infringe a blockade.

Cases of resistance to search and of rendering aid to the enemy need not detain us.

The Allies might have been tempted to stop ships proceeding to hostile ports by declaring the coasts of the Central Empires in a state of blockade. This declaration, however, was dependent for its effectiveness upon the existence of various circumstances which never occurred during the war of 1914–18.

If a blockade is to conform with the requirements of international law it must be effective and bear with equal severity upon all neutrals ; the Allies however were unable to command the Baltic and could not prevent Sweden and Denmark communicating freely with German ports. On the other hand it was impossible from a military point of view to blockade *one portion only* of the German coast. Such a proceeding, moreover, would not have given the Allies the results they required. *The Central Empires, therefore, never were blockaded*, in the legal sense of the word, and if I should happen to use the term in the course of this work, it will be in its ordinary acceptance of " economic encirclement."

The Allies, in their efforts to put a stop to German trade, were therefore induced to extend the meaning of the word "contraband." A definition of this meaning must be sought in the Declaration of Paris of 1856 and in that of London of 1909.

Declaration of Paris, 18th April 1856

According to this Declaration, which confirms the practice adopted by Anglo-French cruisers during the war of 1856, *a neutral flag covers enemy goods with the exception of contraband of war; and neutral goods, with the exception of contraband of war, are not liable to capture under an enemy's flag.*

By this Declaration Great Britain gave up her traditional right which entitled her to confiscate enemy property on board neutral ships: in return for this concession she obtained the abolition of privateering.

"The exception of contraband of war" was not defined in the Declaration: it was the intention of the negotiators that this exception should apply to objects of immediate utility in war such as arms, military equipment, harness or ammunition. But belligerents were inevitably led by their interest on the one hand and by the development of industry in the course of the twentieth century on the other to extend this conception of contraband to an ever increasing number of objects.

The Russo-Japanese war inflicted grave injury upon the interests of Great Britain, which at that time was neutral, owing to the Russian decrees as to contraband, and revealed very clearly the weak points of the Declaration of Paris. An international conference was summoned by the Emperor Nicholas II. and sat at the Hague from the 15th June–18th October 1907. The forty-four States which were summoned to the Hague agreed as to the terms of eight conventions concerning maritime war. The most important of these conventions dealt with the institution of an international prize court whose task it would be to look after the interests of neutrals in time of war.

The creation of this court had been proposed by the representatives of Great Britain, who were still under the influence of the events of the Russo-Japanese war; her delegates however were out of harmony with a large body of opinion in the United Kingdom.

The Hague Convention provided that this international court, in the absence of arrangements to be subsequently agreed upon or of generally recognised rules of international law, should base its findings upon the general principles of law and equity. The British Government, at the request of Sir Edward Grey, who felt that he would be unable to secure the adhesion of his country to this international court unless the powers of the latter were strictly defined, took the initiative in convening a conference in London by his circular note of 28th February 1908, to which Germany, Spain, Italy, Russia, France,

CONDUCT OF THE NAVAL WAR

Japan, Austria, the United States and the Netherlands were invited to send representatives.

Declaration of London, 26th February 1909

The Conference sat in London from the 4th of December 1908 to the 27th of February 1909, and on the 26th of February the delegates of the Powers signed a declaration the rules of which they stated " corresponded in substance with the generally recognised principles of international law " and the provisions of which " must be treated as a whole and cannot be separated."

I will only refer to these rules so far as they affect contraband.

At the Hague Conference in 1907 Great Britain, which at that time was upholding the interests of neutrals, had proposed to suppress contraband, hoping by this radical step to put an end to all uncertainty upon the subject. Twenty-five out of thirty-five votes were cast in favour of the British proposal. The latter, however, was not accepted owing to the opposition of Germany, Russia, France and the United States. The French delegation had maintained that as neutral ships could carry on contraband trade in arms without hindrance from their own Governments the power to put a stop to this traffic under a neutral flag was a genuine right of legitimate self-defence in the hands of belligerents.

As the Powers had been unable subsequently to come to an agreement at the Hague upon the definition of contraband the question was further considered in London.

In considering the liability to capture of merchandise of any kind as contraband, two factors must be taken into account :
  (1) the nature of the merchandise,
  (2) its destination.

The Powers applied themselves at first to the consideration of the nature of the merchandise and upheld the traditional distinction in British law between two kinds of contraband : ' absolute contraband,' which applies to objects " susceptible exclusively of military use," and ' conditional contraband,' which applies to objects " susceptible of use both for military and civil purposes."

The list of absolute contraband comprised eleven articles. It was admitted that as a war proceeded a belligerent would have the right to add further articles to the list provided that these articles also were " susceptible exclusively of military use " and that neutrals were notified thereof. Absolute contraband was in reality neither more nor less than traditional contraband, *i.e.* arms, ammunition, equipment, &c.

The list of conditional contraband comprised fourteen articles, and included amongst other things food, fodder, articles of clothing suitable for military use, fuel and lubricants. It was likewise agreed that a belligerent could make additions to this list in the course of hostilities ; but in order to guard belligerents against the temptation of making unreasonable additions the Conference decided to draw up a third list of articles which could never be declared contraband of war. This third list comprised seventeen articles, including cotton, indiarubber, fertilisers, ore and paper. This free list was of great advantage to neutral trade.

But although merchandise had now been classified according to its nature the question of its detention on account of destination was still unsettled. The Declaration of London (Article 30) states clearly that " absolute contraband is liable to capture if it is shown to be destined to territory belonging to or occupied by the enemy or to the armed forces of the enemy. It is immaterial whether the carriage of goods is direct or entails trans-shipment or a subsequent transport by land."

The Conference, it will be seen, applied to objects of absolute contraband the doctrine of "continuous voyage" "which allows a belligerent to detain arms and ammunition discharged in a neutral port but the ultimate destination of which is enemy territory."

The Conference then decided (Article 33) that " conditional contraband is liable to capture if it is shown to be destined to the use of the armed forces or of a Government Department of the Enemy State."

Article 35. " Conditional contraband is not liable to capture except when found on board a vessel bound for territory belonging to or occupied by the enemy or for the armed forces of the enemy and when it is not to be discharged in an intervening neutral port."

The doctrine of continuous voyage which was admitted as regards absolute contraband was not agreed to in respect of conditional contraband, that is to say, to take a concrete case, according to the terms of the Declaration of London, foodstuffs consigned to the German Government but unloaded at Rotterdam could not have been captured by the allied cruisers in August 1914.

Fate of the Declaration of London

The Declaration of London had hardly been signed by the representatives of the eight Great Powers who had drafted it when a violent agitation against its ratification broke out all over the United Kingdom.

The objections of the opponents of the Declaration may be reduced to three in number.

The most serious of these objections referred, as we have already mentioned, to the establishment of an international prize court on which Great Britain would have only one representative out of eight, and to the detriment which would consequently result to British maritime law of which that country is so very jealous.

The second objection gave rise to the most alarming exaggerations; we have seen that a certain number of articles, foodstuffs amongst others, could be included in the list of conditional contraband and become liable to capture if they were intended for the use of a Government Department of the Enemy State and were in course of conveyance to a hostile port.

The Declaration of London did not however stop there; it had stated that these very articles should be presumed to be conditional contraband "if they were consigned to a contractor established in the enemy country who as a matter of common knowledge supplied articles of this kind to the enemy."

This presumption which was created by the famous Article 34 of the Declaration allowed a belligerent at war with Great Britain to stop all foodstuffs consigned to the United Kingdom. Every large town of the kingdom was covered with sensational posters depicting a neutral ship laden with food for England being sunk by the fire of an enemy ship.

These posters also symbolised the third objection to the Declaration, Article 49 of which allowed the destruction of neutral prizes if the captor's safety would be endangered by bringing them into port; this argument was often pleaded by Germany as an excuse for the behaviour of her submarines, which the Declaration of London had never contemplated.

The British Government defended the Declaration; it replied to its opponents that a distinction must be drawn in the reprovisioning of Great Britain between food coming in under the national flag and that imported under a neutral flag. In the event of war, moreover, Article 24 made no change in the attitude of hostile cruisers with regard to British ships; it only applied to neutral shipping, which in normal circumstances supplied England with only 15% of its food.

Public opinion nevertheless gained the day; on the 13th December 1911, by 145 votes against 53, the House of Lords threw out the essential part of the Declaration, which thus became a dead letter owing to the failure of Great Britain to ratify.

It is fair to add that the instructions given by the principal Powers to their navies were nevertheless closely adapted to the terms of the Declaration. The French instructions drawn up in 1912 contained the principal articles of the Declaration *verbatim,* as did also the German instructions of 1909 which were in force when war broke out.

Intervention of the United States and First Steps taken by the Allied Governments. Decree of 25th August 1914. *Order in Council of* 20th *August* 1914

On the 2nd of August 1914 the French Government appointed Rear-Admiral Moreau and M. Fromageot, legal adviser to the Ministry of Foreign Affairs, to study the problems of international law that were about to be raised by the war. The British Government likewise appointed Admiral Slade and Sir Cecil Hurst.

A further impetus was given to the study of

these problems in international law by the intervention of the Government of the United States which telegraphed on the 6th of August 1914 to the belligerents requesting them to be good enough to inform it as to the attitude they intended to adopt with regard to international maritime law. The United States suggested that the belligerent powers should adopt the Declaration of London as it stood, as everyone was familiar with its provisions. As the Declaration, however, had not been ratified it could not have binding force upon states which were only required to observe the stipulations of international law.

The Allies might possibly have acceded to the American suggestion if they had not been informed during the first fortnight of August by their Ministers at the Hague that whole cargoes of corn were being unloaded at Rotterdam and conveyed to Germany by way of the Rhine.

Holland declined to forbid this transit trade as her hands were tied on the one hand by her declaration of neutrality and on the other by the Convention of Mannheim of 1868 which regulated the navigation of the Rhine.

The Allies took counsel together : it was quite obvious that if the Declaration of London was applied in its entirety Germany, which moreover had anticipated such a state of affairs, would be able to provision herself afresh as conveniently by way of Rotterdam as through Hamburg and thus render nugatory the Allied command of the sea. The latter accordingly answered the United States by the Order in Council of the 20th of August and the French decree of the 25th of August in which they stated that they would apply the Declaration of London but with a very serious departure from it as regards conditional contraband.

According to the terms of Article 35 of the Declaration of London conditional contraband, as we have seen, was only liable to capture upon a ship proceeding to enemy territory or to territory occupied by the enemy or the armed forces of the enemy and was not to be discharged in an intervening neutral port. Paragraph 5 of Article 1 of the decree of the 25th of August laid down, however, that " notwithstanding the provisions of Article 35 of the Declaration, conditional contraband, if shown to be destined as prescribed by Article 33, was liable to capture to whatever port the vessel was bound or at whatever port the cargo was to be discharged."

The destination contemplated by Article 33 was as follows : " Conditional contraband is liable to capture if it is shown to be destined for the use of the armed forces or of a Government Department of the enemy state." On the other hand Article 34 of the Declaration added : " The destination referred to in Article 33 is presumed to exist if the goods are consigned to enemy authorities or to a contractor established in the enemy country who as a matter of common knowledge supplies articles of this kind to the enemy. A similar presumption arises if the goods are consigned to a fortified place belonging to the enemy or other place serving as a base for the armed forces of the enemy. No such presumption, however, arises in the case of a merchant vessel bound for one of these places if it is sought to prove that she herself is contraband. In cases where the above presumptions do not arise the destination is presumed to be innocent. The presumptions set up by this article may be rebutted."

The decree of the 25th of August 1914 (paragraph 3 of Article 1) modified Article 33 in an important particular : " The destination contemplated by Article 33 of the Declaration may be inferred from any adequate proof and (in addition to the presumption prescribed by Article 34) shall be presumed if the merchandise is consigned to or on behalf of an agent of the enemy state or to or on behalf of a contractor or any other person acting under the control of the authorities of the enemy state."

The last line referred to the control to which the German state was subjecting certain articles of conditional contraband as to which the Allies at that time, we are bound to state, were very imperfectly informed.

Although the traditional distinction between absolute and conditional contraband was still recognised, the decree of the 25th of August modified the Declaration of London in such a way as to afford the Allies undeniable facilities for stopping conditional contraband

AUGUST 1914—FEBRUARY 1915

destined to neutral ports of Northern Europe.

As for Germany, she replied to the United States on the 22nd of August 1914 that she was willing to apply the Declaration of London in its entirety : it was obviously her interest to do so.

Protest of the United States against the Order in Council of the 20th August 1914

The United States, upon receipt of these replies, declared that owing to the important reservations made by certain belligerents with regard to the Declaration, it would take no account of it while the present war was in progress and would confine itself to requesting that the existing rules of international law should be observed. At the same time, however, it made vigorous protests at London against the Order in Council of the 20th of August : it seemed to it inadmissible that the Allies should assume the right to capture neutral merchandise while in transit from a neutral American port to a neutral Dutch or Scandinavian port.

The Allies' Reply to the United States. The Order in Council of 30th October 1914 (Decree of the 6th November 1914) *is substituted for the Order in Council of 20th August 1914*

The Allies took counsel together once more. On the one hand they were anxious not to offend the United States ; on the other hand the reports received by them as to the control set up by the German Government over articles of conditional contraband did not concur. They made a practical concession to the American Government by not placing cotton on their contraband list and a further one of a formal nature by the issue of the Order in Council of 30th October which cancelled that of the the 20th of August.

The new Order in Council again recognised the validity of the Declaration of London; but conditional contraband bound for a neutral port only became liable to capture if it was "to order," that is to say unaddressed to any consignee or if it became apparent from the ship's papers that the consignee was resident in an enemy country; but whereas, formerly, it was incumbent upon the Allies to prove that the ultimate destination of the merchandise was in enemy country it was the duty thenceforth of the owner of the captured goods to prove his innocence.

The Order in Council contained lists of contraband goods which had now become very voluminous as compared with those which had been published on the morrow of the declaration of war. Certain articles appeared there, in particular, which the Powers had declared in London in 1909 were never to be made contraband.

Disputes between the Allies and the United States with regard to the Order in Council of the 30th October 1914

The American Government made a further protest on the 26th December 1914 in a lengthy note. The idea that the consignment to order of articles inscribed upon the list of conditional contraband and destined to a neutral port could carry with it a legal presumption of hostile destination seemed to it to be false. Had not, moreover, Lord Salisbury declared during the South African War that "foodstuffs, even if bound for a hostile destination, cannot be considered as contraband unless they are destined for the use of the armed forces of the enemy ; it is not sufficient that they should be capable of being so used ; it must be clearly obvious that such was really their destination at the time of capture "?

The American Government concluded its protest by drawing the attention of the Allies to the deplorable condition of American trade which was being excluded from the markets of neutral nations adjacent to Germany.

The British Government sent a somewhat ironical reply on the 7th of January in which it enclosed a table of the relative exports from New York to European neutral states in November 1913 and 1914. These exports amounted in the case of Denmark to 558,000 dollars in 1913 but exceeded 7,000,000 dollars in 1914. As regards Sweden they amounted to 377,000 dollars in 1913 and 2,858,000 dollars in 1914.

"From the 4th of August last to the 3rd of January the number of steamers proceeding from the United States for Holland, Denmark, Norway, Sweden and Italy, has been 773. Of these there are 45 which have had consignments of cargoes placed in the Prize Court, while of the ships themselves only 8 have been placed in the Prize Court."

In conclusion the British note upheld the lawfulness of the action taken by the Allies in international law. Was it not during the American Civil War that the doctrine was applied for the first time which allowed of the capture of merchandise destined to an enemy viâ an intervening neutral port? And, as regards Germany, what did Prince Bismarck say in 1885 when the point was raised in his presence as to whether foodstuffs which were not destined to the enemy forces could be seized or not? " The measure in question," he said, " has for its object the shortening of the war by increasing the difficulties of the enemy, and is a justifiable step if uniformly enforced against all neutral ships."

Development of the Right of Search during the latter Months of 1914

The decree of the 6th of November, it may be mentioned, was not the only subject of dispute between the Allies and the United States. The decree could only be enforced by the exercise of the right of search.

In order to supervise merchant shipping France and Great Britain immediately after the

AUGUST 1914—FEBRUARY 1915

declaration of war had established various cruising grounds, the most important of which were situated off Scotland, at the mouth of the Channel, and off the ports of Genoa and Barcelona. Their cruisers proceeded at once to put into practice the right of search, which allows any belligerent to verify the nature, ownership and destination of any goods embarked on board a merchant ship irrespective of its nationality, provided that the search takes place outside the territorial waters of a neutral.

Now the Hague Conference had confined its dealings practically to search at sea, that is to say the despatch of an officer and a few men on board a merchant ship with a view to examining its papers. When no later than August 1914 a French warship searched a Dutch passenger steamer, the *New Amsterdam*, under circumstances such as had been previously contemplated and discovered that this steamer was carrying 1,000 tons of contraband and 750 mobilised enemy soldiers, it was felt that the mobilised men and contraband could not be transhipped at sea and accordingly the *New Amsterdam* was ordered to proceed to the nearest French port, in this case Brest. The Dutch Government protested against this compulsory deviation of course: did not the text lay down that the ship exercising the right of search should inflict upon the ship so searched as little inconvenience as possible?

It was a ticklish question. On the one hand

in the case of the *Manouba* during the Turco-Italian war the Hague court had practically found against the Italian navy, which had acted in a manner similar to ours; in view of the situation created by this precedent compensation for deviation of course had to be offered without loss of time.

On the other hand, however, during the wars of the 19th and early 20th centuries search had taken place under very different conditions and the search of a big passenger steamer on the high seas could only be contemplated under exceptionally favourable conditions of weather.

It was the German navy which, quite unintentionally, provided the solution of this difficult problem.

On the 7th of August 1914 the German Government had informed the neutral countries of its intention to lay mines at the points of arrival and departure of British troop transports; it accordingly proceeded on the 22nd of August to lay mines at the mouth of the Tyne and Humber, by which two Danish ships were blown up.

By the 25th of August the British Government had published the following notice :—

" The Admiralty wishes to draw attention to the previous warnings to neutral shipping of the danger of traversing the North Sea. The Germans are continuing their practice of laying mines indiscriminately upon the ordinary trade routes. The Admiralty desires to impress not only upon British but on neutral shipping the vital importance of touching at British ports before entering the North Sea."

The Germans continued to lay mines.

The British Admiralty began to follow suit and started laying mines on the 2nd of October.

At last an auxiliary cruiser, the *Berlin*, succeeded in forcing the British blockade during the last week of October and laid mines upon the West Coast of Ireland, whence she proceeded northwards towards Greenland and was finally interned at Drontheim.

The British Admiralty took advantage of her action to issue on the 2nd of November the following solemn manifesto :—

" During the last week the Germans have scattered mines indiscriminately on the main trade route from America to Liverpool viâ the north of Ireland. Peaceful merchant ships have already been blown up . . . by this agency. These mines cannot have been laid by a German ship of war. They have been laid by some merchant vessel flying a neutral flag which has come along the trade route.

" In these circumstances, having regard to the great interests entrusted to the British navy and the maintenance within the limits of international law of trade between neutral countries, the Admiralty feel it necessary to adopt exceptional measures appropriate to the novel conditions under which this war is being waged."

Henceforth the whole area of the North Sea

was to be considered as forming part of the military zone; from the 5th of November onwards any ship crossing a line traced from the northernmost point of the Hebrides to Iceland by way of the Faroe Islands did so at its own risk and peril. Ships proceeding to Norway, Denmark and Holland were advised to enter the North Sea by the Straits of Dover where they would find reliable guides who would pilot them up the East Coast of England.

Great Britain, it will be seen, took very skilful advantage of the danger entailed by navigation in the North Sea to force all neutral shipping to come-to in the Downs at the mouth of the Straits of Dover; it at once became obvious that ships could be searched there under much safer conditions than on the high seas.

France, on the contrary, continued during the latter months of 1914 to consider enforced deviation of course as an exceptional measure, and set up on the 30th November 1914 a "committee to advise as to the compensation to be paid for enforced deviation of course," with an Admiral as Chairman. The committee was entrusted with the task of allotting compensation to shipowners in cases where deviation of course had been ordered without adequate reason.

Owing, however, to the stormy weather in the winter, search at sea naturally occurred less and less frequently. Vice-Admiral Favereau, who was in command of the cruising squadrons in the Channel, reported that he had searched 28 ships during the first half of November, 16 during the second half, and one only during the first half of December. " In fact," he wrote, " search at sea cannot be contemplated in future," and he advocated most warmly the adoption of British methods of search.

This divergence of practice came to an end as soon as the German submarines started torpedoing merchant ships.

On the 23rd of December 1914 rules were drawn up by an Anglo-French Conference which were in future to govern the question of search. Any ship ordered to come-to in the Channel was to be reported to the Naval authorities at the port to which it was bound; if the latter was in allied territory search would take place there. If, on the other hand, the ship was bound for a neutral port she was to be searched in the Downs.

In the Mediterranean every ship was to be searched on principle at Alexandria or Gibraltar, and its port of destination was subsequently to be reported to the Maritime prefect at Toulon or to the Admiral Superintendent at Malta.

The entry of Italy into the war in 1915 allowed of a considerable restriction of the work of the cruising squadrons of supervision in the Mediterranean, which, incidentally, owing to losses from torpedo fire, was on the point of becoming rather dangerous.

Alexandria, Gibraltar, the Downs (near Dover) and a fourth anchorage at Kirkwall on the Scottish coast sifted the entire neutral commerce; some idea will be afforded of the fineness of these meshes when I state that from January to July 1915, 2,466 ships arrived in neutral ports in the North Sea and that 2,132 were carefully examined by the War Trade Department.

Controversies between the Allies and the United States on the Subject of the Exercise of the Right of Search.

The methods of search and the compulsory deviation of course such as we have described naturally did not fail to elicit protests on the part of the neutral Powers, for whom the United States again acted the part of spokesman. In its Note of 28th of December 1914 it declared that systematic deviation of course was tantamount to a general presumption of contraband which was contrary to international law.

"It is not impossible," Great Britain replied on the 10th of February 1915, " that the course of the present struggle will show the necessity for belligerent action to be taken in various ways which may at first sight be regarded as a departure from old practice. The growth in the size of steamships necessitates in many cases that the vessel should go into calm water in order that even the right of visit, as apart from the right of search,[1] should be exercised. . . . As long ago as the Civil War the United States found it necessary to take vessels to United States ports in order to determine whether the circumstances justified their detention.

"The same need arose during the Russo-Japanese war and also during the second Balkan war, when it sometimes happened that British vessels were made to deviate from their course and follow the cruisers to some spot where the right of search could be more conveniently carried out. . . .

"To do so is not to be looked upon as a new belligerent right but as an adaptation of the existing right to the modern circumstances of commerce."

Before leaving this controversy with reference to the right of search I will quote the words of the final notes exchanged on the subject. The United States replied on the 5th of November 1915:

"In regard to search at sea an examination of the instructions issued to Naval Commanders of the United States, Great Britain, Russia, Japan, Spain, Germany and France from 1888 to the beginning of the present war shows that search in port was not contemplated by the Government of any of these countries. On the contrary the context of the respective instructions shows that search at sea was the procedure expected to be followed by the Commanders. All of these instructions impress upon the Naval officers the

[1] In British law the right of visit is called " right of visit and search."

necessity of acting with the utmost moderation " and only contemplate deviation of course when a regular inquiry is to be held by a Prize Court. On the other hand the British objection as to the material impossibility of search at sea cannot be taken seriously. " The facilities for boarding and inspection of modern ships are in fact greater than in former times, and no difference, so far as the necessities of the case are concerned, can be seen between the search of a ship of 1,000 tons and one of 20,000, except probably a difference in time." If the Allies claim that they are justified by the increase in neutral imports in making such a general presumption of contraband as to allow of their compelling all trading ships to deviate from their course and detaining them for a more or less lengthy period the United States refuses absolutely to admit this point of view and that all the more as the period of detention is often used by the Allies to obtain evidence against the ship under detention.[1]

The British Government replied to this proposition with weighty arguments: on the 14th of April 1916 it wrote as follows:

With regard to search at sea it had consulted two experts, Lord Jellicoe and the French Admiralty.

Lord Jellicoe considered search at sea inadequate and dangerous owing to the risk of ships so stopped being torpedoed by hostile submarines.

[1] The text outside the inverted commas is not the literal wording of the passage but a summary made by the Author of the sense of it. [Tr.]

AUGUST 1914—FEBRUARY 1915

The French Admiralty had written : " The naval practice as it existed formerly, of searching ships at sea, a legacy of the navy of former times, is no longer suited to the conditions of present day navigation. The Americans have anticipated this inadequacy : the instructions issued by the Navy Department on the 28th of June 1898 contained the following directions. ' If the ship's papers show that contraband of war is being carried the ship must be seized, otherwise it must be allowed to go free unless, owing to the existence of serious grounds for suspicion, a more detailed examination appears to be called for.'

" The French Admiralty considers that nowadays a ship to be searched must be diverted from her course to a port whenever the state of the sea, the nature, weight, volume and loading of the cargo under suspicion as well as the unintelligibility or the vagueness of the ship's papers render search at sea practically impossible or a source of danger to the ship being searched. On the other hand, in the absence of the foregoing conditions, the ship must be searched at sea. Deviation of course is also necessary and justifiable when the neutral ship enters the zone or the neighbourhood of hostilities."

The British Government, however, for its part, considered that " The question of the locality of the search was one of secondary importance." " What is essential is to determine whether or not the goods were on their way to the enemy.

CONDUCT OF THE NAVAL WAR

If they were, a belligerent is entitled to detain them, and having regard to the nature of the struggle in which the Allies are engaged they are compelled to take the most effectual steps to exercise that right."

This note put an end to the theoretical discussion in which the Allies and Neutrals had become involved; in practice mining and submarine warfare alone would have compelled the search to be carried out in port even if the Allied arguments had been less satisfactory.

This method of search enabled us to make use of the valuable services of the Customs authorities in examining cargoes right up to the end of the war.

The Organisations in charge of the Blockade from August 1914 to February 1915

The association of the Customs service with the duties of blockade is only one instance among many of the increasing complexity of these duties which necessitated the co-ordination of the work of several departments. To ensure this co-ordination a commission was set up by Great Britain no later than the 15th of August 1914 composed of representatives of the Admiralty, the Foreign Office and the Board of Trade, to whom the task was assigned of co-ordinating the work of such ministerial departments as were concerned in the work of the blockade. On the 22nd of September, moreover, a member of the

Government in the shape of Lord Crewe was appointed Chairman of the War Trade Advisory Committee, a consultative organisation which acted as clearing house for information of every kind in relation to the blockade.

The French Cabinet decided in November at Bordeaux to create a similar Commission entitled 'the Committee for preventing supplies reaching the enemy,'[1] with Rear-Admiral Moreau as Chairman.

The Committee held one meeting in order to define its functions and concluded that it should undertake to centralise all information as to the economic activity of the enemy, and to arrange further what neutral cargoes were to be bought on account of the French Government.

The Minister of Finance agreed to the first part of this programme but was unable to assent to the second in view of the fact that in France the right to authorise expenditure is confined to Ministers alone. Of course the draft decree provided that the liabilities so contracted should be submitted beforehand for approval to the Prime Minister, but how would the latter in the absence of any regular organisation at his disposal be able to shelter himself from personal responsibility in questions of so difficult and serious a nature?

Thus the Committee, which was yet unborn, was forced to forgo the other part it had hoped to play. We shall come across it again in March 1915 when it was finally appointed.

[1] Known later as the Committee of Restriction. See p. 64.

CONDUCT OF THE NAVAL WAR

Alongside of this Committee an important organisation was created in France by November 1914, the 'Commission of Exemptions from the Prohibition to Export.'

On the morrow of the declaration of war the French Government forbade the export of a number of products which were indispensable to the economic life of the country, and the Customs Service was ordered to hold up these products which were classified as 'prohibited exports.' Nevertheless, to avoid unnecessary injury to our foreign trade, the Government decided that special exemptions should be allowed in certain cases, and three officials of the Ministries of War, Foreign Affairs and Finance were empowered to grant them.

They were assailed with demands on such a scale that the Cabinet decided on the 16th of November 1914 to substitute for them an interdepartmental commission which was called the 'Commission of exemptions from the prohibition to export,' with the Director General of Customs as Chairman.

The navy was represented by one member on the Committee.

Early Negotiations with the Neutrals

Although the organisation of the blockade only existed in embryo at the beginning of 1915 there was one Ministerial Department which from that time onward played an important part in that organisation, namely the Ministry of Foreign Affairs.

By the month of October 1914 it had occurred to the Allied Governments to increase the efficiency of the purely naval blockade by initiating diplomatic negotiations with such of the neutral Powers as were able to provide the Central Empires with supplies either directly or across their territory, and through the instrumentality of their ministers who were accredited to these neutral Governments they obtained from the latter, in return for facilities to be granted to their *bonâ fide* trade, securities against the export to Germany of merchandise which the allied cruisers would then allow to proceed.

On the 3rd of November 1914 France and Great Britain presented a memorandum to the Governments of Holland, Sweden, Norway, Denmark, Switzerland and Italy, of which the most important passages read as follows:

The Allied Governments are very anxious to regulate their rights of search as belligerents, as also their rights of inquiry and detention with regard to neutral ships suspected of carrying contraband, and at the same time to cause the least possible inconvenience to *bonâ fide* traffic between neutral countries.

A simple examination of the ship's papers with a description of the cargo would suffice in the case of ships honestly conveying conditional contraband to a neutral country. With this

CONDUCT OF THE NAVAL WAR

object in view it is proposed to come to an understanding with the neutral countries concerned.

Such an understanding might be concluded upon the following basis:

"(*a*) The Neutral Governments would prohibit the export from their respective countries of all those classes of goods and materials comprised in the lists of contraband which they wish or expect to see imported for *bonâ fide* home consumption.

"(*b*) They would also give a guarantee that whenever such goods are addressed to a named consignee in their respective countries the goods will not be allowed on arrival to be declared in transit but will be landed and thereupon fall under the operation of the prohibition to export stipulated for."

Thus only cargoes to order would be considered suspicious.

The materials which the Allied Governments are very anxious to see included in the lists of prohibited exports are mineral oils, petrol, copper, indiarubber, hides and leather, fodder and certain categories of foodstuffs, such as corn, flour and meat.[1]

It was in this spirit that the Allied Governments entered upon negotiations with the neutrals: the details of these troublesome negotiations will be found in Part II of this work. It will be sufficient, at this point, to

[1] See note on p. 36.

AUGUST 1914—FEBRUARY 1915

give a short résumé of the results attained by the action of the Allies by the beginning of 1915.

Results Attained by the Allies by the Beginning of 1915

The confusion into which trade had been thrown all over the world during the first few weeks of the war makes it impossible to appreciate the results of allied action until the month of December 1914.

A. Imports. We find, to begin with, that *direct* imports into Germany from the United States had practically ceased. These imports which in December 1913 had amounted to 32,000,000 dollars were only worth 2,200,000 dollars in December 1914. In January 1915 they amounted to 6,500,000 dollars as against 34,300,000 in January 1914.

The following figures which relate to imports from the United States into neutral countries in December 1913 and January 1914 and December 1914 and January 1915, show very clearly how Germany was receiving fresh supplies indirectly under cover of neutrality.

	December 1913 & January 1914 dollars	December 1914 & January 1915 dollars
Holland	19,300,000	26,800,000
Sweden	2,200,000	17,700,000
Norway	1,500,000	7,200,000
Denmark	3,000,000	14,500,000

Against a fall of 57,600,000 dollars in the direct exports from the United States to Germany for these two months, there must therefore be set an increase of 40,200,000 dollars in the exports of the United States to these four neutral countries.

B. Exports. The direct exports of Germany to the United States for the last five months of 1913 amounted to 81,700,000 dollars. In the corresponding period of 1914 they amounted to 40,000,000 dollars.

It will be seen, therefore, that the German direct export trade suffered less than her direct import trade owing to the Declaration of Paris by which the Allies were bound to respect enemy goods sailing under a neutral flag to the United States.

Moreover the fall in the German exports to the United States was less steep than the foregoing figures seem to show, for during the same period the exports from Northern neutrals to the United States reached a value of 29,700,000 dollars as against only 24,800,000 dollars during the corresponding period of 1913.

In view of the interest of these Northern neutrals in exporting their products to Germany, which was a much more profitable market for them than that of America, we may assume that the exports of these neutrals to the United States represent to a large extent German exports.

The economic life of Germany, accordingly, had only been slightly affected by January 1915; she knew, however, that as the months went by

Allied action would become intensified; she was aware of the increasing severity of the control exercised by the Allied navies; she was receiving information as to the efforts of the Entente diplomacy in neutral capitals and could form a very good idea of the pressure the Entente could bring to bear upon the neutrals to achieve its purpose. She was still breathing normally but was haunted by fears of suffocation; she beheld herself as it were a fortress, already beset, a state of mind which was itself becoming an obsession.

This obsession was one of the reasons which impelled Germany to embark systematically upon the adventure of submarine war.

CHAPTER II

FROM THE FIRST TO THE SECOND DECLARATION OF SUBMARINE WAR: FEBRUARY 1915— FEBRUARY 1917

The first German Declaration of Submarine War

ON the 4th of February 1915 the German Government presented a memorandum to all the neutral Powers on the subject of the reprisals rendered necessary owing to the action taken by the Entente with a view to stopping the maritime trade of neutrals with the Central Empires " in defiance of international law."

The action to which objection was taken was :

(1) The addition to the lists of contraband of war of articles " which are either not at all or only very indirectly employed for military purposes."

(2) The abolition of the distinction between absolute and conditional contraband.

(3) The violation of the Treaty of Paris : German goods which were not of a contraband nature were said to have been seized upon neutral ships.

(4) The proclamation as a war zone of the whole of the North Sea, which amounted, to a certain extent, to an irregular blockade of the neutral

FEBRUARY 1915—FEBRUARY 1917

coasts, which was forbidden by international law.

Germany having thus stated her grievances and pleaded her vital interests, surrendered to the behests of her officers, who longed to escape from the inactivity which had been enforced upon the German squadrons, and launched her first declaration of submarine war: from the 18th of February 1915 onwards any hostile merchant ship encountered in British or Irish waters, including the Channel, would be destroyed without regard for crews or passengers.

Neutral ships themselves navigating these waters would be exposed to danger, as, in accordance with a ruse allowable at sea, hostile ships had on several occasions hoisted neutral colours and mistakes could not always be avoided.

Counter-Measures of the Allies: Order in Council of 11th March 1915 (Decree of 13th March 1915)

The Powers of the whole world were struck dumb with astonishment. The United States in vain intervened between the belligerents: they requested the Entente to allow foodstuffs to pass which were destined to the Central Empires provided that they were addressed to neutral agencies entrusted with their distribution to non-combatants: they requested Germany in return to refrain from using submarines against merchant shipping in the manner contemplated by her.

CONDUCT OF THE NAVAL WAR

Germany replied evasively that she could not entirely refrain from using her submarines; the Entente took note of her reply.

Then when the Central Empires put their threats into practice the Allies took counsel as to what measures of reprisal should be adopted. These measures were the subject of the solemn Declaration of the 1st of March 1915 and of the Order in Council of the 11th of March, which introduced a novel conception into economic warfare. Up to that date indeed France and England had confined their attentions to contraband alone; from the 11th of March 1915 they held themselves free to bring into their ports any goods the destination, ownership or origin of which was presumed to be hostile. In other words all direct trade between Germany and the Powers overseas was put a stop to.

This Order in Council was only made applicable at the outset to European seas lying to the east of the 15th degree of east longitude and north of the 30th degree of north longitude. On the 29th of September 1916 the Allies extended its zone of application to the east of the 30th degree of west longitude to enable them to stop enemy goods on the coast of Africa. Finally on the 13th of January 1917 they declared that the term ' enemy property ' applied to objects belonging to any one domiciled in an enemy country.

This most important Order in Council is the principal document on which was based what has been erroneously termed the blockade of the

FEBRUARY 1915—FEBRUARY 1917

Central Empires. It is rather startling from the point of view of international law because, putting a stop as it did to German foreign trade, it entailed results similar to those which would have been brought about by an official notification of a blockade of the German coast; but no blockade in a legal sense was ever notified. Moreover, and this did not help to simplify matters, the Allies had a very proper respect for the Declaration of Paris of 1856 which prohibits the confiscation of enemy goods sailing under a neutral flag. They accordingly declared that they would seize any goods found under such conditions, but that they would not confiscate them and would confine their action either to sequestrating them or returning them to their owner.

Controversy between the Entente and the United States on the Subject of the Order in Council of 11th March 1915

The United States immediately asked for an explanation as it could find no precedent for holding up goods in this manner. It argued on the following lines : any normal blockade of Germany is impossible, for such a blockade must affect all neutrals equally, and as the Allies have not the command of the Baltic the neutral Scandinavian States trade with German ports as much as they please. The Order in Council of the 11th of March does not therefore prescribe a normal blockade but is equivalent in its results to a blockade which would include not only the German coast but neutral ports and is therefore illegal, for even if the zone to which the Order in Council is applied is confined to European waters, the same is so vast in extent and the ships supervising its enforcement are so far distant from the enemy's coast that it is impossible for neutral ships to reach certain important neutral harbours, which the Entente as belligerents have no right to blockade, without crossing the allied cruising grounds. On the other hand the United States believes that the Allies are too enamoured of justice to attempt to excuse the illegality of their measures of reprisal under plea of the illegalities committed by Germany. The United States concluded by reserving its right to compensation.

The Allies replied several times to these American notes in March, April and July 1915.

" The contention," wrote Sir Edward Grey, " which I understand the United States Government now puts forward is that if a belligerent is so circumstanced that his commerce can pass through adjacent neutral ports as easily as through ports in his own territory his opponent has no right to interfere and must restrict his measures of blockade in such a manner as to leave such avenues of communication still open to his adversary. This is a contention which His Majesty's Government feel unable to accept and which seems to them unsustainable either in point of law or upon principles of international equity."

To counterbalance the liberty possessed by a

belligerent of trading through a neutral country without compromising its neutrality, the other belligerent must, in all justice, be able to stop the trade of its enemy either before it reaches the neutral country or after leaving it, on condition, of course, that he prove that the trade so stopped is really enemy trade and not *bonâ fide* trade going to or coming from a neutral country.

The main object to be secured is the adaptation of the ancient rules of international law to new circumstances in accordance with those general principles upon which it is admitted the right of belligerency is based.

According to the Government of the United States the rights of a belligerent at sea should be confined to the sole right of capture and condemnation for affording assistance to the enemy, transport of contraband or breaking a blockade. But the practice of nations has never been uniform nor very clearly laid down even in these three respects. The forms and conditions of a lawful blockade have often varied but it has always been unanimously admitted that a belligerent has the right by means of a blockade to prevent his enemy trading by sea.[1]

Although the position of the Allies was quite arguable in equity it was somewhat ambiguous in point of law, as will be perceived from the tone of Sir Edward Grey's reply.

The French Government, wedded as always to logic, took advantage of the entry of some

[1] See note on p. 36.

CONDUCT OF THE NAVAL WAR

British submarines into the Baltic in September 1915 to advise its allies to proclaim a normal blockade of the entire German coast.

The British Admiralty at once raised two objections : it was dangerous at the time we were protesting against German methods of submarine warfare to urge the control of merchant shipping in the Baltic by British submarines as a justification for a normal blockade ; on the other hand the approach of winter would put the British submarines out of action.

The Allies accordingly confined themselves to the strict execution of the Order in Council of the 11th of March, and the United States again protested on the 21st of October 1915 : England had declared that she could easily draw a distinction as regards traffic to neutral ports between enemy trade and really neutral trade. The experience of six months proved that the Allies were unable to draw this distinction. Their blockade was ineffective owing to the German coasts being accessible from the Scandinavian countries. Was not Great Britain herself exporting large quantities of goods to Norway, Sweden, Denmark and Holland while holding up American goods which were destined to these same neutral countries ? The United States concluded as follows : " The task of championing the integrity of neutral rights against the lawless conduct of belligerents the United States unhesitatingly assumes."

The Allies replied to the Government of the United States in two notes dated 13th of

December 1915 and 24th of April 1916 respectively. It was quite true that British commerce with neutrals had increased. But what was this increase in comparison with the waxing prosperity of American trade? To give but one figure: from June 1913 to June 1914 the cotton exports of the United States to neutrals had amounted to 5 million dollars, and from June 1914 to June 1915 to 60 million dollars! How could British trade be suspected under these circumstances of endeavouring to supplant that of America? During the first nine months of 1913 American exports to the three Scandinavian countries and to Holland had amounted to 126,763,000 dollars, and during the same period of 1915 to 274,037,000 dollars! It appeared, therefore, that the United States was hardly in a position to complain.

To the latter, on the other hand, the Order in Council of the 11th of March seemed to be worthless because it failed to conform to the ordinary rules of blockade which are summarised in concrete form in the first twenty-one articles of the Declaration of London. But, again, the Allies had no intention whatever of setting up a regular blockade of the German coast; when they had established blockades of this nature on the coasts of Asia Minor, Syria or Africa, they had always observed the regular formalities.

With regard to the German coast there was no question of putting a stop to the entry or egress of ships to and from enemy ports. What the

Allies wanted to stop were goods destined to or produced by the enemy. Indeed the United States seemed to consider illegal any measures of reprisal which were liable to injure neutrals; that was a very complex matter but His Majesty's Government could hardly conceive that the point of view of the United States could be upheld in every instance.

In conclusion, the British Government took note with sincere satisfaction of the wish of the United States to champion the rights of neutrals; had not the first act of the present war been the unjust invasion of Belgium to the accompaniment of abominable acts of cruelty? Had not this contempt for the rights of neutrals been subsequently extended to naval warfare by the destruction of merchant shipping?

"His Majesty's Government would welcome any combination of neutral nations under the leadership of the United States . . . and they cannot believe that they or their Allies would have much to fear from any combination . . . which takes an impartial and comprehensive view of the conduct of this war."

The Order in Council of the 11th of March emerged intact from these endless discussions and was even, as we shall see, strengthened by Great Britain very drastically in February 1917, subsequently to the proclamation of unrestricted submarine warfare.

This Order and the enactments relating to contraband were the two chief documents which up to the armistice governed the economic encirclement of the Central Empires.

Extension of the Lists of Contraband

The conception of contraband itself, moreover, continued to expand as the war went on. In the course of 1915 the Allies on several occasions made additions to their lists of absolute and conditional contraband and kept the neutrals informed to this effect. The recapitulatory lists of the 14th of October 1915 included already 42 articles of absolute and 14 of conditional contraband.

The article the inclusion of which entailed the most troublesome negotiations was cotton, primarily because cotton was one of the articles which according to the Declaration of London could not be declared contraband, and subsequently because it was essential for the Allies to keep on good terms with the United States, who were the chief exporters of cotton to Europe. The French Government approached the British Government as early as September 1914 in order to point out to the latter the necessity for declaring cotton contraband.

Great Britain was prevented by the unsurmountable opposition of the American Government from adopting this course. The discovery in December 1914, however, of contraband articles inside bales of cotton led to the Allies, with the concurrence of the United States, setting up a service of inspection of cotton cargoes in American ports prior to sailing : Allied inspectors issued to neutral ships certificates which were held, in law, to afford preliminary proof of the lawful nature of their cargoes.

At the beginning of 1915 the French Government, being unable to add cotton to the lists of contraband, proposed to include linters—that is to say the long and fine down which is yielded by the final process of stripping and is used in the manufacture of gun-cotton. This suggestion, however, was not followed up.

The Order in Council of the 11th of March had at least the advantage of stopping the direct importation of cotton into Germany, but as the importation went on under cover of the neutrals Sir William Ramsay, chairman of the Foreign Office Committee of Explosives, took British public opinion into his confidence.

His efforts were immediately successful, in as much as by an Order in Council of 26th of April 1915 the export from Britain of raw cotton to foreign ports other than those of France, Russia, Portugal and Spain was forbidden : Egyptian and Indian cotton were prevented by this means from reaching neutral ports adjacent to Germany.

In July 1915 information reached the Allies that the German Government had taken over the control of the entire cotton industry and put an end to their scruples. They went further and proposed to the United States to buy their cotton crops by means of a loan which was floated in New York.

FEBRUARY 1915—FEBRUARY 1917

On the 22nd of August 1915 raw cotton and linters were at last added to the list of absolute contraband.

Other additions to the lists of contraband, although giving rise to less difficult negotiations, were as numerous in 1916 as in 1915; every two or three months fresh notifications were sent to the neutrals on the subject. The recapitulatory lists of the 14th October 1915 were so largely supplemented that it became necessary towards the end of the war to draw up fresh recapitulatory lists, which were published on the 25th of October 1918: 62 articles were included in the last French list of absolute contraband and 22 in that of conditional contraband.

In other words practically every single article of commerce at the end of the war had become contraband.

Inadequate Results of the Decree of 6th November 1914, *and of the* 13th *March* 1915

The results, however, which had been obtained by the enforcement of the Decree of the 6th of November 1914 in conjunction with perpetual additions to the lists of contraband, and by the application of the Decree of 13th of March 1915 to all goods emanating from, destined to or owned by the enemy, seemed to the Allies to be but moderate when the statistics of neutral imports came to be examined at the end of 1915.

The following comparative statement based

upon official statistics shows the imports of neutral countries for the years 1913 and 1915.

Imports

	1913	1915
Sweden	£47,000,000	£62,000,000
Norway	£3,000,000	£48,000,000
Denmark	£38,000,000	£64,000,000
Holland	£326,000,000	£176,000,000

Now for a comparative statement of the exports of these neutral countries to Germany for the same two years.

	1913	1915
Sweden	£10,000,000	£33,000,000
Norway	£5,000,000	£11,000,000
Denmark	£10,120,000	£27,040,000
Holland	£113,000,000	£70,000,000

Although these figures show a clear falling off in the case of Holland, which had a considerable transit trade in time of peace, they reveal an alarming increase of exports to Germany from the Scandinavian countries.

In order to stop goods which very often could not be brought before a prize court on account of their being dispatched to a neutral trader the Allied Governments began, about the middle of 1915, to entertain an idea which was based neither upon the usual conception of contraband nor upon that of a semi-blockade which is really at the bottom of the Decree of the 13th of March, namely that of the quota.

FEBRUARY 1915—FEBRUARY 1917

First Appearance of the Quota

The Commission of Exemptions from the Prohibition to Export whose rôle we have explained, very soon created a standard for limiting French exports to neutral countries during the war : it examined the pre-war commercial statistics of the neutrals and stated that it would only allow exemptions to the extent of neutral imports prior to 1914 ; and French exports to neutrals were rationed accordingly.

When, in June 1915, the Allies arranged for holding one of their earlier economic conferences the French delegation proposed the application to trade " between neutrals " of the system in force as regards the economic relations " between neutrals and Allies." The advice of M. Fromageot legal adviser to the Ministry of Foreign Affairs was sought, but the application of the quota system, in a general way, seemed to him impossible ; he suggested, however, that advantage should be taken of the Order in Council of 11th of March to consider all imports of a neutral which exceeded its normal requirements as being destined for an enemy ; by this means a more or less adequate presumption of hostile destination would be created.

The idea was again taken up at the Conference of London in August 1915. Sir Eyre Crowe, the British delegate, formulated the following objection. " Let us assume," he said, " that bacon, for example, is imported into Sweden in excess of the needs of the country and you order your cruisers to stop any ship carrying bacon to Sweden. The cargo will be unloaded and brought before the prize court. Will the court declare the capture good and valid simply because Sweden for three or six months has imported a greater quantity of bacon than she needs ? It is extremely doubtful."

Sir Eyre Crowe asked if there were not grounds for publishing a fresh Order in Council as had been done in order to put a stop to trade destined for or emanating from the enemy. The other delegates objected and pointed out that it was unnecessary to add fresh protests from neutrals to all those which had already been occasioned by the Order in Council of the 11th of March.

Certain jurisconsults then put forward the following solution : the Allies would stop such ships as, according to pre-war statistics, were carrying goods to neutrals in quantities notoriously in excess of their normal consumption. Probably if the circumstances of each ship were scrutinised the Allies would discover further reasons tending to strengthen the original presumption. At the worst the prize court would order the ship to be released, but the original presumption would be sufficient cause for refusing any compensation to the neutral shipowner who would think twice before again incurring the loss he had suffered.

It so happened that while the Allies were seeking for a solution of the problem they were unexpectedly helped by the judgment given by the

FEBRUARY 1915—FEBRUARY 1917

British prize court on 16th September 1915 in the case of the *Kim*.[1] The *Kim* with three other steamers had been stopped by the British fleet in November 1914 because they were carrying nineteen million pounds of lard from New York to Copenhagen. Now Denmark had only imported 1,459,000 lbs. of lard in previous years and lard was included in the list of conditional contraband. The court began by declaring that it had the right and the duty to find out if the consignment of these goods to the port of Copenhagen was not a fictitious one. It held then that it ought to be told whether these goods were destined for Denmark in order to be " incorporated in the general stocks of the country," and it agreed that the introduction of such a quantity of lard into Denmark, which was an exporter of food products, made it a practical certainty that the major portion was destined ultimately for Germany. By the judgment of the court, which was very ably stated, the *Kim's* cargo was confiscated " on account of the extreme probability of its being destined for the enemy."

Thus the quota system was placed upon a legal basis, and that too, independently, we may observe, of the Order in Council of the 11th of March 1915, which moreover would not have applied in the case of the *Kim* as this ship had been stopped in 1914. It only remained for the Allied delegates to agree as to its application, and

[1] See *Jurisprudence britannique en matière de prises maritimes*, by Fauchille and Basdevant (publishers : Arthur Rousseau).

CONDUCT OF THE NAVAL WAR

this concurrence was secured at the Conference of London in October 1915.

International Quota Commissions were set up in London for Holland and the Scandinavian countries and in Paris for Switzerland, to discuss either with the neutral Governments themselves or with syndicates of neutral importers the amount of raw material that the Allies would allow to go through by land or sea.

Protests of the United States against the Quota System

The Government of the United States, however, again gave utterance to the most vigorous protests. It held that commercial statistics, which were anyhow very difficult to elucidate, could not constitute a proof of hostile destination and maintained its right to sell goods with a view to increasing the stocks of a neutral country irrespective of their ultimate destination. Would not, moreover, this quota system lead to all kinds of abuses and would not Great Britain endeavour, under cover of it, to convey the largest amount possible of British goods into a neutral country adjacent to Germany and then stop American goods on the plea that the fixed quota must not be exceeded?

It would be unfair, Great Britain replied, not to admit that since the beginning of the war enemy interests have been served by neutral ports. The question of ascertaining whether goods sent to a neutral port are meant or not to be incorporated in the stocks of the neutral country to which they are destined is one of fact. But the circumstances under which goods have so often been dispatched do not allow of these consignments being assimilated to *bonâ fide* transactions—when whole cargoes of meat are sent to a dock worker and thousands of tons of cotton are consigned to business houses at a neutral port which are non-existent can it be contended that consignments of this kind are meant to be incorporated in the national stocks of a neutral country?

The dispute went no further, and was only revived in respect of individual instances. It must be remembered in all these discussions that the United States could not push matters to a rupture with the Entente without seriously compromising its own industry and trade; the Allied orders for arms and ammunition were increasing month by month, and if the United States felt some bitterness at its exclusion from the German market it was much too sensible to lose all its foreign markets except South America and China.

The Machinery of the Blockade in 1915 and 1916

While, as we have just explained, the ideas of the Allied Governments with regard to the blockade were gradually expanding, the committees or commissions which had grown up around them to advise and inform the responsible Governments with regard to decisions about the lists of contraband, for instance, or as to fixing the various quotas, had increased in number also.

In London, the War Trade Advisory Committee, whose appointment in August 1914 we have mentioned, was supplemented in 1915 by the Contraband Committee and the countless sub-committees of the War Trade Board. It was the task of the Contraband Committee to keep card indexes comprehending the five continents on which the cargo of every ship bound to a neutral port was entered; as soon as a ship appeared in view of the British coasts, its case had already been examined by the Committee and the latter could make its decision merely on the strength of the information forwarded by the port of search. The sub-committees of the War Trade Board specialised in raw material: one of them was concerned with the banking blockade, another with stopping leather, another with stopping corn.

At Paris the Committee of Restriction which had failed to materialise in November 1914 was finally set up on the 22nd of March 1915. The Departments of Foreign Affairs, War, Marine, Public Works, Agriculture, Commerce and Colonies were represented upon this Committee, which was usually known as the R. Committee. An admiral was appointed chairman, Rear-Admiral Moreau being the original holder of that office. The general secretary of the Committee was appointed by the Ministry of Foreign Affairs.

This committee was an advisory organisation to which the draft of every inter-allied agreement or convention with neutrals was submitted. It also received and focused every kind of information, documentary or otherwise, about enemy and neutral trade.

At Paris the Commissions of Exemptions from the Prohibition to Export and the International Quota Commission worked alongside this Committee.

And so the end of 1915 was reached.

People in France whose opinion was entitled to respect stated publicly that a blockade of this kind which was lacking entirely in unity of direction was against common sense. The Commission of Exemptions from the Prohibition to Export, whose existence we may say had no legal basis, consisted of eight members and had to decide at each sitting as to 400 to 500 applications for exemption; it had neither the machinery nor the information to enable it to undertake the necessary preliminary inquiries; its actual work was carried out by 18 Customs officials, whereas the corresponding organisation in London, the Licensing Committee, consisted of more than 300 persons. The Committee of Restriction, however hard it worked, could only express desires which were forwarded to the Ministerial department that was competent to deal with the subject, which either carried them out or let them drop, as the case may be.

Certain economists were anxious for the Under Secretary of State for Food and Commissariat, who had recently been attached to the Minister of War, to be appointed Minister of Economic Defence. Others wished to appoint a " Committee to Direct the Blockade," a kind of triumvirate, consisting of representatives of the Departments of War, Navy and Foreign Affairs directly under the Prime Minister. Public opinion in France, however, was not aware in 1915 of the discussions that were going on : in Great Britain on the other hand the subject was exciting the most passionate controversy.

On the 4th of January 1916 the Foreign Office published a White Book explaining its policy of blockade, which it decided up to then had been entirely effective in stopping German exports and partially so in stopping hostile imports owing to the difficulty of distinguishing between merchandise imported by neutrals for their own consumption and that imported by them for re-exportation to the enemy.

On the 13th of January Admiral of the Fleet Lord Jellicoe wrote a letter to the Lords of the Admiralty in which he took up the various points as to which the Foreign Office had shown so much satisfaction. The commander-in-chief of the British naval forces compared the neutral imports of 1913 with those of 1915. He was surprised that Germany should have the liberty of supplying herself with stuffs which practically all of them went through British hands. "It seems evident," he concluded, "that the blockade is not producing the results which should accrue from the number of vessels intercepted and that we are not using to the full a weapon which might materially shorten the duration of hostilities. If the rationing policy . . . were introduced generally the blockade should at once become effective."

In a reply to Admiral Jellicoe, Mr. Harwood, the head of the War Trade Department, defended the Foreign Office theory; no doubt the figures of neutral imports were impressive: but had the Admiral interpreted them properly? For instance a great deal of glycerine entered Holland and oil into Norway, but they went thither for purposes of refinement and subsequently returned to Great Britain. It was quite true that the Netherlands imported a great deal of oleaginous grain, but that was used for manufacturing margarine in large quantities which were destined for England. Last of all political considerations had to be taken into account. Recently, said Mr. Harwood, a ship was let through laden with 600 tons of copper consigned to the telegraph service of the Swedish Telegraphic Bureau. Sweden had already received her normal quota of copper, but it would have been an insult to the Swedish Government to stop this ship, and what would our Russian allies have said who are so anxious to maintain the sole line of communication which connects them through Sweden with the Western States?[1]

The controversy became the subject of a debate in the House of Commons; and under pressure of public opinion the British Government on the 23rd of February 1916 created a regular Ministry of Blockade with Lord Robert Cecil as its responsible head.

Fired by this example the French Government endeavoured to unify the various organs of the blockade; it only however took one half measure in the shape of a decision on the 23rd of March 1916 that a Minister of State, M. Denys Cochin, whose powers were not defined, should be placed at the head of the Committee of Restriction; furthermore representatives from the Allied Embassies were to be entitled thenceforth to be present at the sittings of the Committee.

It was not until the 23rd of August 1916 that the Cabinet recognised that this state of uncertainty could not go on. In the meantime, moreover, M. Denys Cochin had proved what efficient services could be rendered by a more rational organisation. It was therefore decided that he should be entrusted with the task of bringing before the Cabinet any question relating to the blockade, that the various Ministerial departments were to consult him before coming to any decision on these matters and that, in the event of a difference of opinion between the various services, he should decide as umpire

[1] Author's summary.

between them either directly or after making his report to the Cabinet.

As regards the diplomatic side of his work, M. Gout, a minister plenipotentiary whose ability and capacity for work had been most noticeable at the inter-allied economic conferences, was ordered to hold himself at M. Denys Cochin's disposal. The latter continued to bear the title of Minister of State.

During the second half of 1916 opinions as to the organisation of the blockade developed in a most curious manner. Two widely divergent sets of views with regard to the blockade were held indeed at this time.

The Navy claimed to be entrusted with the entire direction of the blockade. " What is needed," asked its protagonists, " for the conduct of a blockade ? Surely instruments only possessed by the Navy and a warlike spirit, of which a military department has not of course a monopoly but at any rate is the fountain-head. The Navy has always been made responsible for naval blockades, and it could not be otherwise."

" The economic war," wrote a sailor, " consists in effecting the isolation of the Central Empires despite their defensive belt of neutral States whose lawful interests must be respected, within certain defined limits ; we must keep our heads clear and show ourselves inexorable with regard to any other claim, no matter whence it proceeds, particularly as regards Allied trade, for it is a question of life or death ; these trading profits which are temporarily suspended will be restored to us a hundredfold by victory, whereas defeat would dry up the well springs of our profits and render those which are so eagerly sought for in the midst of war, and secured sometimes in defiance of public interests, problematical."

We may infer from these words, to confine ourselves merely to a psychological analysis, that upon every commission composed of representatives of the military departments and of the Ministry of Foreign Affairs, the former were inclined by their professional bias to take vigorous action, and the latter, also for a similar reason, to deal gently with the neutrals who bemoaned their sad lot or with the Allies who were taking the lion's share in one branch of trade or the other ; caution of this kind appeared to its advocates as in keeping with the real interests of the country.

Aiming as I do at being impartial I shall refrain from taking part in the controversy ; but it seems fair to point out that there is another side to all these questions relating to the blockade. A few years ago Rear-Admiral Consett, C.M.G., published a book entitled *The Triumph of Unarmed Forces* in which he described the behaviour of British traders up to 1916 as disgraceful. The author, who was formerly British naval attaché at Copenhagen during the war, adduced figures to prove the extent of the assistance as regards provisions and raw material

FEBRUARY 1915—FEBRUARY 1917

that had been afforded to Germany by the Scandinavian countries, and added that this assistance had only been rendered possible by means of British imports into Scandinavia which took place in considerable quantities during the first two years of the war and were, to say the least of it, authorised by the British Government. As against this assumption, which in any case is in accordance with the facts, it is fair to remind my readers that England was the banker of the Entente and that the maintenance of a part of her trade was closely connected with the protection of the pound and ultimately, moreover, with that of the franc. I cannot judge how far Admiral Consett's assumption is upset by an argument of this kind. I will confine myself to pointing out that divergent tendencies were being pursued in 1916 by the various organisations which were responsible for the blockade and that M. Denys Cochin agreed with the view of the Ministry of Foreign Affairs. At his own request he sacrificed his title of Minister of State and became attached to that Department as Under-Secretary of State for the Blockade on the 16th of December 1916, being at last possessed of effective powers and entrusted with the conduct of any diplomatic negotiations with a view to ensuring the restriction of enemy supplies.

It was well understood that, as regards Departments other than that of Foreign Affairs, the new Under-Secretary of State would continue to be furnished, as in the past, with any reports or information relating to the blockade and that he would collaborate with them in drawing up whatever instructions might be necessary, and that he would be kept continually informed as to any executive action that was being taken.

" I am convinced," wrote M. Aristide Briand at the time, " that the creation of the new Under-Secretaryship will enable the various public services to carry on the economic war in due touch with one another and with all the energy that is required. The considerable results yielded up to now by the policy of blockade are already perceptible. While preserving the rights of neutrals the Allies must pursue this policy without respite. In view of obtaining a final decision all the public services must extend and unite their efforts to one purpose, that of action."

To ensure greater cohesion between the various services M. Denys Cochin, who had been holding weekly conferences of the representatives of the Departments connected with the economic war, decided on the 20th of February to give legal status to these conferences. Thus was created the French Committee of Blockade, of which M. de Lasteyrie, an Inspector of Finance, was appointed secretary.

Attempts to Organise the Blockade on an inter-Allied Basis

There was one step more to be accomplished, and it was the most difficult of all.

FEBRUARY 1915—FEBRUARY 1917

From June 1915 onwards the French Government had never ceased requesting that the blockade should be conducted by means of a permanent inter-Allied organisation. But all attempts in this direction on the part of ministers, especially those of M. Clemenceau who was the moving spirit at the earlier inter-Allied economic conferences, had been wrecked by the contradictory nature of the commercial interests of the Allied nations, which were only kept in touch with one another by means of intermittent conferences and by the fact that members of the diplomatic body could sit upon the various national committees.

Owing, of course, to the excellent relations prevailing between M. Denys Cochin and Lord Robert Cecil the number of questions which gave rise to friction between France and the United Kingdom had been considerably lessened. Both capitals, however, complained of not being informed of decisions taken upon the other side of the Channel: Paris, for geographical reasons, had become the centre of negotiations in connection with Switzerland, whereas London was in charge of those relating to Holland and Scandinavia, and methods, as we shall see, were different. We will only say this much, that Great Britain regarded the blockade from a commercial point of view; it had seemed natural to her during the first two years of the war to try to take Germany's place in several neutral markets, to sell her manufactured goods there, and to take agricultural produce in exchange. France had a more legal conception of the blockade : she was ready to sacrifice her trade interests in their entirety to the complete isolation of the Central Empires.

This divergence of view had betrayed itself by a considerable difference of practice in the supervision of neutrals. Great Britain was in favour of general understandings with the Powers or with certain neutral organisations, the principle of which was to entrust neutrals with their own supervision ; but this was a dangerous principle, as the traffic to be suppressed was illicit only in the eyes of the belligerents.

France would have preferred to organise the supervision of each neutral Power in its own country through agents who would control on the spot the use to which the imported stuffs were put ; but to make this organisation effective would have required unremitting efforts, much spade work and a large number of agents, and secret work of this kind was very unsympathetic to the diplomatic services of the Allied nations who preferred general agreements with the neutrals.

Notwithstanding these differences the Allies had created on the 20th of June 1916, at the conclusion of a Conference presided over by M. Clémentel, a "Permanent International Committee of Economic Action."

This Committee, which sat at Paris, had indeed no executive authority ; it confined itself to the very useful task of co-ordinating the lists of prohibitions to export, but played no part in bringing about unity of direction between the Allies.

This unity which had not been brought about by the end of 1916 was imposed by the sheer force of events in 1917.

Abandonment of the Declaration of London (7th July 1916)

The appearance of Lord Robert Cecil as head of the British Ministry of Blockade had an important effect on the attitude hitherto assumed by the Allies from the point of view of international law. The Declaration of London had been used as a façade for all the measures taken by them; but the structure so raised by the Allies was only distantly connected with the monument of law erected by the Powers in 1909, and was in certain respects entirely out of keeping with it.

This state of affairs, in the opinion of the British Government, constituted a weak point in the work of the Allies; it seemed to it to be illogical to proclaim by the Order in Council of the 30th of October 1914 which was still in force that the Declaration of London would be applied with certain reservations and at the same time to take measures in direct defiance of the aforesaid Declaration, which stated in one of its articles that it was to be treated as an inseparable whole.

CONDUCT OF THE NAVAL WAR

When a building is finished the scaffolding which made its construction possible is removed, and the first idea of Lord Robert Cecil when he was appointed Minister of Blockade in 1916 was to pull down the scaffolding, a task which was the more congenial to him as, in the opinion of quite a large section of the British public, the Declaration of London was responsible for the inadequate results of the so-called blockade.

The French Government, on the contrary, in spite of having taken exactly the same action as its ally, was frankly unwilling to declare the Declaration abrogated, and one of its arguments was not lacking in force. " The Declaration," it said, " is a text known to every Power. On the other hand it binds the Allies to identity of action. If we give it up England and France will each revert to their own maritime law and the neutrals will be all at sea."

The controversy between the two Governments assumed a very lively character and lasted throughout the spring of 1916.

Although the Foreign Office had been won over to the French point of view Lord Robert Cecil was not unmindful of the vigorous opposition he had formerly offered to the Declaration as a Member of Parliament, and was anxious as Minister of Blockade to put into practice the ideas he had advocated seven years previously. The greater part of British public opinion wanted to revert to its old time-honoured law and took exception to the drafting of the Declaration as unduly narrow in form. Lord Robert ultimately announced that Allied unity of action was unaffected by the wording of the British Orders in Council. "As a matter of fact," he said, "in France, when the President of the Republic makes a decree your prize court is obliged to enforce it. In England the prize court judges in accordance with what it holds to be international law and need not pay any attention to Orders in Council if they appear to it to be contrary to what it believes to be the usage of international law."

The French Government replied to these arguments as follows: "Of course, in international law, more than anywhere else, narrowness of drafting is a serious defect. But all the same, a rule in black and white, whatever its limitations prove with regard to neutral trade, is preferable to the uncertainty in which the Powers lived up to 1909. Furthermore if it seems advisable to make the Declaration more flexible why should it not be remodelled ? True it is, indeed, that it is stated in one of its articles that the Declaration is to be treated as an inseparable whole, but as the Declaration has not been ratified this article has only a relative value. Lastly, we were not surprised to be informed of the British doctrine concerning the scope of Orders in Council in England. The French state is bound by the rule it has decreed and which can be modified by it ; but any private individual can contend that the rule thus enforced by decree does not conform to international law and can claim to be entitled to the more favourable treatment ensured him by the latter."

Eventually Lord Robert Cecil found it necessary to come to Paris in person on the 28th of May 1916, when he won the day. It was arranged that the Allies were to send the neutrals a joint memorandum explanatory of their attitude :—

At the beginning of the present war the Allied Governments, in their anxiety to regulate their conduct by the principles of the law of nations, believed that in the Declaration of London they would find a suitable digest of principles and compendium of working rules. They accordingly decided to adopt the provisions of the Declaration, not as in itself possessing for them the force of law but because it seemed to present in its main lines a statement of the rights and the duties of belligerents based on the experience of previous naval wars. As the present struggle developed, acquiring a range and character beyond all previous conceptions, it became clear that the attempt made at London in time of peace to determine, not only the principles of law, but even the forms under which they were to be applied, had not produced a wholly satisfactory result.

As events progressed the Germanic Powers put forth all their ingenuity to relax the pressure tightening about them and to reopen a channel for supplies; their devices compromised innocent neutral commerce and involved it in suspicions of enemy agency. Moreover, the manifold developments of naval and military science, the invention

FEBRUARY 1915—FEBRUARY 1917

of new engines of war, the concentration by the Germanic Powers of the whole body of their resources on military ends, produced conditions altogether different from those prevailing in previous naval wars.

The rules laid down in the Declaration of London could not stand the strain imposed by the test of rapidly changing conditions and tendencies which could not have been foreseen.

The Allied Governments were forced to recognise the situation thus created and adapt the rules of the Declaration from time to time to meet these changed conditions.

These successive modifications may perhaps have exposed the purpose of the Allies to misconstruction; they have therefore come to the conclusion that they must confine themselves simply to applying the historic and admitted rules of the law of nations.

The Allies solemnly and unreservedly declare that the action of their warships no less than the judgments of their prize courts will continue to conform to these principles; that they will faithfully fulfil their engagements and in particular will observe the terms of all international conventions regarding the laws of war; that mindful of the dictates of humanity they repudiate utterly all thought of threatening the lives of non-combatants; that they will not without cause interfere with neutral property, and that if they should by the action of their fleets cause damage to the interests of any merchant acting in good faith they will always be ready to consider his claims and to grant him such redress as may be due.

Immediately following on this proclamation of principles a Decree and Order in Council appeared on the 7th of July 1916 in Paris and London respectively by which the Declaration of London was cancelled. The French decree was very short and merely adapted our regulations as to prizes of 1778 to the conceptions of contraband and the quota system as evolved in the way we have shown.

In practice the orders given by the Allied Powers to their navies were not modified in any way, and the variations between French and British law as regards lawful blockades which might have caused difficulties at certain points of the coasts of Asia Minor and Africa did not in any way affect the unity of action of the admiralties.

General Survey of the Negotiations with Neutrals during 1915 *and* 1916

The action taken by the Allies with regard to contraband, the quasi-blockade and the quota system obviously only affected neutral imports by sea. No such action could have directly affected the home production of neutrals or prevented for instance Dutch cattle or Swedish iron ore entering Germany.

The Allies had two means available of preventing the home products of neutrals being

FEBRUARY 1915—FEBRUARY 1917

disposed of in Germany : they could either look indulgently on such production and purchase the greater part of it or discountenance it by preventing fodder from reaching Holland and mineral oils from reaching Sweden.

The latter step, however, was a double-edged sword : as soon as the Allies began to talk about stopping fodder and oil cake coming into Holland the Dutch agriculturists took care to point out that they would be forced to kill their cattle and send the results of this hecatomb to Germany.

The Allies resorted to both the methods we have mentioned, but different problems arose in connection with each neutral country, some of which had not been solved when the war ended, others were only cleared up by dint of very difficult negotiations which as the war went on brought into ever increasing relief the important part played by the Ministry of Foreign Affairs in matters relating to the blockade.

At this point three stages can clearly be distinguished in Allied action with regard to neutral trade.

(1) To stop the arrival in neutral countries of an undue quantity of imports by sea.

(2) To ensure the imports which the Allies had allowed to go through being retained in the neutral country where they were landed.

(3) To divert from the Central Empires the home production of the neutrals.

The first stage called for action on the part

of the Allied admiralties alone; the second and third were the concern of their diplomatic services.

The methods used by the Allied diplomacy varied with each country :—

In Holland, for instance, it formed a syndicate of importers, the Netherlands Oversea Trust, or N.O.T., which offered to give a guarantee to the Allies that it would not re-export the goods imported by it. This syndicate became the general consignee of Dutch imports and the Allies made their quota agreements with it.

In Switzerland as we shall see a somewhat analogous syndicate was evolved : the Swiss Society of Economic Supervision, or the S.S.S., which was organised by the Federal State itself and acted mainly as the machinery for working the quota.

In Denmark and Norway the Allies dealt with private syndicates such as the Company of Notable Traders in Copenhagen or the Associated Norwegian Importers of Mineral Oils.

In Sweden, last of all, the Allies found the greatest difficulty in dealing either with the Government or official syndicates.

But whatever the methods employed the quota system introduced in 1915 had been widely extended as regards all these neutral countries by the end of 1916.

FEBRUARY 1915—FEBRUARY 1917

Survey of the Results of the Blockade at the End of 1916

The results obtained are shown by the following figures of the American exports to neutrals.

	July 1913 to July 1914 £	1st year of war July 1914-15 £	2nd year of war July 1915-16 £	Third year of war July 1916-17 £
Holland	22,400,000	28,600,000	19,400,000	6,400,000
Sweden	2,800,000	15,600,000	10,400,000	4,800,000
Norway	1,800,000	7,800,000	10,600,000	1,400,000
Spain	6,000,000	7,600,000	10,400,000	15,400,000

It will be seen that whereas the value of the imports from the United States into Spain which was unrationed increased steadily in value, there was a perceptible fall in the amount of these imports into other neutral countries from July 1916 onwards when the quota system really came into force.

Now this falling off in neutral trade during the second half of 1916 made Germany very anxious. Indeed the winter of 1916-17 began under circumstances most critical for her. She termed it the "turnip winter," on account of the enormous quantities of this vegetable which she was forced to consume owing to a fall of over 50% in the potato crop in 1916, upon which she mainly depended for food: only 25 million tons were produced instead of 50 millions.

CONDUCT OF THE NAVAL WAR

Of course the encirclement of the Central Empires was, as yet, by no means complete. Roumania had been invaded and Germany anticipated finding there, notwithstanding the ravages of the soldiery, considerable quantities of petroleum and wheat. On the Eastern Front the doors of the Russian granary were still closed, but the false hopes founded thereon enabled Germany to carry on patiently through the winter of 1917–18.

The German harvests began to diminish in yield for lack of the necessary fertilisers. The wheat harvest fell from 4,400,000 tons in 1913 to 2,999,000 tons in 1916, that of rye from 11,200,000 tons in 1913 to 8,900,000 tons in 1916.

The consumption of meat which had amounted to a kilogram per head per week previously to the war fell by 50% in the country and by 75% in the majority of the towns of Germany : Germany, as we shall see, was rationing herself systematically in the hopes of saving her livestock. But this livestock she was thus endeavouring to save was but ill fed : Berlin only received 486,000 litres of milk daily in 1916 instead of the 840,000 litres she had been accustomed to in 1914.

As regards the raw material which was essential to her industry, the stocks of copper which had been accumulated in 1914 were exhausted and the imports from neutral countries had not exceeded 13,000 tons in 1916, although she normally used as much as 200,000 tons of copper.

Germany was short of nickel and tin ; it was at

the end of 1916 that the shortage of manganese first began to be felt, and she could not make steel without it.

The stocks of cotton which had been accumulated prior to the war and during 1915 were getting low; the powder factories got over the difficulty by using cellulose, but the clothing problem had still to be solved.

Germany's Reasons for Declaring Unrestricted Submarine Warfare

In short, Germany at the end of 1916 was very much inconvenienced—and this state of affairs told the more heavily on a people which liked the good things of this world—owing to the stabilisation of the land fronts, more especially in the west, and the consequent impossibility of foreseeing any end of it.

It was not surprising that the German people were anxious to be rid of their discomfort. We must bear in mind that a large political and naval party had been telling them for months past " There is only one means of doing so. The soul of the hostile coalition is England; the reason why the submarine war as waged by us has not yet forced her to sue for peace is that this war is being carried on under all the restrictions imposed by international law and that we respect, on principle, neutral shipping. Let us abolish these restrictions and play the card of submarine warfare for all it is worth."

What had been the economic results of submarine warfare up to the end of 1916 upon which these hopes were based?

The Position of Allied Tonnage at the End of 1916

The world tonnage of merchant steamships of more than 500 tons displacement amounted in August 1914 to 46,700,000 tons.[1]

Owing to the war the German, Austrian, Turkish and Russian merchant shipping, 7,000,000 tons in all, was unavailable for oversea traffic.

On the other hand British and French merchant shipping to the amount of 4,000,000 tons had been requisitioned for war purposes and was therefore equally unavailable.

We find then that by the end of 1914 25% of the world's shipping was of no further use for trading purposes.

This loss of 25% was in reality much more considerable, for it must be borne in mind that the Allied admiralties had requisitioned the fastest passenger steamers as auxiliary cruisers, and that the return yielded by the tonnage still available was diminished by the various hindrances put in the way of navigation, such as search and the difficulties of loading.

Submarine warfare made its appearance at the beginning of 1915. The following figures give

---

[1] The figures given by the Author on page 9 would indicate a world tonnage, in August 1914, of 43,200,000. [Tr.]

FEBRUARY 1915—FEBRUARY 1917

the amount of tonnage sunk quarterly during the years 1915 and 1916.

	1915	1916
1st quarter	321,000 tons	523,000 tons
2nd ,,	381,000 ,,	525,000 ,,
3rd ,,	530,000 ,,	592,000 ,,
4th ,,	494,000 ,,	1,160,000 ,,

The tonnage thus sunk amounted to 1,726,000 tons in 1915 and 2,800,000 tons in 1916, or to 4,526,000 tons altogether.

The Allies had one means at their immediate disposal of making good this loss of tonnage, namely to accelerate the rate of shipbuilding. The year 1915, however, showed a marked falling off in shipbuilding all over the world. In 1913 Great Britain had launched 1,932,000 tons, but in 1915 she only launched 651,000. The total tonnage of new ships that were put into service all over the world in 1915 amounted to 1,202,000 tons.

The year 1916 was marked by a renewal of activity in the shipping yards; the tonnage of new ships put into service that year amounted to 1,688,000 tons.

The net deficit of world tonnage, if we take the new ships into account, amounted therefore in January 1917 to about 1,600,000 tons.

This deficit might have been of no great consequence if the needs of France and England as regards imports had not continually increased and if the risks incurred by merchant shipping from submarine warfare had not diminished the return yielded by each voyage to such an extent that the general naval staff considered in 1916 that the tonnage available for the exchange of goods was less than one half of that employed in the transport trade in 1913.

This state of things is very clearly illustrated by the freight tables :—

The freight charges for a ton of coal from Cardiff to Havre rose from 14/8½ in January 1915 to 23/3½ in December of the same year, and would have exceeded the 25/2 charged in December 1916 had they not subsequently been controlled.

The freight charges for a ton of wheat from America to England rose from 12/0½ in July 1914 to 37/2½ in March 1915, 68/4 in December 1915, and £6 in December 1916.

Apart from the vigorous prosecution of the campaign against the submarines and stimulating the activity of their shipyards the Allied Governments had only two ways open to them of overcoming the crisis :—

(1) By securing the best possible return of services from their own merchant fleet,

(2) By inducing neutral merchant fleets to come into their service.

We have already shown what had been achieved so far by the shipyards in 1916; we will now explain briefly how the merchant fleets of France and Great Britain were organised in 1916 and how the Allies brought pressure to bear upon neutral shipping.

Organisation of the Merchant Fleets in Great Britain and France from 1914 to 1916

Prior to the war British commercial shipping was controlled, in theory at any rate, by the Board of Trade. When the British Government had to arrange for transports for its own service it used to apply to an unassuming branch of the Admiralty, the Transport Department. On the 2nd of August 1914 a civil director was placed at the head of this service with an advisory council of shipowners to help him, and he set to work; his task up to the middle of 1915 consisted in requisitioning ships, mobilising the personnel and organising innumerable transport offices.

At this point the Board of Trade, which still retained the economic direction of the United Kingdom, perceived the dangers of the freight crisis; losses had risen from a monthly average of 55,000 tons to one of 87,000. In true British fashion it set up a Committee called the 'Ship Licensing Committee' which was composed of shipowners, whose duty it was to see that the shipping belonging to Great Britain was utilised in the most effective way; the Committee issued the necessary licence to any British ship about to undertake a voyage, and France and Italy applied to it when they required British tonnage, which was often the case.

CONDUCT OF THE NAVAL WAR

As matters grew worse a super-committee in the shape of the 'Shipping Control Committee' was appointed in January 1916 with plenary powers as to the utilisation of all merchant shipping.

The super-committee met with a disagreeable surprise as soon as it took up its duties; in 1915 Great Britain had requisitioned for her own needs and those of her allies 7,000,000 tons of shipping, or to put it differently fifteen to sixteen hundred vessels, which had brought $49\frac{1}{2}$ million tons of goods from overseas. Suddenly, at the beginning of 1916, France applied for a further 600,000 tons and Italy for a further 800,000 tons of shipping.

The needs of the Allies and Great Britain were added together and it was found that there was a deficit of $3\frac{1}{4}$ million tons of shipping, which meant that the Allies in 1916 would have to go short of 13 million tons of goods. Although goods of any kind which were not indispensable were ruthlessly excluded, freight charges which at the beginning of 1916 amounted to 18 shillings went up to £2 at the end of the same year.

In December 1916 unrestricted submarine warfare was felt to be impending; Great Britain considered that the Admiralty would have its hands full in fighting the submarines: she separated the by now famous Transport Department from the Admiralty and created a Ministry of Merchant Shipping with the Shipping Controller at the head of it. The various Committees either ceased to exist or exercised purely advisory functions. The Shipping Controller had full powers as to shipbuilding, chartering of every kind, and allotment of tonnage to the Allies. He was assisted in his work by two other Controllers, one of equipment, the other of food. The former was appointed in 1915, the appointment of the latter was the outcome, following the usual British practice, of the formation of various committees.

It had, indeed, become necessary for the British Government as far back as August 1914 to give serious attention to the question of its sugar supplies. England had imported 2,200,000 tons of sugar in 1913, of which 1,800,000 had come from the Central Empires; a Commission had to be set up to organise the transport and sale of the sugar which she had acquired in the Antilles, Cuba, and the Dutch East Indies. Some weeks later a Frozen Meat Commission was appointed to supply the needs of the British squadrons and armies in this respect: 1915 gave birth to the Corn Commission, and when, at the end of 1916, the danger became urgent, a Food Controller was appointed as chairman of all these commissions.

By the beginning of 1917 the two British Ministries of Food and Munitions, under the supervision of the Shipping Controller, were exercising effective control over 70% of the imports of Great Britain.

At the beginning of 1915 the French became

aware of the need for organising sea transport on the assumption that the war was likely to last a long time; in fact, owing to the invasion, the production of cast iron by our industry had fallen by 80%, our trade by land had practically ceased to exist, and our merchant fleet, which in peace time did not effect one quarter of our imports, had been seriously diminished by requisitions.

The Ministry of War, upon whom the needs of the artillery as regards ammunition acted as a spur, was first in the field and inaugurated a policy of maritime transport by setting up on the one hand commissions at the ports and on the other at Paris a branch at the office of the Transit Maritime et Affretements Généraux.[1]

The Under-Secretaryship for Merchant Shipping which had been abolished in August 1914 was revived on the 13th of March 1915, but its functions were mainly administrative and its influence upon merchant shipping was practically nil.

Other ministerial departments had found it necessary to requisition fleets of shipping in the performance of their duties; while the Ministry of War was operating the fleet under the management of its branch at the Transit, the Ministry of Public Works operated the so-called coal fleet

---

[1] Sea Trade and General Charterers. This branch of the Transit was undertaking the management of 140 ships in the middle of 1916; it was therefore, at this time, the largest French chartering company.

which supplied our needs in fuel; the Ministry of Marine operated its own fleet of supply ships, and the Ministry of Commerce directed the operations of the so-called Hudson's Bay fleet which furnished the civilian population with supplies.

On the 29th of February 1916 an advisory Committee called the 'Committee of Maritime Transport' was appointed at the request of the Minister of Marine, and was assigned the task of discovering how to secure a better return of services from our means of transport. The Committee endeavoured to harmonise more or less the views of the various services which employed merchant shipping. It was abolished at the end of 1916 and replaced by an Under-Secretaryship of State for Transport which was attached to the Ministry of Public Works, M. Claveille being the first holder of this office.

The Under-Secretary of State for Merchant Shipping, who had been separated from the Ministry of Marine and attached to that of Public Works, continued to deal with questions of administration, and the various merchant shipping services were only consolidated in France in 1917.

Allied Pressure upon Neutral Shipping

In spite of all the efforts up to this point on the part of the Allies to secure the best possible results from their own merchant fleets the co-operation of neutral tonnage had been found indispensable.

CONDUCT OF THE NAVAL WAR

This tonnage, which amounted to 13,000,000 tons, was mainly distributed as follows:

United States ..	5,500,000 tons
Holland	1,300,000 ,,
Norway	2,450,000 ,,
Sweden	1,500,000 ,,
Denmark	700,000 ,,
Spain	800,000 ,,

Coal afforded the Allies the best means of exercising pressure upon neutral shipping, securing the best return from its services and dissuading it from embarking upon indirect but remunerative ventures on behalf of the Central Empires. Long sea voyages were notoriously difficult unless the good offices of British coaling companies in Allied or neutral ports were resorted to. The idea naturally occurred of making the measure of confidence felt by the Allies in the captains or shipowners the grounds for granting or withholding bunker coal ; in the meantime, however, it was essential to draw up a black list.

The idea of drawing up a black list of ships originated in the summer of 1915 when the question arose of the transfer to neutral flags of German ships which had taken refuge in neutral waters at the outbreak of hostilities. The Allies at that time objected strongly to transfers of flag and it was decided that any ships so transferred were not to be supplied with coal if they entered Allied ports.

Furthermore, the inspectors of navigation who

inventoried the stores of ships about to sail from Allied ports were given orders to fix the amount of coal needed for each impending voyage and only to allow a fixed quantity to be laden " in order to prevent bunker coal being employed for purposes other than that for which it had been put on board."

While keeping its eye on individual units of the merchant fleets the British Government felt that it was better in October 1915 to appeal to the neutral shipping companies themselves.

If you want bunker coal, the Foreign Office declared in its circular note, you must supply us with a list of all your ships and their charter parties and bind yourselves not to allow any of them to trade with an enemy of Great Britain. Furthermore, you must direct your ships to call at British ports of search, refuse to carry any cargo ' to order ' or goods which are liable to be stopped by the British authorities.[1]

The ships of any company which agreed to these terms were entered upon the white list, whereas those of other companies appeared on the black list.

In November 1915, however, it was decided that bunker coal should be withheld even from ships on the white list if the latter, when sailing from the United Kingdom, preferred to sail in ballast rather than take a cargo of coal to some intermediate port slightly off their direct route.

We have no desire, the British Government

[1] Author's summary.

stated, to impose these restrictions with a view to hampering or inconveniencing neutral trade of a lawful character, we are trying to discourage shipowners who are undertaking voyages in ballast solely in order to take advantage of abnormal freight charges.[1]

With a view to securing the strict application of these rules the English Government in December 1915 set up an 'Advisory Coal Committee' at the Admiralty. To ensure the enforcement of the measures in question not only in the ports of the Entente but at all coaling stations under London control every Allied coaling depôt was furnished with a copy of the black and white lists.

The pressure the British Government was thus enabled to bring to bear upon neutral shipping companies with a view not only to withdrawing their ships from contraband trade but using them to carry supplies for the Allies may well be imagined. The black and white list system, moreover, was not applied to shipping only; as far back as November 1914 the Allies had directed their agents in neutral countries to draw up black lists of traders suspected or convicted of furnishing the Central Empires with supplies. The cruising squadrons were furnished with these black lists, but the attention of the officers in command was drawn to the fact that owing to the methods employed in compiling them the latter could not be considered alone as proof of unlawful traffic.

[1] Author's summary.

Side by side with these semi-official black lists the British Government had published by 1916, in the *London Gazette,* official black lists termed ' Statutory Lists ' containing the names of persons or companies domiciled in neutral territory with whom commercial dealings of any kind were strictly forbidden ; the very fact of trading with any one whose name appeared upon these lists rendered the offender liable to severe penalties.

Up to July 1916 France confined herself to semi-official lists ; the Ministry of War drew up its own lists and the Ministry of Foreign Affairs composed others. This gave rise to friction, as the Ministry of Foreign Affairs claimed to be alone in a position to make accurate lists by reason of the sources of information at its disposal in neutral countries.

The Ministry of Marine intervened in May 1916 and declared that an ' official ' list of enemy agents in neutral countries was an indispensable weapon in the economic war ; it often happened indeed that neutral cargo boats were diverted by ship commanders on the strength of information derived from semi-official black lists ; as soon as the cargo boat had been brought into port and the question arose of proving hostile destination before the prize court the latter would request to be informed why the consignees had been entered upon the black lists ; reasons for doing so could hardly be stated without giving away our own intelligence agents ; if the ship was released in consequence, heavy compensation had to be paid by the Government for deviation of course.

At the request of the Ministry of Marine and conformably with the conclusions of the inter-Allied Conference of 1916, the French Government accepted the suggestion of publishing an official black list, and entrusted this task to the inter-Ministerial black lists commission. The commission used the British Statutory List as a foundation for its work; its first official list appeared on the 6th of August 1916, and the very fact of a trader being entered upon it afforded preliminary proof of his hostile character.

It is obvious that these lists were subject to frequent variations: the black list commissions which worked in conjunction with London and subsequently with Washington endeavoured to keep them up to date and amalgamate them; one trader who had been entered upon a list would give proof of future good behaviour and upon affording security would have his name erased from the lists; another, again, would at once change the name of his firm in the hope of enjoying a few months' immunity pending the discovery of the fraud.

There can be no doubt that the plan of making black lists of ships and traders both official and secret was of yeoman service to the cause of the Allies, the real merit of which ought by rights to be ascribed to the unseen and often dangerous work of our intelligence agents.

FEBRUARY 1915—FEBRUARY 1917

Germany's Calculations

Germany was well aware of the pressure that was being put upon neutral shipping by the Allied Governments, but she reckoned that her declaration of unrestricted submarine warfare would be the one means of rendering it ineffectual. She had not the slightest doubt that the threat of torpedoing neutral merchant ships without warning would paralyse them with terror and keep them in port. The Allies would then be reduced to their own resources in tonnage. She reckoned, too, at the end of 1916, upon England only having $10\frac{3}{4}$ million tons of shipping available for her own supplies of food, and in this reckoning she was not far out, for the total available tonnage of the British merchant fleet did not amount to 13 million tons.

The Chief of the German Naval Staff wrote in person to the Emperor as follows:

"The very perceptible shortage in the world production of corn and foodstuffs gives us an unique opportunity this year. North America and Canada will probably hardly be able to send corn to England after February 1917. She will then have to apply to the Argentine, India and Australia, and will have to use three quarters of a million tons more shipping than in 1915 for corn alone. Now according to our calculations England has only $10\frac{3}{4}$ million tons of shipping available to supply her with food.

"If Germany by means of unrestricted

CONDUCT OF THE NAVAL WAR

submarine warfare succeeds in sinking 600,000 tons of shipping a month, and if we can count upon neutral traffic being stopped by the terror our methods inspire, British commerce must be reduced mathematically by 39% in five months; the United Kingdom cannot stand this and will be forced to sue for peace.

"In a word," concluded the Chief of the General Naval Staff, " unrestricted submarine warfare is the best and only means of bringing the war to a victorious conclusion."

The decision as to unrestricted submarine warfare was made in October 1916.

Germany, therefore, was about to play her last card at sea; but she played it, not as she claimed in a defensive spirit in order to avoid death from starvation, but animated entirely by the spirit of offence with the object of striking at England's heart; just as a gambler plays double or quits with the firm conviction that he is going to win.

CHAPTER III

FROM THE SECOND DECLARATION OF SUBMARINE WAR TO THE END OF THE WAR: FEBRUARY 1917—NOVEMBER 1918

Declaration of Unrestricted Submarine Warfare and Entry of the United States into the War

On the 19th of January 1917 at a conference held at Pless the Emperor signed the following order :

" I hereby order unrestricted submarine war to be commenced on the 1st of February and to be prosecuted with the utmost energy."

Germany committed two errors of psychology when she launched her declaration of submarine war ; firstly in under-estimating the vigour of the Allied counterstroke, and secondly in not allowing in her forecast for the attitude of the United States. Our surprise at these mistakes is to-day as great as ever.

It is of course quite true that in August 1914 the United States had exchanged some very tart notes with the Allies on the subject of the economic war ; but it could easily be inferred from the tone of the notes sent by it to Berlin on the subject of the torpedoing of individual American merchant ships

CONDUCT OF THE NAVAL WAR

that it would never stand systematic torpedoing, within a well defined zone, of ships protected by the Stars and Stripes.

On the 3rd of February 1917 President Wilson read to the American Senate his message in which he announced that diplomatic relations had been broken off with Germany; at Berlin the news was received with overwhelming astonishment.

On the 28th of February the House of Representatives authorised the President to provide American merchant ships with defensive armament. The scandal which was occasioned by the publication on the 1st of March of a letter from the German Government to Mexico and Japan containing proposals of alliance against the United States increased tension almost to breaking point.

When at last three American steamers had been torpedoed President Wilson on the 6th of April declared a state of war to exist between the United States and Germany: this was the first result of the counter-blockade which had been declared by the Central Empires, and was to be followed by inter-Allied co-operation with regard both to the blockade and sea transport.

New Aspect of the Blockade subsequently to the Entry of the United States into the War

April 6th 1917 is the turning point in the history of the blockade, in as much as up to that time the United States had acted as the main reserve of the raw material used by the belligerents; but whereas this raw material had reached the Entente Powers directly, it had only reached the Central Empires after passing through neutral hands. The Allies had succeeded by a long series of efforts in reducing these imports to a considerable extent; their anxiety to remain on good terms with the United States is the only explanation of the time that elapsed before their efforts became effective.

The moment the United States itself became a belligerent Germany's principal reservoir was completely dried up: thenceforward the policy of blockade became a very simple one as is proved by an examination of the question which was made at the time by the Committee of Restriction.

As far as the Entente countries were concerned there were merely two things to be done:

(1) To forbid any exportation whatever to neutral countries adjacent to Germany,

(2) To proceed to exchange products with these same neutrals if the latter were able to supply the Allies with goods which would be useful to them.

The second of these measures reduced trade between the European Allies and neutrals to the truck system. As regards the United States the Committee of Restriction submitted the following policy to them:

(1) To forbid the export of any goods not consigned to organisations having authority to supervise their consumption in neutral countries

or destined to firms entered upon the black lists,

(2) To adhere to the agreements which were already in force with neutral countries adjacent to the enemy.

There were very great practical difficulties in the way of the adoption of this simple policy : Great Britain, whose exports to the neutrals in the North Sea had amounted to £42,000,000 in 1913, to £66,000,000 in 1915, and £76,000,000 in 1916, would have been inconvenienced by total prohibition of trade with neutrals.

On the other hand the United States had a much more radical conception of the economic encirclement of the Central Empires than the European Allies, and this was to become very apparent as time went on ; but it was anxious to judge for itself as to the position in each neutral country and declined to accept blindfold the agreements concluded by the Allies with the neutrals.

Last of all, Great Britain was haunted not only by the fear of the ruin of a part of her trade in the space of a few weeks but by that of losing for good and all the foodstuffs she was receiving from Holland and the Scandinavian countries.

For these various reasons May and June 1917 went by without any decision being reached. It was only at the very end of the latter month that President Wilson appointed a Committee of Exports called the 'Export Council,' whose duty it was to prevent any American products being supplied to the Central Powers. The Council was composed of the Secretaries of State, Agriculture and of Commerce and of Mr. Hoover, who previously had been entrusted with the feeding of Belgium.

The Council was to be guided in its action by the following principles : firstly to retain for the United States as many of its products as it needed, then to supply the most urgent needs of the Allies, and finally to send the balance to neutrals on condition that the amount so sent did not exceed the quotas already fixed by the Allies.

General Embargo of 9th July 1917

In conformity with these principles President Wilson on the 9th of July 1917 signed the Proclamation which was known as ' the general embargo,' by which corn, fodder, petrol, cast iron, steel, fertilisers, arms, ammunition and explosives were forbidden to leave the ports of the United States without a special licence from the Export Council.

To begin with, and in order to allow the American experts time to examine the situation of each neutral, it was decided that not a single cargo of foodstuffs should be sent to neutral countries adjacent to Germany prior to December 1917 ; it was calculated that these countries would not suffer from famine till then and that ample time was being given them to prove their requirements.

CONDUCT OF THE NAVAL WAR

It was decided also on the 10th of August 1917 to set up at once an international council of blockade in London of American and Allied delegates : the Export Council in the meantime, owing to the energy displayed by Mr. W. Vance MacCormick, had become practically a ministry of blockade.

It was up to the Allies at this point to bring their policy into line with that of the United States, and conferences were held in London with this object in September 1917 between M. Métin, who had succeeded M. Denys Cochin, and Lord Robert Cecil.

It was there settled that the French and British Governments should assist the policy of embargo upon exports to neutral countries by every means in their power, until the import quotas, which were absolutely essential to these countries whose national resources had been completely exhausted, should have been agreed upon with the United States : " Although the French and British Governments are prevented by prior obligations from at once applying a general embargo in every instance they will in future be governed in their action by the principle of not allowing any exceptions to the embargo, save in the form of truck, in exchange for products which are indispensable either for the National Defence or as foodstuffs for countries which have been invaded by the enemy."

In accordance with this principle the French and British Governments forbade the export of goods of any kind to Holland and the Scandinavian countries after the 9th of November 1917. The Allied Governments issued, however, a further statement to the effect that they had no intention of refusing to consider individual applications as regards goods the export of which had previously been permitted and upon which an interdict had just been laid, but exporters were informed that they would in future " be unable to assume that such applications would be favourably entertained as a matter of course."

In the meantime the control of raw material by the United States was daily becoming more effective. The control of any industrial products which might be used for military purposes was exercised by an influential committee called the War Purchasing Commission or W.P.C., which had the right to requisition through the agency of the War or Navy Departments, and to place an embargo upon the shipment of goods through that of the Export Council and its branches. The W.P.C. controlled the whole industrial system in all its ramifications and its output at every stage of manufacture.

" On principle," wrote M. Tardieu, our High Commissioner in the United States, " the war needs of the United States are given preference, but exceptions are made in cases of proved urgency on behalf of the Allied armies in action.

" The needs of the civilian population of the

United States are subordinated to the war requirements of the Allies.

"The requirements of private individuals whether Allied or neutral are considered last of all, which means that they will not be satisfied.

"Even to-day foreign private firms are finding it very difficult to place fresh orders and are only able to obtain delivery of, or leave to export, orders which are in course of execution, with the greatest difficulty. All these difficulties will to-morrow be insurmountable, for the machinery we have described is working with increasing rapidity and very shortly control will become absolute and universal."

On the 28th of November 1917 the system of licences which was already in force as regards exports from the United States was made applicable to imports into that country: licences to import being issued by the War Trade Board. The object of this measure was to make it impossible for commercial business houses in the South American Latin republics which were controlled by German capital to continue their operations in the United States.

The embargo upon imports was a weapon for use against certain states who were looking indulgently upon German propaganda and also against the European neutrals, who, it was calculated, would prove in consequence more amenable in the negotiations relating to their intercourse with the Entente and the Central Powers.

FEBRUARY 1917—NOVEMBER 1918

Development of the Organisations which directed the Blockade in London and Paris between the Beginning of 1917 and the End of the War

At the end of 1917, then, the machinery which M. Tardieu has referred to was working at full pressure. Nothing remained to be done but to ensure that the exertions of the Allied and Associated Powers were directed to a single purpose. Let us first of all see how the organisations which directed the blockade in London and Paris developed between the beginning of 1917 and the end of the war.

In March 1917 the weakness displayed by the French and British Governments in the conduct of the economic war was the subject of debates both in the House of Commons and the Chamber of Deputies. In the House of Commons the Foreign Office was very severely attacked; it was blamed, especially, for allowing British merchants to export to neutrals, on the pretext that they were receiving in exchange from those very same neutrals raw material which was vital to Great Britain. It was a bad bargain as Great Britain only received from the neutrals an infinitely small amount as compared with Germany. The supporters of the motions went so far as to demand the complete cessation of the export of goods of any kind to neutral countries adjacent to the Central Empires, and that, with a view to the more active prosecution of the economic war, the direction thereof should be taken out of the hands of the Foreign Office and transferred to the Admiralty.

Lord Robert Cecil defended his policy and stated that it was impossible to entrust the blockade to the Admiralty, as negotiations with the neutral Powers were perpetually going on. The First Lord of the Admiralty stated that Lord Robert Cecil's policy was that of the entire Cabinet, and the motions were withdrawn.

At the Palais Bourbon the Government was interpellated by M. Tardieu, who quoted the following figures from the tribune :—

Holland had exported 195,000 tons of food commodities to Germany in 1913, 425,000 tons in 1915, and 491,000 tons in 1916.

The exports from Scandinavian countries to the Central Empires had increased by 25% as regards copper, 104% as regards fats, 177% as regards fish and by 312% as regards coffee.

"There are three remedies," he said; "we must first of all fix the quotas of neutral countries very carefully; then organise within these same countries our policy of purchase; and finally ensure unity of direction of the blockade, in France to begin with and then as between the Allies. . . . In the war we are carrying on," he concluded by saying, " there is only one unit of expense; that unit of expense is the life of our soldiers and it is of that which we ask you to be sparing."

M. Denys Cochin in his reply made use of the

same arguments as Lord Robert Cecil. He likened the quota system to one of guardianship under which neutral countries were allowed just what they needed but nothing to make free with outside their own boundaries and pointed out the obvious defect of a system which could only apply to the imports of neutral countries and was entirely ineffective as regards their internal production.

"It is obvious," he concluded, "that we have not got a complete blockade but only a partial one; but were we to apply force to the neutrals we should irritate every one. If we exercise a little more patience before taking strong measures, if we find, as we hope to do, that the greatest and most powerful of the neutrals is going to make common cause with us, will not the others change their attitude?"

In spite of the favourable reception which was naturally given to a statement of this kind, on the eve of the entry of the United States into the war, the Chamber adopted the following Order of the Day: "The Chamber finding that the blockade of Germany in respect of foodstuffs is not completely assured, relies on the Government to adopt, or secure the adoption of, whatever measures may be necessary, more especially the assessment of quotas generally, periodical revision of the same with a view to their suppression in the event of proved infringement, the organisation of its policy of purchase on a better footing, a more effective concentration

CONDUCT OF THE NAVAL WAR

of the French blockade services and proper co-ordination of inter-Allied action, and passes to the Orders of the Day."

After this debate M. Denys Cochin persuaded his colleagues to empower him, subject to their previous assent, to take immediate executive action in matters concerning the blockade.

A few weeks later when M. Denys Cochin felt that his machinery was in working order he left the Ministry, for reasons unconnected with the economic war, and was replaced by M. Métin, who as Secretary of State had the same powers as his predecessor. In November 1917 the latter's place in the new Clemenceau ministry was taken by M. Lebrun, not as Under-Secretary of State but as Minister of Blockade and the Liberated Districts.

M. Lebrun's new powers stood in need of definition and he was accordingly entrusted, by the decree of the 14th of December 1917, with the duty of directing and co-ordinating the various public services in charge of the blockade; he was also empowered to co-operate with the Minister of Foreign Affairs in initiating and carrying on any negotiations which might be expedient in connection with the economic war. The province of the ministry was very extensive, and accordingly a sub-department of blockade was formed under M. Delavaud, a minister plenipotentiary, which absorbed the various services dealing with the economic war. M. Lebrun accordingly directed the economic war staff, properly speaking, which drafted instructions and did the preliminary work of negotiations in general, the organisations which dealt with the financial blockade, exemptions from the prohibition to export, and control, and the general secretariats of the Committee of Restriction, and of the Quota Commission. This organisation underwent no further change.

The Allies achieve Unity of Direction of the Blockade

The attempts made to bring about unity of direction between France, Great Britain and Italy had hitherto been unsuccessful : it is of course true that at the end of 1915 the Allies had set up in London a Committee of Blockade composed of twenty members : the Committee however was too big a one and British particularism was too much to the fore to allow of the Committee doing good work : it only held about a dozen sittings and ceased to meet towards the middle of 1917. Unity of direction which France had always asked for and which had been so conspicuously lacking was forced upon the Allies by the economic policy of the United States.

In December 1917 the Allies Blockade Committee, commonly known as the A.B.C.[1] met for the first time : it consisted of four members only. Mr. Leverton Harris, the British Under-Secretary

---

[1] This was the inter-Allied committee, the appointment of which had been agreed upon on the 10th of August 1917.

of State for the Blockade, was chairman, and Mr. Sheldon, Signor Giannini and M. Charpentier represented the United States, Italy and France respectively upon it.

Great Britain deputed two representatives, Sir Eyre Crowe on behalf of the Foreign Office and Mr. Amery on behalf of the War Trade Board, to place at the disposal of the A.B.C. two marvellous intelligence organisations in the shape of the Contraband Committee and the Statistical Department, upon which the Allied nations were subsequently represented. Moreover, in every neutral capital the preponderant part hitherto played by the British Legation was undertaken by sub-committees of blockade which were formed on the model of the A.B.C.

Such was the system of inter-Allied co-operation which began to function in March 1918, at the very time more or less when the single command was established, the principle of which, however advisable from the military point of view, was obviously inapplicable to economic warfare.

However, just about the time that inter-Allied co-operation in the economic war really became effective the blockade ceased to occupy the first place in the economic anxieties of the Allies. The German counter-blockade, which had already caused the United States to enter the war and achieved unity of action on the part of the Allies as regards the blockade, was about to produce a further result—united Allied action

FEBRUARY 1917—NOVEMBER 1918

in respect of maritime transport, and thereby give them the victory in the economic war.

The Economic Effects of the Submarine War and their Alleviation

In the light of our knowledge as to the position of Allied tonnage at the end of 1916, the extreme anxiety felt by the Allied governments at the results of the first few months of the submarine war can well be understood. 540,000 tons were sent to the bottom in February, 578,000 tons in March and 875,000 tons in April 1917; moreover neutral shipping for the most part refused obstinately to leave port. Although from the point of view of the policy of blockade Germany had been cruelly undeceived by the entry of the United States into the war, there was every appearance that her scheme of submarine warfare was about to prove successful. During 1917 the loss of Allied sea-going tonnage amounted to 6,100,000 tons. As before, three means of salvation were open to the Allies: to build fresh tonnage, make the best possible use of what they already owned and bring once more into service the neutral trading fleets which were standing idle in port.

In 1916 Great Britain had built only 608,000 tons, but as 1,163,000 tons were delivered by her yards in 1917 her losses in shipping, which had amounted to 7,079,492 tons since the 1st of August 1914, had been reduced by 3,031,555 tons. The

CONDUCT OF THE NAVAL WAR

United States, which had launched 228,000 tons of shipping in 1913, launched 821,000 tons in 1917; Japan also launched 350,000 tons, as against 65,000 tons in 1913.

The second means at their disposal was to employ the Allied merchant fleets to the very best possible advantage.

By the beginning of 1917 the whole of the British merchant shipping was under Government control.

It was not so in France, where, as I have already pointed out, dual control was exercised at the end of 1916 by the departments of the Under-Secretary of State for Merchant Shipping and that of Transports, the latter of which indeed was converted in April 1917 into the Ministry of Food and Maritime Transport.

In June 1917 the Prime Minister, M. Ribot, decided to put an end to this rivalry and concentrate in the hands of the new Under-Secretary for Merchant Shipping, M. de Monzie, every single organisation connected with maritime transport.

M. de Monzie's first proceeding was to subject the whole of the French merchant shipping to control, which was effected on the 17th of July 1917 : a separate licence for every voyage was to be issued to any French ship exceeding 100 tons displacement. It may be as well to remind our readers that in the middle of 1917 the French merchant fleet amounted to 4,167,000 tons, of which 3,214,000 were being operated on behalf of Government departments. After deduction of hospital ships and mail boats there only remained 365,000 tons of shipping available.

These 4,167,000 tons of merchant shipping moreover satisfied our requirements only to the extent of 35%; the deficit was made good by British help (9,000,000 tons) and by chartering neutral shipping.

So strict did the state control of the merchant fleet become in the course of the last six months of 1917, that when orders were given in January 1918 for the requisitioning of the entire French merchant fleet it merely confirmed a state of affairs which was already existing.

Joint Organisation by the Allies of Maritime Transport

Up to the end of 1917, however, there was no co-operation between the Allies in respect of merchant shipping, although some attempts had been made to effect it.

In April 1917 M. Tardieu had been sent to the United States to co-ordinate the requirements of the various ministerial departments, and by August 1917 had come up against the Shipping Board, a body which exercised sharp control over shipbuilding of every kind in the United States, on the question of merchant shipping.

In April 1917, likewise, the French Government had sent M. Guernier to London for six months as High Commissioner to co-ordinate the various French organisations working in that capital.

CONDUCT OF THE NAVAL WAR

Nothing more was done in the way of fusion than to hold meetings from time to time of the French officials at the head of the organisations which dealt with maritime transport, chartering, corn and coal supplies, under the chairmanship of a counsellor of Embassy.

Owing to the shortage in the harvests of 1917 in France and Italy, which entailed abnormal demands upon the Allies for shipping, the latter were compelled in November 1917 to enter upon negotiations with a view to a more rational distribution of tonnage. These negotiations, in which the United States took part, resulted in the Conference of Paris (29th November 1917) at which every economic question affecting the Allies and Associated Powers was carefully studied. The conference decided to create an all important organisation under the name of the 'Allied Maritime Transport Council,' or A.M.T.C. This Council, which was composed of the responsible Ministers of Food and Transport in each Allied country, held regular meetings, subsequently, in London or Paris; every Minister who sat on the Council received full powers from his Government. The Council also was equipped with a permanent secretariat entitled the Executive Section of the A.M.T.C.

Great Britain was represented on the A.M.T.C. by the Under-Secretary of State for Foreign Affairs and the Shipping Controller, France by her Ministers of Commerce and Munitions, Italy by her Ministers of Transport and Food, and

FEBRUARY 1917—NOVEMBER 1918

America by the Vice-President of the American Shipping Board.

The principal work of the A.M.T.C. was to prepare plans for supplying the allied nations with food on a rational basis.

Pressure upon Neutral Navigation. Order in Council of 16th February 1917

Concurrently with their attempts to prepare a rational plan for the provision of food supplies the Allies, from the moment unrestricted submarine war was declared up to November 1918, were unceasing in their efforts to bring back into service the neutral tonnage which had been immobilised by the submarine war, and to retain control over such neutral shipping as had put to sea.

The Germans had declared that they would torpedo any merchant ship in waters adjacent to Great Britain. Neutral shippers therefore requested that the Allied regulations which required ships proceeding to Holland or the Scandinavian countries to touch at a port of the United Kingdom should be modified, and proposed that search stations should be established at Halifax, Bermuda and Bathurst.

The position of the new stations, however, and also the diminution of activity on the part of the cruising squadrons on account of the submarine danger, acted as an incitement to fraudulent conduct on the part of neutral shipping. Accordingly in 1917 the British Government, with a view to checking fraudulent behaviour of this kind, decided to extend the application of its Order in Council of the 11th of March 1915. Up to that date any ship carrying goods of enemy origin or destined to an enemy was stopped but not captured. The British Government now proposed that any such ship should be liable to be seized and condemned merely for carrying such goods. It went even further : it proposed that any ship encountered at sea bound to or coming from a neutral port which had means of reaching enemy territory without touching at a port in British or Allied territory should be held to be carrying goods destined to an enemy or of enemy origin, in other words be liable to capture.

This proposal received a lukewarm reception from the French Government; even though it was justifiable as a measure of reprisal it constituted none the less a partial abrogation of the Declaration of Paris of 1856 and a direct attack upon neutral property at sea. The Government of the United States had just afforded the Allies moral support by breaking with Germany. It might be that she would enter the war on their side. The French Government therefore requested London to wait and see what impression would be made at Washington by the publication of a document of the kind.

The Allied ambassadors at Washington were consulted, and advised the adoption of the tactics advocated by the French Government.

Lord Robert Cecil, on the other hand, attached

very great importance to the publication of the Order in Council. "To allow neutrals to be searched at Halifax without taking strong action of another kind is tantamount to recognising the validity of the German blockade. We shall have the appearance of yielding and the impression upon neutrals will be deplorable. There does not really seem much likelihood, moreover, of the situation in the United States being much affected by this Order in Council."

Lord Robert Cecil carried the day. Ships leaving the United States for the North Sea and *vice versa* were allowed to be searched elsewhere than in the United Kingdom on the following conditions :—

(1) They were not to carry mails or postal parcels.

(2) Their entire cargo was to be 'approved' prior to departure, in other words be reported item by item to London before they received a pass.

An additional precaution was taken in the case of ships leaving Scandinavia or Holland, which had to provide themselves on sailing, as regards their cargo, with a certificate of origin to be furnished by a British consular agent. This procedure was sanctioned by the Order in Council of the 16th of February 1917 which rendered liable to capture " any vessel which is encountered at sea on her way to or from a port in any neutral country affording means of access to the enemy territory without calling at a port in British or

Allied territory." Goods discovered under these circumstances "which were of enemy origin or of enemy destination" became liable to capture.

The German declaration of the 1st of February 1917 with regard to unrestricted submarine warfare set all rules of law at defiance and was a plain infringement of the Declaration of Paris of 1856. The measures of reprisal adopted by Great Britain were therefore justified.

After several weeks' hesitation the French Government considered that no object would be served by issuing a decree to the same effect as the British Order in Council and took no action.

Survey of the Negotiations between the Allies and Neutrals on the Subject of Tonnage

The Allied and Associated Powers did, however, carry on joint diplomatic negotiations from April 1917 up to the Armistice with a view to compelling neutral tonnage to proceed again to sea. These negotiations were of a very complicated nature, in as much as they were closely connected with the question of reprovisioning the neutrals during the last two years of the war. The latter were not entirely dependent upon the Allies for all their supplies; they were also dependent upon Germany for goods as will be explained in the second part of this work. Negotiations were not always successful and the Allies in certain cases revived the law of angary, which enables a belligerent to make use of neutral tonnage in his ports for his own ends.

An agreement was signed with Sweden on the 29th of May 1918 by which the latter placed 400,000 tons of shipping at the disposal of the Allies. Norway alone never failed under any circumstances to place her 2,000,000 tons of shipping at the disposal of the Allies in spite of the serious losses sustained by her merchant fleet in the course of the submarine war.

Denmark by a special agreement dated the 20th of June 1917 placed 200,000 tons at the disposal of Great Britain, but the general agreement which affected an additional 285,000 tons was only signed on the 18th of September 1918.

No agreement with Holland was possible, and on the 20th of March 1918 President Wilson was forced to exercise the law of angary with regard to the whole of the Dutch shipping in American ports. 700,000 tons of Dutch shipping was placed by this means at the disposal of the Allies.

Final Attempts on the Part of Germany to interfere with the Economic Policy of the Allies

The combined effect of the arrangements made by the Allies and the successful conduct of their anti-submarine campaign afforded them reason for hoping, from the spring of 1918 onwards, that the economic war would turn in their favour. In the first place there was a diminution of activity on the part of the enemy submarines: this is

CONDUCT OF THE NAVAL WAR

clearly shown by the statistics of ships torpedoed in 1918 : whereas in 1917 the submarines had sunk 6,100,000 tons of shipping they only sunk 3,230,000 tons in 1918. The output of the allied shipbuilding yards on the other hand was steadily increasing. The United States, which had launched 228,000 tons in 1913 and 821,000 tons in 1917, launched 2,600,000 tons in 1918. Japan built 490,000 tons in 1918 as against 350,000 tons in 1917. From July 1918 onwards the tonnage of ships sunk was exceeded by that of new constructions.

By April 1918 Germany realised that she could not overcome her enemies by submarine warfare. She had every intention, nevertheless, of turning it to the best account up to the very end; and in the hopes of appearing still to exercise a partial control over neutral shipping and of improving her position in the economic negotiations she was carrying on with the neutrals, and of putting difficulties in the way of the Allies who were negotiating with these very neutrals, she resolved on the 27th of April 1918 to aggravate, in theory at least, the conditions of submarine warfare by publishing what is known as the supplementary clause to Article 55 C of the German Ordinance as to prizes.

According to this Article " any merchant ship which is chartered by an enemy Government or is being operated on behalf of enemy organisations directing the conduct of the operations of war is to be destroyed."

The supplementary clause to Article 55 C stated that "A neutral ship is to be considered as being operated with a view to furthering enemy operations of war . . . and therefore sunk . . . if the State under whose flag it is sailing has made an agreement with the Allies, or if, in default of such official agreement, the greater part of the merchant fleet of that State is being operated on behalf of the Allies."

This notorious supplement to Article 55 C amounted in practice to permitting the German submarines to sink every ship they met. As, however, the aforesaid submarines had not shown themselves so very discriminating during the previous year, we may be allowed to suspect that in publishing the supplementary clause Germany was pursuing another aim than that of facilitating the task of her submarines.

She hoped in reality, owing to the terror caused by the supplementary clause, to force neutral shippers, one and all, to ask for safe conducts and to issue them on the dearest terms possible. Accordingly at the end of April 1918 the German Consuls in neutral ports were found to be imposing increasingly strict conditions upon shipowners, who were besieging them with demands for safe conduct : obligation to carry goods for merchants who were entered upon the Allied black lists—prohibition to carry absolute contraband[1] or to put into an Allied port—in fact every kind of condition that was likely to

---

[1] As specified in the German lists of contraband.

disorganise radically the maritime trade of the Allies.

The German Government was aware that the submarine war was abating in severity, but it was anxious to strike the imagination of neutrals and prove to them that in spite of all Germany was still controlling commercial navigation. It would thus kill two birds with one stone : it would make it more difficult for the Allied and Associated Powers to obtain supplies, and at the same time would give a strong hint to neutral shippers that if their ships were not torpedoed it was because they were furnished with safe conducts, and not as the Allies claimed, because the German submarines were decreasing in numbers weekly.

In France the Minister of Marine saw through Germany's game and gave immediate orders for enforcing deviation of course, with a view to thorough search, upon all neutral shipping and particularly, as we shall see in the chapter dealing with Spain, upon Spanish ships that were furnished with German safe conducts.

The French Government considered, however, that the German manœuvre should be countered by measures of reprisal to prevent neutral tonnage from coming to a standstill and the system of safe conducts being generalised. It accordingly suggested that any neutral ships which were provided with an enemy safe conduct should be liable to capture.

FEBRUARY 1917—NOVEMBER 1918

Great Britain did not favour this proposal; it contended that severe measures of this kind would confront neutral shipping with the alternative either of being sunk by an enemy submarine if they were unprovided with a safe conduct or of being stopped by an Allied cruiser if they had one, and that under these circumstances neutral shipping would probably remain in port. She considered, moreover, that the question of safe conducts was of relatively small importance and would only become serious if the German submarines were able to control neutral navigation, and this was not the case.

As a matter of fact, Great Britain was of opinion that the Order in Council of the 16th of February 1917 rendered any further pressure upon neutral shipping unnecessary. France had not adopted the Order in Council and therefore lacked the necessary means of putting effective pressure upon neutral ships which were furnished with safe conducts.

At the suggestion of the United States, however, whose attention had been drawn to the question of safe conducts, the Powers in July 1918 took into consideration the question of taking diplomatic action with regard to the neutrals: not by any means an easy matter on account of the different problems presented by each neutral country.

The Allied and Associated Powers had actually given official recognition to German safe conducts in the case of ships carrying supplies for Switzerland,

and the curious sight was witnessed several times in the port of Cette, which was specially reserved for Swiss traffic, of a neutral ship refusing to put to sea and occupying valuable berthing space because its German safe conduct had not arrived.

In Sweden, for reasons connected with internal politics, the Allied ministers were entirely opposed to the adoption of severe measures with regard to safe conducts. In Norway, on the other hand, they were in favour of them. In Holland they suggested that in order to detract from the value of German safe conducts the Allies should issue counter safe conducts to neutral shipping.

The question came several times before the Committee of Blockade, but the latter was unwilling to come to a decision as opinion was so much divided upon the subject.

The French Government decided to leave no doubt as to its attitude, and on the 27th of August 1918 issued the following decree : " Any neutral ship which places itself under enemy control by the acceptance of a safe conduct, which is not recognised by the Allies and is incompatible with the exercise by them of their rights as belligerents, will be considered, failing proof to the contrary, as being operated in the interests of the enemy state and as such will be liable to capture and confiscation as well as any goods forming part of its cargo that belong to, have originated with, or are destined to, the enemy."

FEBRUARY 1917—NOVEMBER 1918

Thus Great Britain considered that she was entitled to bring before the Prize Court any ships which declined to enter a British port for purposes of search, and France those which were holders of safe conducts and did not comply with the conditions prescribed by the Decree of the 27th of August 1918.

Preparation of a General Scheme for Provisioning the Allies during the Year 1918–19

It must be confessed that the question of safe conducts was mainly important from a theoretical point of view.

From the summer of 1918 onwards the attention of the Allies was concentrated, primarily, upon the efforts of the Allied Maritime Transport Council to ensure supplies for what might have been the fifth year of the war. When the A.M.T.C. met in August 1918 to discuss the question, it learned to its satisfaction that new ships had been built in sufficient numbers since the 1st of January to compensate the losses due to submarines during the first half of the year.

The problem of transport, however, was none the less acute, for the statistics as to newly built ships comprised those of the United States, which needed the whole of its tonnage for its own requirements; moreover the European Allied Powers alone had been short of a million tons of shipping since August 1917. Now a shortage

CONDUCT OF THE NAVAL WAR

of 2 million tons of shipping was equivalent to one of 8 million tons of goods.

Again, American troops had been carried to France on a scale which had never been anticipated; in fact, 637,879 soldiers had been conveyed to Europe during the three months of April, May and June, 305,000 in July, and 313,000 in August. The transport of these troops was effected both in American ships and in those of the Allied Powers. In August 1918 for instance the 313,000 American soldiers had been brought over by 100,000 tons of Franco-American, 116,000 tons of British, and 40,000 tons of Italian shipping.

If, as the Allies estimated, the transport of each soldier was equivalent to that of 2 tons of goods we shall easily understand their being faced with a shortage of a million tons in August 1918, before any fresh estimates had been drawn up.

At this moment the Allied Ministers submitted their requirements in imports which were absolutely essential to them for the campaign of 1918–19, amounting in all to 85 million tons. The A.M.T.C., however, could only transport $72\frac{1}{2}$ million tons.

The demands so made were divided into four categories: coal, raw material, food and ammunition.

The Council first of all allotted 25,200,000 tons in the shape of coal supplies for France and Italy. It then allotted 7,500,000 tons to the raw

FEBRUARY 1917—NOVEMBER 1918

material essential to industry. Only 39,800,000 tons remained over for food and ammunition against a joint estimated requirement of 49 million tons.

The Council proceeded to take into account the improved yield of the harvest of 1918 as compared with that of 1917, and only allotted 22 million tons for food, and the balance of 17,800,000 tons to ammunition. It was arranged that the transport of ammunition should take place during the autumn and winter and that food should await the spring to ensure the Allied armies having the necessary material at their disposal for the offensive of March 1918.

It was no longer a question of the Allied Powers trading with neutrals and thus protecting the private interests of their traders; the very lives of these Powers were at stake, and if the French and British States had requisitioned the whole of their merchant fleets they had obviously not done so in order to convey food to Rotterdam or Stockholm.

The Results of the Blockade in 1918

We can only here give a general survey of these results, as they will be set forth in detail as regards each neutral country and Germany in the second and third parts of this work.

The following table shows the American

CONDUCT OF THE NAVAL WAR

exports to neutral countries during the last two years of the war :—

	1st July 1916 to 1st July 1917 £	1st July 1917 to 1st July 1918 £
Holland	6,400,000	1,240,000
Switzerland	4,440,000	4,200,000
Sweden	4,800,000	840,000
Norway	1,400,000	5,040,000
Spain	15,400,000	13,400,000

The second table shows the exports of European neutral countries to Germany during the last two years of the war, the figures of 1913 being also given for purposes of comparison.

	1913 £	1917 £	1918 £
Holland	113,000,000	25,280,000	12,640,000
Switzerland	12,240,000	30,840,000	17,880,000
Sweden	10,000,000	18,320,000	15,160,000
Norway	5,000,000	7,840,000	4,400,000
Denmark	10,120,000	25,360,000	15,960,000

Bearing in mind the fact that German imports in 1913 amounted to £560,000,000 it will be seen that in 1918 they only amounted to £66,000,000 apart from imports from Austria, Bulgaria, Roumania, Serbia, Turkey and Russia. We shall find, however, that the resources derived from Russia by Germany after the peace of Brest-Litovsk were very insignificant in amount, and although we are quite unable to estimate the value of the resources derived by Germany from countries allied to her or conquered territories, it must be remembered that the assistance afforded by her to her allies much exceeded the resources she received in return.

The above estimate is more or less confirmed by the receipts of the German customs, which amounted in 1914 to £34,000,000, but fell in 1918 to £6,600,000.

On the other hand an examination of the Allied statistics as regards American imports into France and Great Britain reveals the following picture :—

	1st July 1913 to 1st July 1916 £	1st July 1916 to 1st July 1917 £	1st July 1917 to 1st July 1918 £
England	118,800,000	409,200,000	399,200,000
France	30,600,000	202,200,000	176,600,000

The total of British imports which in 1913 amounted to £760,000,000 amounted in 1918 to £1,320,000,000.

The total of French imports rose from £480,000,000 in 1913 to £800,000,000 in 1918.

The weight of goods landed in French ports varied between 31 million tons in 1913, 51 million tons in 1916, 45 million tons in 1917 and 49 million tons in 1918. The only decrease that took place occurred in the case of the tonnage of ships entering French ports with cargoes of imported goods, which fell from 34 million tons displacement in 1913 to 26 million tons in 1917. This was due to the more rational use made of shipping during the war.

CONDUCT OF THE NAVAL WAR

These various figures show that in November 1918 what has been termed the blockade of Germany had become a reality, and that the Allies had acquired and retained liberty of action at sea. Many tentative methods had been employed and had added to the protracted nature of the task, but the navies of the Entente had played their twofold part successfully, in as much as by the end of the war they had secured the economic encirclement of the Central Empires and were able, in spite of the submarine war, to keep the Allied communications open with the rest of the world.

PART II

HOW THE ECONOMIC NAVAL WAR AFFECTED THE NEUTRALS

CHAPTER I

THE THREE SCANDINAVIAN COUNTRIES

I HAVE included under this heading the three countries of Sweden, which was dependent upon industry, Norway, upon the sea, and Denmark, upon agriculture—three countries, moreover, whose economic policies differed very widely during the war. They have, however, some features in common, and Germany was anxious on several occasions between 1914 and 1918 to re-establish Scandinavian unity for her own ends and use it as a diplomatic weapon against the Entente.

The three countries, drawing as they did the greater part of their coal from England, their petroleum and cotton from the United States, and fertilisers, precious metals, india-rubber and all kinds of colonial wares from overseas, were dependent to a great extent for their supplies upon the attitude of the Allies with regard to the maritime trade of neutrals. Denmark stood in a peculiar relationship to the other two countries, as large quantities of goods were landed at Copenhagen and subsequently re-exported to Norway and Sweden.

The first inter-Scandinavian Conference met at Stockholm on the 24th of October 1914 and resulted in the delivery of a joint note to the belligerents protesting against the manner in

NEUTRALS AND THE NAVAL WAR

which the Entente and the Empires were exercising their rights as belligerents at sea. The Allies vouchsafed no reply to this note, as they were unwilling to start a controversy which was bound as it proceeded to arouse feelings of solidarity among the Scandinavian states.

The three Scandinavian Kings met subsequently at Malmö and sent representatives to a conference at Copenhagen on the 20th of January 1915 to discuss the arrangements to be made for the protection of neutral shipping. Although a considerable measure of agreement was attained the divergent tendencies of the various countries became obvious as the conference proceeded. Sweden desired to secure the adoption of resolutions favourable to Germany, Denmark was apprehensive of appearing to compromise herself in the eyes of that Empire, while Norway seemed inclined to play an independent part and evinced British sympathies tempered only by the fear of finding herself excluded from the concert of Scandinavian countries and having alone to bear the brunt of Germany's resentment.

The conference at Copenhagen agreed to suggest to Great Britain that neutral shipping should be convoyed by neutral warships when crossing the North Sea.

No proposal could have been more unwelcome from the point of view of British naval policy, as ships under convoy of their flag escape to some extent from the exercise of the right to search.

SWEDEN

The wishes expressed at the Copenhagen conference were consequently not followed up, as Norway from the spring of 1915 onwards deliberately declined to have anything further to do with inter-Scandinavian union.

Scandinavian solidarity was never again displayed in the course of the war, save as regards matters of an entirely economic nature. Denmark agreed, for instance, in 1918 to supply Sweden with wheat in return for an offer by the latter to assist her industrially.

SWEDEN

Political and Economic Situation in Sweden in 1914

Geographically speaking Sweden's back was turned to the Allies : her eyes were riveted upon the Baltic, which was practically an inland sea, and, in spite of the exertions of the Russian navy and the heroic cruises of a few British submarines, never came under Allied control at any time during the war.

Sweden, thanks to her agriculture, was more or less self-supporting. Out of a total area of 45 million hectares 18 million were unproductive, 21 consisted of forest land, and only 6 were under cultivation ; her population, however, which only amounted to 20.8 inhabitants per square mile, was so scattered that she had no difficulty in maintaining a more or less even balance between the resources of the country and the food requirements of its inhabitants.

Sweden nevertheless was in the habit of importing 180,000 tons of wheat, and 70,000 tons of rye. She also had to import one-fifth of the fodder required by her cattle in the form of cake and was dependent upon Germany for her potash fertilisers.

In time of peace she obtained her coal from Great Britain and her mineral oils from the United States; Germany, however, was in a position to supply her with coal although of an inferior quality; in fact, from 1915 onwards Germany almost entirely supplanted Great Britain in the Swedish coal trade.

The means at the disposal of the Allies for putting pressure upon Sweden were, therefore, relatively ineffective; and moreover they needed help from her. They had to go very carefully, primarily because of the need for keeping in certain touch with Russia : once the Dardanelles were closed and before proper arrangements had been made at the White Sea ports—and these arrangements were never to be depended upon owing to ice and difficulties of navigation—there was no other way of sending ammunition to Russia except through Sweden.

The second reason which compelled the Allies to proceed cautiously was connected with maritime trade : the shipping which had been chartered by the Allies was obliged to use Swedish

SWEDEN

territorial waters, and especially the Kogrund passage, in order to avoid German cruisers.

Now Sweden took her neutrality very seriously and was horror-struck at the very idea of her railways carrying war material for the Allies and had established a barrage of mines in the Kogrund passage to prevent any action being committed there in defiance of international law. The result was that war material on the way from France and Great Britain to Russia accumulated at the frontier and about twenty British ships remained in the ports of the Baltic.

Negotiations between Sweden and the Allies (November 1914—February 1917)

Action of this kind was not calculated to further economic negotiations between Sweden and the Allies. These negotiations had commenced in November 1914 about the time exports from the United States to the Scandinavian countries had increased almost tenfold. Reference has been made in Part I of this book to the general circular note sent by the Allies to the neutrals on the 3rd of November 1914, in which the former declared their willingness to allow neutral shipping to proceed freely provided neutral Governments gave the two following guarantees: that they would prohibit the re-export of goods which were included in the Allied lists of contraband, and would also prohibit goods addressed to a consignee being declared 'in transit' as soon as they had been discharged, a fraudulent method frequently used by neutral importers in order to get over the prohibition to re-export.

The Swedes began by refusing to publish their customs statistics and then fell back upon dilatory tactics. By June 1915 the Allies had merely succeeded in limiting the amount of cotton imported by Sweden to 6,300 tons quarterly.

The Allied ministers at Stockholm frequently requested Sweden to add one product or another to the lists of prohibited exports. The Swedish Government, for instance, laid a partial interdict upon copper and no twisted copper wire nor copper plates exceeding 3 millimetres in thickness were allowed to leave the kingdom. The very next day Swedish manufacturers began to make nothing but drawn wire and copper plates of less than 3 millimetres in thickness: the big prices offered by Germany and the consequent profits proved irresistible.

The ministers of France and Great Britain were obliged, moreover, in the course of negotiations to bear in mind Russia's desire to remain on good terms with Sweden in the hope of thereby removing the difficulties in the way of effecting Russian imports by the Swedish railways.

This became very apparent in the *Nike* affair. The *Nike* was a Swedish steamer which was captured on the 8th of October 1915 by a British submarine while engaged in transporting magnetic iron ore from Lulea to Germany. The

SWEDEN

submarine took her prize into Reval. Great Britain demanded the application of the Order in Council of the 11th of March 1915, *i.e.* the condemnation of the cargo. Russia, on the other hand, laid stress on the fact that magnetic ore was not included in the Allied lists of contraband, and in the end secured the release of the *Nike*, a precedent which forced the submarines in the Baltic to confine their attention to such ships as carried contraband.

Moreover the British Admiralty heard, more or less about the same time, that not a single Swedish ship was leaving the Baltic without undergoing control by the German Admiralty, and that a Swedish ship was only allowed to pass through the Sound if it promised not to carry goods which were included in the German lists of contraband.

Throughout the whole of 1915 Sweden pursued the policy of including in her lists of goods debarred from transit every single kind of product which the Allies had succeeded with great trouble in persuading her to add to her lists of prohibited exports: for instance, Sweden promised the Allies not to permit any further export of the rubber which had been allowed to reach her, and when, just about that time, the Allies were anxious to send rubber to Russia, replied that this article could not be sent by her railways as she had included it in her lists of prohibited exports. The delicate nature of negotiations which these practices gave rise to is obvious.

NEUTRALS AND THE NAVAL WAR

In the spring of 1916 various Swedish merchants, at the suggestion of the Allies, endeavoured to come to a compromise. As the Swedish Government refused to sign economic agreements could not private individuals of Swedish nationality form themselves into importing syndicates and perhaps give the undertakings required by the Allies? The syndicate was in process of formation and was intended to become the Swedish branch of a group of American importers known as the ' American Overseas Corporation.' The Swedish Government got wind of the affair and secured the passage of a law forbidding Swedish subjects to make arrangements of any kind with a foreign Power which might place hindrances in the way of the free import, export or transport of goods.

This put an end to the Allied plans. Great Britain at last got angry and in May 1916 stopped all copper and mineral oils which were bound for Sweden. Her action proved effective, and on the 7th of August 1916 the quota of Swedish imports of mineral oils was fixed at 22,500 tons of petroleum and 3,000 tons of naphtha per quarter.

With the commencement of unrestricted submarine war at the beginning of 1917, the quotas of Swedish imports became automatically fixed, as Swedish merchant vessels refused to leave their ports.

From the Allies' point of view two issues only were involved at that time in the Swedish question: those of tonnage and ore. These two points

SWEDEN

were the subject of troublesome negotiations, which although carried on simultaneously must for the sake of clearness be dealt with separately.

Swedish Tonnage (1917–18)

On the 1st of January 1917 the Swedish merchant fleet consisted of 2,801 ships of a gross capacity of 1,128,000 tons, 220,000 tons of which were employed in coastal trade and 50,000 tons in trade with Germany. The Allies could count upon using one half of the remaining 800,000 tons of shipping, the balance being required to supply the needs of Sweden.

As soon as the submarine war was proclaimed the Swedish merchant fleet ceased operations and the Government of the kingdom requisitioned the whole of the stocks in the country in order to be ready for any eventuality. Moreover, the shipowners who had safely in pocket the enormous profits they had made in 1915 and 1916 were very disinclined to run the unknown risks of this novel kind of warfare; their inactivity was fostered by the refusal of the insurance companies to insure vessels proceeding from Sweden to Great Britain and by the concession of special terms to ships wishing to return home; public opinion, too, in Sweden was convinced that Great Britain would soon succumb to submarine warfare.

It took a ministerial crisis in the Ryksdag to clear up the situation; Admiral Lindemann, the new Minister of Foreign Affairs, began conversations with Great Britain in April 1917 on the

NEUTRALS AND THE NAVAL WAR

subject of the resumption of sailings. The question was full of difficulties : for if on the one hand about forty Swedish ships were detained in British ports by the British Government, which felt that if it were to allow these ships to leave it would run great risk of never seeing them again, on the other hand about twenty British ships had been held up for nearly a year in the Baltic, owing to the difficulty of getting through the well-known Kogrund passage.

An agreement was concluded in May 1917 whereby 80,000 tons of Swedish shipping were allowed to leave British ports and an equivalent amount of British ships were conducted by Swedish pilots into the North Sea. The agreement, however, was of an imperfect nature. as the remainder of the Swedish merchant fleet still refused to move and took up space in the ports of the Allies, till the latter at last had recourse to strong measures and requisitioned several Swedish ships under the law of angary, which allows belligerents under certain conditions to use neutral ships for their own purposes.

During the summer of 1917 the effect of the stoppage of imports began to be felt in Sweden : there was a shortage of cotton, phosphates and oil, and food had to be rationed, much to the popular discontent.

At the General Election of September 1917 a liberal and socialist majority was returned to the Swedish Parliament, and the Ministry of the Right, which had been presided over by Mr.

SWEDEN

Schwartz, was succeeded by one of national union under the leadership of Mr. Eden. On the 6th of December 1917 negotiators left Stockholm for London.

By the end of 1917 the shipowners could figure out what their inertia had cost them; 400,000 tons of shipping had been standing idle for 219 days on an average, entailing upon the shipping companies unremunerative expenditure to the tune of 16 million crowns and the very serious loss of the profits they had forgone in the meantime.

Negotiations went on during the first three months of 1918, the Swedish Government invariably pointing out to the Entente, whenever the latter proved intractable, how unpleasantly its interests would be affected if the Eden Ministry were to fall and be succeeded by one of the Right.

The Agreement between the Allies and Sweden was signed on the 29th of May 1918. By the first part of the Agreement Sweden was allowed to import goods of various kinds in which she was to be rationed afresh every three months: in return the Swedish Government promised to forbid the re-exportation of such goods under any circumstances whatever. The British Government agreed to deliver to Sweden 150,000 tons of coal monthly, provided that Swedish ships came and fetched it.

The second part provided that 400,000 tons of Swedish shipping were to be detailed for the service of the Allied and Associated Powers, of which half were to be used within and the remainder outside the war zone.

The remainder of the Swedish merchant fleet, amounting to about 400,000 tons, was to continue to carry supplies to Sweden, but to a large extent under Allied control. The names of such Swedish ships as had hitherto appeared on the shipping black list were removed from it.

The Question of Swedish Iron Ore

The real reason for the protracted nature of the negotiations in London was due to the presence behind the scenes of a third party to whom every single paragraph of the Agreement had been submitted by the Swedes before they signed it. The third party in question was none other than Germany, who attached the greatest importance to the Agreement, not so much on account of the articles dealing with tonnage or supplies as of Article 12, which related to iron ore. The latter was, indeed, a matter of paramount importance for Germany, as she had been cut off by the declaration of war from the iron ore of Spain, and the only country which could furnish her with ore of the kind was Sweden, who had an exporting capacity of about 5 million tons per annum. This quantity may seem unimportant in view of the fact that in peace time Germany produced 36 million tons of iron ore and had, thanks to the fortune of war, secured control of the entire output of the Briey basin. By 1916, however,

SWEDEN

she was absolutely dependent upon Swedish help, as the whole of the ore at her disposal contained a rather high percentage of phosphorus. Another metal, manganese to wit, was needed by her if this ore was to be converted into steel, and she ran out of manganese towards the end of 1916. Steel suitable for military purposes could only be manufactured from Swedish iron ore : in fact it may be said that from 1917 onwards German steel of good quality came exclusively from Sweden.

When the draft of the general agreement with the Allies was submitted to Germany by the Swedish Government in April 1918, the former raised no objection thereto provided that an invariable minimum of 3,500,000 tons of iron ore was exported, of which 750,000 tons were to be of the first category, that is to say of the finest quality. Now Article 12 of the Swedish-Allied Agreement stated precisely that Sweden was not to export more than 6 million tons of ore annually, of which Germany was to receive only $3\frac{1}{2}$ million tons, and that the balance, amounting to about 2 million tons, was to be purchased by the Allies from Sweden. At the same time, the Swedish Government credited the Allies with $6\frac{1}{4}$ million crowns monthly, with a view to facilitating their purchases.

The Agreement of the 29th of May 1918 reduced the exports of Swedish ore to Germany by about one-third as compared with the figures of 1917 ; in fact it was in reality merely a compromise between the needs of the Allies, to whom the question of tonnage was vital, and those of Germany.

Final Discussions between Sweden and the Allies

It might have been thought that a circumstantial treaty of this kind when once ratified by the Swedish Parliament, as it was upon the 17th of June 1918, would put an end to all the difficulties which since the outbreak of war had been the cause of strained relations between Sweden and the Entente. But this was by no means the case. It is true that the food position in Sweden improved in June; the daily ration of bread was raised to 180 grammes per head when it became clear that the actual shortage of corn was less than had been feared at the beginning of the year : Denmark, moreover, had a surplus of corn at its disposal and offered 15,000 tons to Sweden in a fit of Scandinavian solidarity.

The Allies, unfortunately, soon found out that Sweden was not in a position to observe strictly the terms of the Agreement of the 29th of May ; as a matter of fact, prior to negotiating with the Allies, she had treated with Germany in April 1918 and had secured deliveries of coal amounting to 150,000 tons per month. In return for this coal Sweden had undertaken to supply the Central Empires with a certain number of articles produced by her the export of which had been forbidden by the Swedish-Allied Agreement.

SWEDEN

Involved as she was in two contradictory treaties, Sweden tried to satisfy both parties ; but when the Allies at the end of August 1918 got wind of the deliveries of Swedish pyrites to Germany (25,000 tons in May, June and July 1918) they decided to present a joint note of protest.

Sweden stated that she regretted the delivery of the pyrites as the result of a private contract between a manufacturer and the German Government, and ended by admitting that she could not help it.

The United States requested to be put in possession of the Swedish trade statistics and the terms of the Swedish-German Agreement, and further stated that the Handelskommission, which centralised the importation into Sweden of any goods that were authorised by the Allies, inspired it with no confidence whatever.

These stormy debates continued up to October, when the military successes of the Allies brought about a complete revulsion of opinion in Sweden as in every other neutral country. The sale of contraband to Germany became a secondary consideration to Sweden and her whole attention was concentrated upon the happenings in the Baltic. What attitude would Finland take up with regard to the question of the Aaland Islands ? Might not Sweden be infected by the Bolshevism that had been let loose in Russia ? With the rout of the German armies would not the Allied armies become the sole defence of Europe against a contamination which would imperil not only the principles of civilisation but the profits made during the war, which peace, as the neutrals hoped, would surely consolidate?

Such were the questions asked by the Swedish public when the Allied fleets entered the Baltic.

NORWAY

Political and Economic Situation in Norway in 1914

The coastline of this power faces Great Britain, and her two national industries are fishing and navigation: the hall-mark of prosperity in Norway is not so much the possession of a ship as of carrying trade. Furthermore 71% of her 32 million hectares of soil was unproductive, 20% consisted of forest land, and only 2% was under cultivation in the South.

In spite of the low density of her population (13 inhabitants to the square mile) Norway was not self-sufficing as regards food; the produce of her fishing industry, which before the war yielded half a million tons of fish, of which four-fifths were exported, was of course an important adjunct in this respect.

But it was by means of the profits made by Norway out of the carrying trade that she was able to import corn, coal, mineral oils, and whatever else she needed. The Norwegian merchant

NORWAY

fleet consisted in 1914 of 2,100 ships of a total capacity of 2,835,000 tons ; it was larger than the combined Swedish and Dutch merchant fleets.

It can well be imagined that under these circumstances this power felt very small sympathy for the German methods of submarine warfare, and the horror felt by her at the submarine war was the more intense as Germany, who was aware that Norway was concluding importation agreements with the Entente, had given orders to her sailors to deal unsparingly with Norwegian vessels. The consequence was that the Norwegian war losses exceeded those of any other merchant fleet and amounted to 45% of her tonnage in 1914. It must be borne in mind, however, that in spite of the horror felt by the Norwegians at these dastardly outrages the country never wavered in its desire to remain neutral in every respect, which is tantamount to saying that she practically always put up with what she could not prevent.

In December 1914 Sweden, at Germany's suggestion, had endeavoured at the meeting of the three Scandinavian Kings at Malmö to form a federation of the Neutrals of Northern Europe as a weapon for possible use against the Entente. Under pressure from Great Britain, Norway, whose merchantmen could not use the North Sea without British leave, dissociated herself from this diplomatic scheme, which never came to fruition. Nevertheless, like her neighbours, she acted for a long period as go-between for American imports to the Central Empires, thanks to her geographical position, which enabled her to evade British control, as regards her land frontiers on the one hand, and her sea frontier of the Skager Rack, which British destroyers could only patrol with difficulty and at great risk, on the other. Even if the British destroyers had gone up the Skager Rack, contraband traffic could have still reached the Belts by keeping within Norwegian and Swedish territorial waters.

The Rationing of Norway

The Allies accordingly were anxious as far back as 1915 to ration Norwegian imports and, finding it impossible to deal with the Norwegian Government which was afraid of failing in its neutrality, signed agreements with a large number of importing syndicates composed of private individuals. As the latter did not find their Government authorities so easy to deal with as those of some of their neighbours, we may assume that Norwegian imports were rationed by the end of 1915.

Doubtless some export permits were granted, but, in the majority of cases, this was only done with a view to obtaining certain goods, such as sugar or dyes, from Germany in exchange, which she claimed alone to be in a position to supply.

From the beginning of 1916 the main object of the Allies was to limit definitely the export to

NORWAY

Germany of the principal products of the country, such as fish, nitrates and copper pyrites.

On the 5th of August 1916 an arrangement was made by which 85% of the products of the Norwegian fisheries was reserved for the Entente. The exports of fish to Germany, which had amounted to 146,000 tons in 1915, were to be limited, nominally, to 50,000 tons.

Under a further agreement a fixed quantity of ammonium and calcium nitrates was allotted to the Allies: it must be remembered that at certain times Norway was supplying the French powder factories with more than one-fifth of their material.

Finally the annual production of copper pyrites which amounted to 600,000 tons, was definitely apportioned between the belligerents by an Agreement dated the 28th of August 1916. The Entente was to purchase 400,000 tons annually. The balance, amounting to about 225,000 tons, was only to be allowed to be sent to Germany in exchange for articles containing an equal amount of copper. This was equivalent to a prohibition to export as Germany was short of that metal, and accordingly the Central Empires, which had obtained 211,000 tons of copper pyrites in 1915, only received 84,000 tons in 1916.

Norway and Unrestricted Submarine Warfare

Germany merely continued to get from Norway the products obtained by companies owned by

German capital, such as nickel and calcium carbide. This was the position in Norway when the unrestricted submarine war broke out.

The Norwegian merchant fleet at the time amounted to 2,560,000 tons, as her losses which up to date amounted to 382,000 tons of shipping had been made good to the extent of 110,000 tons.

Great Britain had been engaged, since the beginning of 1917, in difficult negotiations with Norway with a view to securing a complete cessation of the export of pyrites to Germany : she had even had recourse to strong measures in order to gain her point and had stopped the export of British coal to Norway.

The situation was altered by the courage of the Norwegian sailors, who alone of all the neutrals still put to sea in spite of Germany's declaration of submarine war. So vigorously indeed was war waged against them that in the first quarter of 1917 240 Norwegian ships of a total capacity of 356,000 tons were sent to the bottom.

Great Britain resumed her exports of coal to Norway and sent them across the dangerous North Sea in her own ships in order to spare Norwegian shipping too disastrous losses, and the whole of the Norwegian shipping so set free was transferred to the Atlantic and the Mediterranean.

The torpedoing of Norwegian ships and the incident of the 'bombs' which were intended to be placed on board Norwegian ships but were discovered among the luggage of a diplomatic

NORWAY

messenger at Oslo, put such a strain upon the relations between Norway and Germany that the Allies had, for a short time, to reckon with the possibility of Norway coming into the war; a rather unwelcome contingency from their point of view as the defence of the kingdom would have entailed upon them the creation of several auxiliary naval bases, which would have absorbed a greater amount of tonnage than they would have been able to supply, and as there was also a likelihood of military complications should Sweden in turn abandon her neutrality and attack her neighbour.

In point of fact Norway preferred to remain neutral. She continued to place her merchant fleet at the disposal of the Allies and made considerable profits by doing so; she also, in order not to exacerbate further her relations with Germany, endeavoured to furnish the Central Empires with supplies so far as it was in her power to do so. She accordingly supplied Germany during the first half of 1917 with 80,000 tons of pyrites, 60,000 tons of fish and 15,000 tons of calcium carbide.

Events which Led to the Conclusion of the Agreement of 30th April 1918

As soon as the United States got to know of these figures it stopped all its exports to Norway; the Allied Governments, too, in order to give America a free hand, decided on the 15th of

September to put an end to the more important agreements they had made with Norwegian associations.

The Norwegian Government informed the United States in reply that the kingdom was bound to be attacked by Germany if it ceased exporting to the Central Empires, and the discussion, carried on as it was under these conditions, threatened to become interminable.

By December 1917 the effects of the American embargo were being severely felt by Norway, and the year closed for that country under very sombre auspices. Since the commencement of the submarine war 477 ships of a total capacity of 736,000 tons had been sunk. Food, which in 1914 could have been bought for 100 crowns, now cost 228 crowns; bread, meat, sugar and coffee had to be rationed, and coal had become eight times dearer than in peace time. The Norwegian Government sent the explorer Nansen to Washington to plead its cause, and for several months he fought his case point by point with the War Trade Board.

An understanding was rapidly reached on the question of fish. The agreements with the Allies had not been observed as Germany had received 150,000 tons of fish in 1917. Norway consented to reduce her exports of fish to 48,000 tons. The Allies furthermore required Norway to forbid the export to the Central Empires of any material which could be used in war industries, and claimed also to be granted pre-emptive rights over calcium carbide, calcium nitrates and nickel.

Negotiations broke down in February. Public opinion in Norway had become more exasperated than ever against the United States owing to the requisitioning by the latter for its own needs of 480,000 tons of Norwegian shipping which were under construction in American yards. Norway was thus practically checkmated in her valiant attempt to make good the losses sustained by her in the submarine war.

Negotiations were only renewed with great difficulty owing to the deterrent effect of the threats and promises of the German Minister at Oslo. It was not until the 30th of April 1918 that her doubts were overcome under pressure from America. That day Dr. Nansen signed a Convention fixing, on the one hand, the annual amounts of corn, cake, fats, mineral oils and phosphates which were to be received by Norway and, on the other, the maximum quantities of industrial products she was to be allowed to export to Germany: among the latter the principal items were 10,000 tons of calcium carbide, 8,000 tons of calcium nitrates, 1,000 tons of zinc and 400 tons of aluminium.

Once agreement had been reached, so far as principles were concerned, the Allies spent the whole of the summer of 1918 in redrafting the various conventions which had been concluded with Norwegian associations in 1915 and 1916 and denounced ten months previously.

On the other hand, the Norwegian Government was forced to negotiate with the German Government, subsequently to the addition of the supplement to Article 55 of the German prize ordinance, in order to obtain safe conducts for ships laden with food from the United States, and so protect the latter from torpedoes. In exchange for these safe conducts Germany obtained in September 1918 a loan of 30 million crowns from Norway; she also forced the Norwegian shipowners to bind themselves contractually not to employ in the service of the Allies either the 93,000 tons of shipping which had been chartered by the Norwegian Ministry of Food, or the 164,000 tons which were employed in inter-Scandinavian trade.

As soon as the Armistice had been signed Norway, with characteristic tenacity, turned her whole attention to making good the losses sustained by her merchant fleet; she still retained in November 1918 1,745 steamers of a total capacity of 1,484,000 tons, 658 sailing-ships (292,000 tons) and 869 motor-ships (88,000 tons).

Very arduous negotiations were begun at London with a view to securing the execution of a definite amount of work by British shipyards on Norwegian account; Great Britain bound herself to build 260,000 tons of shipping annually for Norway during each of the three years following the signature of the treaty of peace. She was not, however, able to carry out her undertaking to the letter.

DENMARK

The part played by Norway during the war has now been told. It is quite true that she made a considerable profit out of her shipping up to 1917 at any rate; but the Allies have no right to forget that 835 Norwegian ships were sunk by German submarines, and that 1,162 sailors of that country lost their lives between 1914 and 1918 in ships that had been torpedoed.

DENMARK

Economic and Political Situation in Denmark in 1914

Prior to the war Denmark used to supply Great Britain with a large proportion of her agricultural produce in the shape of ham, butter and eggs. As soon as the war broke out, Germany, who was to prove a very unpleasant neighbour, endeavoured to divert to herself the whole of the agricultural produce of Denmark, for which, moreover, she was prepared to pay very high prices. Denmark, accordingly, began to provide Germany with food and, like her Scandinavian neighbours, imported from the United States for re-sale to the Central Empires everything that the Allies allowed to come through.

The soil of Denmark is distributed between the various branches of agriculture in a proportion similar to that of the Netherlands, more than one half of the land under cultivation being devoted to cattle breeding; but whereas the Netherlands have 280 inhabitants to the square mile Denmark has only 120, and accordingly not only possesses large resources in food for her home population but is in a position to export agricultural produce in abundance. Before the war Denmark consumed 220,000 tons of meat annually and exported 200,000 tons. She also exported 24,000 tons of butter out of a total production of 117,000 tons. She imported 390,000 tons of corn, in spite of a home production which amounted to 540,000 tons, but this she did with a view mainly to ensuring the prosperity of her cattle breeding industry. She also imported a fifth of her fodder with the same object. 69% of surplus agricultural produce was exported to Great Britain in peace time and 31% to Germany.

In the light of these facts the extent of the profits made by her agricultural industry during the early years of the war may well be imagined. Her merchant fleet was another source of gain to her. It consisted in 1914 of about 750,000 tons of steam-ships, 100,000 tons of motor-ships, and 140,000 tons of sailing-ships, and the profits realised by this industry between the 1st of August 1914 and the 31st of December 1916 amounted to £21,080,000 and yielded an annual dividend of 35%. She also carried on a very extensive transit trade.

DENMARK

The Rationing of Danish Imports

It was the latter of these industries that the Allies were most successful in regulating. Their attention had been drawn not only to the abnormal increase in Danish imports but to acts of contraband of a definite nature. A Danish steamer, the *Skjolborg*, for instance, was found to have left Baltimore with a cargo of wheat and two sets of papers, the first of which gave Frederikshavn in Denmark as her port of destination and the second the German port of Lübeck. Thanks to her first set of papers this steamer succeeded in reaching Frederikshavn safely and after stopping there 48 hours proceeded to Lübeck, where she discharged her cargo. The incident became the subject of a good deal of comment, public indignation was aroused and the Danish Government compelled to order an inquiry, which resulted in a compromise. The shipowner paid a fine of 10,000 crowns, but must have made 200,000 crowns by the sale of his wheat at Lübeck.

Contraband trade also assumed another form. A Danish shipper was anxious to carry some corn from New York to Stettin. He chartered a steamer called the *Ruby* which sailed from New York with Copenhagen as her official destination. The shipowner sent telegraphic orders to her to put in at the Norwegian port of Stavanger : when she got there she received fresh orders not to call at Copenhagen but to proceed directly to Stettin. The captain, being an honest man, disregarded these directions and as his papers required him to proceed to Copenhagen he did so. The Danish Government was absolutely forced to confiscate the cargo of wheat but refused to impose any further penalty.

As soon as the French and British Ministers at Copenhagen were informed of facts of this kind they made their protest to Mr. de Scavenius, the Minister of Foreign Affairs; such protests however were rarely effective. Importers of French and British goods into Denmark were required to give an undertaking not to re-export them: this undertaking, however, was not upheld by the Danish courts and was, consequently, not invariably observed.

In order to clear Danish trade from the suspicions it had aroused in the belligerent countries the 'Association of Notable Traders of Copenhagen,' which was an institution corresponding to our Chamber of Commerce, undertook at the end of 1915 to give security for such Danish firms as would undertake not to re-export and to compel the latter to pay a large fine should they fail to observe their undertakings. Thus a contract between Danes was substituted for the earlier contracts between Danes and foreigners. Great Britain gave her consent and on the 17th of November 1915 signed an Agreement with the Association of Notable Traders of Copenhagen and with the Chamber of Danish Manufacturers.

On the 16th of March 1916 France followed suit.

DENMARK

These Agreements were extremely complicated as they applied not only to the consignment of goods but to a certain number of products, such as cotton, wool, sulphur, phosphates, pyrites, cake, &c., quotas for which had to be fixed. The rationing of Danish imports, moreover, was no easy matter. In the case of each product the quantity necessary for home consumption had to be determined. Due allowance had also to be made for the fact that by virtue of her geographical position Denmark played the part of a broker between countries overseas and the two other Scandinavian kingdoms, and the quota had therefore to be increased accordingly. Denmark then asked for a further increase to enable her to exchange the goods so acquired with Germany and obtain dyes or drugs in return. She also, in some cases, asked for yet another increase in order to meet the requirements of her converting industries and particularly of her breweries.

Denmark, it will be seen, was very generously treated with regard to the quotas. The consideration which Great Britain, moreover, was alone in showing her did not in any way put a stop to contraband. Hardly a day passed without some scandal either great or small being brought to light: on one occasion rubber was discovered hidden in herring barrels; on another food, the export of which had been prohibited, was sent across the German frontier with the complicity of a Danish station-master; and German sailing vessels used mysteriously to take on board cargoes of tin and oleaginous grain in a Danish port on the Jutland coast without being interfered with. When the Allies threatened to become seriously annoyed Germany would display feverish activity all along the Danish frontier, construct trenches, build railways, and spread abroad reports of an intended British landing on the coast of Jutland. The Danish Government was thus in a position to play off the German danger against the British and the British danger against the Germans.

If the official figures are accepted as correct, and they are certainly very far from representing the facts, it will be seen that under cover of these manœuvres Danish exports to Germany increased in value from 178 million crowns in 1913 to 300 millions in 1914, 487 millions in 1915, and 690 millions in 1916, whereas Danish exports to Great Britain underwent the reverse process and fell from 410 millions in 1913 and 431 millions in 1914, to 385 millions in 1915 and 351 millions in 1916.

The figures of the Danish exports to Great Britain would have fallen still further but for the constant fear of famine on the part of the latter, which caused her to have a clause inserted in every quota agreement under which a considerable proportion of Danish agricultural produce and half the produce of the Danish fisheries were reserved to her.

Even so Great Britain only took 31% of the Danish agricultural exports in 1916, whereas in

DENMARK

1913 she had taken 69% of them, and Great Britain's loss was Germany's gain. That being so, Denmark's sole object when the submarine war broke out in February 1917 was to preserve her neutrality.

Denmark and Unrestricted Submarine Warfare

The Danish Government weighed up the risks it was incurring : it was very unlikely that Great Britain would land troops, whereas it had every reason to believe that an invasion of Schleswig on the part of Germany was impending, as a big concentration of troops on the Danish frontier had taken place in February 1917. Since 1864, moreover, the kingdom had lived in fear of its redoubtable enemy, who tried by means of her usual methods of economic penetration to lay hands upon the Belts which were the keys of the Baltic, and the irredentist Danish associations received very moderate encouragement from their former fatherland in their endeavours to keep German Schleswig faithful to it.

The Danish ships, like those of Sweden, refused to leave harbour in February 1917 ; the immediate result of this game was to put a complete stop to the export of butter and bacon to Great Britain ; the entire agricultural produce of Denmark went to Germany and contraband trade was carried on to such an extent that for some months the Danish German frontier ceased to exist. It may be taken that during the month of February

1917 Denmark supplied our enemies with a million rations of meat per diem.

The British Government, which was still anxious to receive the agricultural produce it had been promised, seemed inclined to exhaust every means of conciliation; after having exercised its rights of angary over some Danish ships in full agreement with their owners it could not do less than stop Denmark's supplies of coal. In April 1917 the Danish Government, finding that its stocks of coal were getting low, decided to send negotiators to London.

Negotiations between Denmark and the Allies in 1917

The negotiations bore upon four points :—(1) the export of agricultural produce to Great Britain; (2) the Danish imports of corn, fodder and fats; (3) the distribution of the products of the Danish fisheries; (4) the supply of British coal to Denmark, which was closely connected with the question of Danish tonnage.

It was impossible to come to an agreement as to the first two points : the Danish negotiators refused to restrict their exports of cattle to the Central Empires.

An agreement as to the third point was reached in September : the Danish exports of fish to Germany were not to exceed 25,000 tons, but in return Great Britain was to supply the fishermen with the mineral oils necessary for their industry.

DENMARK

" What a funny agreement," a certain Frenchman observed, " which places at the disposal of the Danes the petroleum they need in order to send fish to Germany ! " " The agreement is unavoidable," replied the British authorities. " If we don't supply the Danish fishermen with petroleum, Germany who controls the wells in Galicia and Roumania will supply them with it, and so gain command of the Danish market in that respect." This was only another instance of the impossibility of reconciling the legal and commercial conception of the blockade.

The fourth point was settled in the following manner : Denmark was to allow the Allies to charter 200,000 tons of her shipping and Great Britain in return was to supply Denmark with 100,000 tons of coal monthly.

The Danish Government then applied to Germany and the United States.

The negotiations with Germany led to the Agreement of the 8th of December 1917 : Germany undertook to provide 100,000 tons of coal and 4,000 tons of steel monthly, and Denmark was to continue, as heretofore, to export her agricultural produce to the Central Empires.

Negotiations between Denmark and the United States in 1918

The negotiations with the United States however dragged on for a long time. The United States was anxious in the first place to ration Danish imports, then to limit Danish exports to

Germany, and lastly to secure the transfer of 300,000 tons of shipping. This latter claim was the rock upon which negotiations split, as Germany declared that she would consider a further cession of 300,000 tons to the Entente as incompatible with Danish neutrality.

Denmark accordingly went back to the United States and stated that she was forced by her requirements in the way of supplies to retain 450,000 tons of shipping, which meant that only 190,000 tons would be left over for the United States. The statement with regard to tonnage was contained in a note addressed to Washington on the 29th of December in which the economic situation in Denmark was dealt with in all its aspects. The note was couched in rather sharp language: the Danish Government began by requesting that any imports it needed should be let through and then made the Entente entirely responsible for its exports of agricultural produce to the Central Empires. The farmers could no longer feed their cattle owing to the stoppage of cake and maize, and were being forced to sell them to Germany.

The Danish press was getting irritated. When on New Year's Day, 1918, the British allowed a ship to arrive at Copenhagen laden with what they called a Christmas present for the neutrals, to wit 5,000 tons of rice, tea, pepper and cocoa, the Danes consumed the present but omitted to thank Great Britain, who was very annoyed in consequence.

DENMARK

The year 1918 commenced therefore under unfortunate auspices. The Allies had decided to remain inexorable knowing full well that the cattle exports to Germany were bound to diminish as Denmark was no longer getting either fodder or fertilisers. Denmark on the other hand persisted in her refusal to give way as she knew she had enough corn to last her till the next harvest and reckoned that her obstinacy would keep Germany well disposed towards her.

By the beginning of 1918, however, Denmark was feeling the effects of the embargo : butter and coffee had to be rationed, the stock of fertilisers was inventoried, and maximum prices were fixed for milk and sugar. Mineral oils too were scarce, and only one litre of paraffin was allowed to each Danish family for the month of January.

The note sent by the United States on the 17th January 1918 in reply to the regrettable memorandum of the 29th December 1917, gave no sign of any change in its attitude.

Denmark, at the suggestion of Germany, replied on the 21st of February in a further memorandum which met with as ill a reception as that of the previous 29th of December. " The United States' note relative to the figures of the Danish quota would of course be taken into consideration, but the figures put forward appeared to the Danish Government to be so low that there certainly must be some telegraphic error ; obviously 5,000 tons of mineral oils were meant and not 50, and similarly the United States must surely have meant to write 3,000 tons of rice instead of 300."

Having delivered itself of this preface the Danish Government agreed to restrict to some extent its agricultural exports to the Central Empires; but in exchange for these concessions, which it qualified as " very considerable," it demanded the immediate dispatch of nitrate from Chili on the grounds as usual that the impoverished condition of the Danish soil was responsible for the cattle exports.

Lastly, Denmark offered the Allies 50,000 tons more shipping than in December, an offer which still fell short by 60,000 tons of the demands of the United States.

The latter declared the Danish proposals to be unacceptable; spring was coming on and there was no merit on the part of Denmark in proposing to restrict her exports of livestock, as her farmers could leave their beasts out at grass and were much less anxious to sell them than during the winter.

A census of cattle was carried out in April 1918 which showed that the number of horned beasts had fallen since the 1st of July 1917 from 2,458,000 to 2,142,000, that horses had decreased from 572,000 to 511,000, and swine from 789,000 to 513,000.

The Danish Government then proposed to the United States to deal with the various problems *seriatim* and begin by settling the various agricultural questions and then come to a friendly

DENMARK

agreement on the question of tonnage. The Allies, for instance, could agree with the owners to charter Danish ships for a single voyage; this the owners were entitled legally to do without applying for leave to the Government. The arrangements thus made between the Allies and owners could be renewed for each successive voyage and kept secret so as to avoid incurring the anger of the German Government.

The United States turned a deaf ear to these crafty proposals; there was no question that secret chartering of this kind would soon have come to the knowledge of Germany.

The Allies were on the point of wondering if they would not have to requisition the entire Danish merchant fleet under the law of angary when the Danish Government resumed negotiations in July 1918, and this time admitted that it was anxious to conclude an agreement.

The Agreement of 18th September 1918

Thus after eighteen months of tergiversations a general agreement was concluded between the Allies and Denmark on the 18th of September. It contained, in the first place, a complete list of the imports to which she was entitled, which amounted in all to 352,890 metric tons. Then came the agreement as to tonnage: the United States had demanded 300,000 tons when negotiations first began: it secured 285,000 tons of shipping which were to be chartered at the rate of $10 75c. per ton in the so-called danger zones, and $8 50c. elsewhere. Denmark was to retain 340,000 tons for her own needs.

The third part of the agreement fixed a maximum quota for Danish exports to Germany, consisting of 400 tons of farm produce per week from September to April and 600 tons from May to August, and of 226,000 head of cattle and 30,000 horses a year. It was also stated in one of the schedules that the Agreement of the 18th of September was to be substituted for the Anglo-Danish Agreement as to tonnage and coal of the 20th of June 1917.

The Agreement was approved by the French Cabinet on the 15th of October.

Too little time was to elapse to enable an opinion to be formed as to its real value, but even so the Armistice was not concluded in time to prevent further friction between the Allies and Denmark. The latter was anxious to make good the losses sustained by her merchant fleet in the submarine war at the earliest possible moment, and accordingly the Danish yards began the construction of about 100,000 tons of shipping in 1918, and imported a considerable amount of Swedish iron. For iron plates and timber however they were entirely dependent upon Germany. Nevertheless, in order to receive iron from Germany the builders had to deposit with the central office of the Dansk-Jern, which acted so to speak as commercial agent for Germany, a declaration whereby they undertook not to commission the

DENMARK

ships which were under construction till the end of the war. They further bound themselves by the same declaration to recognise the German courts as competent in the event of any disagreement between themselves and Germany.

As soon as the Allied Ministers got to know of this latter clause they handed a note to the Danish Government on the 26th of October 1918 in which they requested further information as to this act of interference on the part of a foreign country in Danish affairs. Victory intervened before they could receive a reply.

The effects of the economic war are shown very clearly by the statistics of trade between Great Britain and Denmark. We will confine ourselves to giving the following figures, which can only be appreciated really if the fluctuations in prices between 1914 and 1918 are taken into account.

In 1913 the Danish exports to England amounted to £22,960,000, but had fallen by 1918 to £4,040,000.

The variations of the Allied policy of blockade are faithfully reflected in the curve of British exports to Denmark.

	£
1913	5,800,000
1914	6,000,000
1915	7,800,000
1916	11,400,000
1917	6,800,000
1918	3,300,000

These exports may be compared with advantage

NEUTRALS AND THE NAVAL WAR

with the French and American exports to Denmark during the same period.

	France £	United States £
1913	1,160,000	4,800,000
1914	920,000	5,240,000
1915	720,000	17,400,000
1916	1,040,000	17,520,000
1917	720,000	2,040,000
1918	240,000	

CHAPTER II

THE NETHERLANDS

Economic Situation in the Netherlands in 1914

HOLLAND was very differently situated from the other neutrals by reason not only of her financial influence and her geographical position at the mouth of the Rhine valley, but also of her commercial importance and the riches of her East and West Indian colonies. Her main line of business was the re-export trade : she imported iron and steel to the value of £24,000,000 and re-exported two-thirds of it ; she imported tin to the value of £1,400,000 from her colonies and re-exported nearly all of it ; her imports of copper amounted in value to £12,000,000 and she retained hardly one-tenth of them.

Her own staple industry was that of cattle breeding, the produce of which she exported to Great Britain and Germany, and to this extent she resembled Denmark. Unlike Denmark, however, the density of her population was so great that sufficient corn could not be produced at home to meet the needs of the country.

She was dependent upon the neighbouring basin of the Ruhr for her supplies of minerals, with which she was ill provided at home : but in respect of corn, fertilisers, concentrated fodder and mineral oils on the other hand, she was at the mercy of the Allies.

First Attempts to Control Dutch Imports

Holland, as we have seen, had refused as far back as August 1914, on the strength of her duties as a neutral and of the Rhine Convention of 1868, to hinder the transit of corn through her territory, and her refusal had been the origin of the very important modifications made by the Allies in the application of the Declaration of London.

Although the Dutch Government published a list of prohibited exports on the 20th of August 1914 it did not do so to oblige the Allies but solely to make sure that it would have sufficient food to meet the needs of the inhabitants of the kingdom till what it was pleased to call ' the crisis ' was over. The Government defined its attitude in the following terms : " The observance of an attitude of strict neutrality means that no exceptional measures will be enforced with regard to either of the two parties in the conflict."

It was in this spirit that the Government of the Netherlands acted when it agreed in September to import ' to order of itself ' (in other words to give the Allies a guarantee against re-export) certain indispensable articles such as corn, copper and petroleum.

THE NETHERLANDS

When Sir Edward Grey proposed to allow the other products included in the list of conditional contraband to be imported under a similar guarantee of the Government of the Netherlands he met with a refusal. The Government of H.M. the Queen was apprehensive of failing in its duties as a neutral if it gave the guarantee demanded of it. With a view, however, to protecting the interests of its merchants and importers it suggested that agreement might be attained if the importers were to form themselves into syndicates which could give the guarantee without let or hindrance from the Dutch Government.

Creation of the N.O.T.

Neutrals were accordingly to be allowed for the first time to keep a check on themselves, a solution of the difficulty which was at once agreed to by the British Government. A syndicate was formed in December 1914 under the name of the 'Netherlands Overseas Trust,' which was soon to be known invariably in diplomatic correspondence by its initials as the N.O.T.

The agreement between the French and British Governments and the N.O.T. was signed on the 27th of December 1914, and the Dutch Government signified its approval only two days later. By the terms of this agreement contraband goods of every kind, with the exception of corn, copper and petroleum, which we have already dealt with, were allowed to enter Holland provided they were consigned to the N.O.T., the members of which bound themselves, under security, not to re-export them.

It seemed, however, inadvisable to the Allies, credulous though they were, to let the N.O.T. function without any check upon its activities, and accordingly Sir Francis Oppenheimer, the British commercial attaché at the Hague, was appointed controller on behalf of France and Great Britain jointly.

As a mark of their privileged position and in order to avoid interference by cruisers, ships carrying goods consigned to the N.O.T. carried at the masthead a cone 6 feet high and 4 feet wide. This system of consignment to the N.O.T. appeared so attractive to the Allies that in April 1915 they allowed it to be extended to copper and petroleum : wheat and wheaten goods alone continued to be consigned to the Government of the Netherlands.

Although the Allies were under no misapprehension as to the absolute good faith of the managers of the N.O.T., they saw by the summer of 1915 that the guarantee of 'internal consumption' given by the Trust still left open a number of loopholes for Dutch exports. Indeed, the expression 'internal consumption' applied not only to the Dutch colonies but to any other neutral European country. The Trust was not only furnishing Holland with supplies in accordance with its Statutes, but was exporting food in many cases to Switzerland and Denmark.

THE NETHERLANDS

A ton of copper or india-rubber inside a cone 6 feet high could be forwarded to Basle with impunity : sometimes it reached its destination.

The Allies were assailed with doubts. Great Britain, who had already once modified the Convention of the 27th of December 1914 with the consent of the N.O.T. on the 11th April 1915, in order to bring it into line with the Order in Council of the 11th of March, decided to subject it to a thorough revision and concluded a new agreement with the N.O.T. on the 19th of July. She succeeded in securing the prohibition of any further re-exports of food, fodder, leather and hides to neutral countries. Other raw material could be re-exported provided it did not pass through enemy territory. The N.O.T. further promised to do its best to prevent its imports of raw materials exceeding the normal Dutch consumption, and by so doing opened the door to the quota system.

France refused to sign the Agreement of the 19th of July in its original form, as she felt it to be unduly lax. She concluded a new Convention with the N.O.T. on the 7th of December, by which petroleum, metals and cotton were added to the list of products that were not to be exported to other neutral states, and the Trust was compelled to keep a check upon the products of the Dutch East Indies, which up till then had not been subjected to any control whatever. Finally the Agreement provided for the rationing of Holland, which must now be dealt with.

NEUTRALS AND THE NAVAL WAR

The Rationing of Holland

Holland had imported a considerable quantity of goods in 1915 under cover of the N.O.T., the greater part of which, in spite of the control exercised by the Trust, had been sent to Germany. The favourite tricks of the smugglers were to alter or break up consignments and to hold fictitious sales, but they had innumerable others at their command. We must remind our readers, in explanation of the term 'fictitious sales,' that the N.O.T. was not required by its rules to continue to exercise control of imported goods after the latter had changed hands a certain number of times. Goods which had thus been sold several times became assimilated to the national produce and crossed the frontier in defiance of the N.O.T. which could only at the best inflict penalties, in the shape of fines, immediate payment of which was not usually required. By this means the Trust made itself the protector of Dutch trade and became a sort of economic state within the political state of Holland.

The French R. Committee, which for some months had been in favour of rationing imports into Holland, stated in September 1915 that it was impossible to settle the quota with the N.O.T., which would have been both judge and party in the same cause. M. Allizé, our Minister at the Hague, thought otherwise : the Trust was extending its operations, the staff had risen from five employees in January 1915 to 600 in

THE NETHERLANDS

September of the same year, and it was bound to gain in authority as time went on.

Great Britain went ahead and took advantage of the presence of M. van Vollenhoven, the chairman of the Trust, in London, to discuss the conditions which were to form the basis of agreement. Preliminary tables were drawn up in London specifying the quantities in metric tons of maize, rye, oleaginous grain, oil, petroleum, and raw wool that Holland was to be allowed to import each quarter. These tables, which formed the original quota agreement, were communicated to the R. Committee with a request for its observations upon them.

The Committee had two criticisms to make. It objected in the first place to the unduly small number of products that had been rationed and the rough and ready way they had been designated. " Since the beginning of the war," the R. Committee said, " the Dutch have displayed such ingenuity in cheating and have practised methods of substitution on such a large scale with a view to outwitting the Allies or to deceiving their own Customs that precautions must be taken. They are much too clever at substituting kapok, which contains more explosive matter, for cotton waste, and solidified linseed oil for the liquid oil, for us to be satisfied with so simple a system of nomenclature."

It took exception in the second place to the manner in which the quotas were allotted; it was urged that the British and French Governments should come to an understanding on this point as soon as the quotas had been fixed, otherwise the British restrictions would put an end to French trade. For instance, " from January to September 1913 France had supplied Holland with 5,998 tons of cocoa beans and Great Britain had supplied her with 8,060. During the same period of 1915 France had supplied Holland with 57 tons and Great Britain 18,425. For months previously Holland had only been getting British tyres, and when the French Government gave permission for the export of two train loads of Michelin tyres, provided they were consigned to the Trust, British cruisers had stopped them."

The grievances thus set forth by the R. Committee remained a dead letter, as no inter-Allied organisation existed at the time which could insist upon attention being paid to them. The British Government recognised, however, that its original quota agreement was susceptible of improvement and in March 1916 rationed cocoa, rice, tin ore and leather.

Complaints were made in France with regard to various articles. The British Government had forced the Dutch to agree to take 104,000 tons, or 80% of the annual quota, of rice from British India : in this rather cavalier way rice from Indo-China was excluded from the market in direct violation of the principle of the quota and of liberty of transactions. It also appeared to the French oil manufacturers that the quota

THE NETHERLANDS

of 200,000 tons of oleaginous grain that had been assigned to Holland was unnecessarily large.

The question of the quota of coffee also gave rise to endless discussions; first of all because the Dutch consumed it in considerable quantities (their annual *per capita* consumption exceeded 7 kilograms) and secondly because it was produced in their colonies and coffee from the colonies was not controlled by the Trust. The British Government proposed to fix the quota of coffee at 72,000 tons of foreign and 24,000 tons of Dutch colonial coffee. The R. Committee insisted that these amounts should be reduced to 43,200 and 23,040 tons respectively, or to 154% of the normal peace time consumption. A proof of the generous scale upon which these quotas were calculated.

By the end of 1916 the number of products imported into Holland under the quota system amounted to twenty-seven.

Purchase by the Allies of the Agricultural Produce of Holland

These various questions arising out of the quota system, difficult as they already were, became still more complicated in 1916 when Great Britain started negotiations with a view to obtaining half of the Dutch agricultural produce. In March 1916 the British Government had become very disagreeably impressed by the amount of meat and farm produce of Dutch origin which was entering Germany. It communicated this impression to the French Government in a note the tone of which betrayed a certain amount of embarrassment :—

"Holland is importing considerable quantities of fodder which is not re-exported directly to Germany but is used to produce meat, butter and cheese, the greater part of which goes to our enemies. . . . The problem of ascertaining the amount of fodder which is strictly necessary to supply the needs of the Dutch population in meat, milk and butter, without allowing for any exports, has hitherto been considered too involved to allow of our asking the Prize Court to condemn a cargo of fodder solely because it forms part of the food of an animal which at some time or other may perhaps be sent to Germany in the shape of meat."

What was then to be done? A mathematical solution of the problem was ready to hand. The agricultural produce of Holland in peace time was estimated at 200,000 tons of meat and 2,704,000 tons of milk; of the latter 46% and 44% of the former was exported. Roughly speaking 1,000 tons of agricultural produce could be taken as the equivalent of 3,000 tons of fodder. The mathematical solution would, therefore, have been to reduce the quota of fodder which was allowed to enter Holland by 40%. This, however, would have entailed a rise in the price of Dutch fodder, farmers would have killed their cattle, and Germany would have obtained meat

THE NETHERLANDS

for the next few months in considerable quantities.

The British Government rejected this solution and proposed to the French Government to leave the quota of fodder untouched and to buy a part of the Dutch farm produce on behalf of the Allies.

France had an agricultural industry of her own and therefore did not receive this proposal with much enthusiasm; she was not in need of Dutch farm produce, and furthermore was apprehensive of Great Britain getting into the habit of buying from Holland the butter and milk with which France had supplied her hitherto. The R. Committee assented, however, in principle, and Great Britain was asked to carry the transaction through independently, it being understood that she was to hand over subsequently to France whatever might be due to the latter.

Accordingly it was arranged as a result of negotiations between the British and Dutch syndicates that the Dutch agricultural produce should be purchased at a price which was higher than that obtaining in the home market but lower than that received by exporters to the Central Empires. Under the agreement which was signed on the 1st of November 1916, from 25–50% of the surplus agricultural produce of every kind which was available for export was reserved for Great Britain. The balance was exported to Germany, which supplied the Netherlands, in exchange, with 350,000 tons of coal monthly.

NEUTRALS AND THE NAVAL WAR

Consignments of the Dutch Government

One other economic question was to disturb the relations between Holland and the Entente in 1916. The Dutch Government, as we have seen, had reserved to itself the sole right of importing certain indispensable products as far back as August 1914, and had subsequently assigned its rights to the Trust in respect of copper and petroleum and had only retained the monopoly of corn imports. In the course of 1916, however, the Queen's Government claimed the right of importing a certain number of other products and of avoiding any control by the Allied fleets by the mere offer of an unofficial guarantee to the Allies that these products would not be re-exported.

A claim of this kind, in the opinion of the French law officers, could have been allowed if it had referred solely to articles which could only be used by the state, such as war material or coinage. The Dutch Government, however, meant to apply the system not only to corn but also to certain metals and to fertilisers.

On the 10th of March 1916 a decree was published in the Dutch Official Gazette under which maize, barley, oats and cake were only to be consigned to the Government, and the Trust was forbidden to accept consignments in respect of these various products.

This one-sided decision was a direct infringement of the charter of the N.O.T. " The state,"

THE NETHERLANDS

so the R. Committee pointed out, " can either act as the national authority when it takes executive action, or as a party in administrative law when it acts administratively. Now the chartering of ships or the purchase of materials to meet the needs of one of the many services of which states nowadays have undertaken the management and which have increased in number since the war began, the importation of wares into a country to prevent famine or to regulate prices, are administrative acts; and the state under circumstances such as these is subject to the jurisdiction of the courts like any private individual. There is nothing which renders the state independent of the conditions imposed by that belligerent which has the command of the sea."

Negotiations were begun on the subject between Holland and the Allies, and thanks to the firmness displayed by the latter an official Agreement was concluded on the 19th of August 1916. Corn was in future, as in the past, to be consigned to the Dutch Government alone; but it was understood that the Government of the Hague, acting through the Trust, would inform the Allies of the amount of corn required for home consumption by the Netherlands and so enable a quota to be fixed. Imports of fodder and cake were to be consigned in equal quantities to the Government of the Netherlands and the Trust, but were only to be distributed by the latter: by the adoption of this procedure the principle of the quota was maintained intact. In con-conclusion the Dutch Government undertook, in giving its orders, to select its contractors overseas from a list to be drawn up by the Allies.

Such in its main outlines was the economic system which prevailed in the Netherlands at the beginning of 1917 : and a very profitable one it was too for farmers, shipowners and merchants who were engaged in the re-export business.

Holland and Unrestricted Submarine Warfare

The Dutch merchant fleet continued to carry on its trade as 'the waggoner of the seas.' Only one-tenth of its ships had been chartered by the Entente and those at rates which were very advantageous to the Nether-land companies.

The action taken by the Allies began, however, to bear fruit. Germany soon became conscious of the fact when she found the Dutch trade becoming month by month less valuable from the point of view of her food supplies. As usual she became abusive and let it be known that it would very much suit her convenience to lay violent hands upon the Dutch stocks that were still in being, and to occupy the mouth of the Scheldt before beginning unrestricted submarine war.

In view of this aggressive attitude Holland

THE NETHERLANDS

sought to give her redoubtable neighbour a proof of her good will, and as at the time she was having trouble with Great Britain on the question of permitting Allied merchant ships which were armed for defence to enter her territorial waters, allowed negotiations to drag on.

The British Government at length lost patience and resolved to take strong measures, for which the hostile attitude of the Dutch Government with regard to the chartering of its merchantmen by the Allies afforded a very good pretext. It accordingly informed the Hague on the 29th of January 1917 that if permission was not given for a portion of the Dutch merchant fleet to be employed by the Entente it would stop all exports of coal to Dutch ports. Holland it may be mentioned imported 220,000 tons of coal monthly from Great Britain in addition to the 350,000 tons she received from Germany.

Notwithstanding this threat not a single Dutch ship would put to sea and enter the forbidden zone when unrestricted submarine war was declared three days later. In consequence exports of agricultural produce to Great Britain ceased entirely.

An incident then occurred which rendered the position still more serious. Six Dutch ships which had left Falmouth for Holland on the 22nd of February, on receipt of an assurance from the German Government that they could return home unmolested, were torpedoed that very day off the Scilly Islands. Months of negotiations were needed to induce Germany to sell six German steamers, which had taken refuge in the Dutch East Indies, to replace the ships thus sunk. The only result of the torpedoing of these six ships was to confirm the Dutch shipowners in their attitude of inertia.

Great Britain was as anxious to get butter from Holland as she was to use the Dutch fleet and made very marked advances to the Government of the Netherlands : she even went so far as to allow Dutch ships to be searched outside the danger zone at Kingston, Freetown and Alexandria. Still the Dutch merchant fleet declined to move, and trade would have been at a standstill in the port of Rotterdam but for the arrival in May of some German ships which came to load coal for Hamburg and the Scandinavian countries in order to relieve as far as possible the congestion on the German railways.

A raid by British destroyers which captured four of these enemy ships put an end to this trade during the summer of 1917, and the whole of the maritime trade between Germany and Holland was carried on subsequently through the port of Delfzyl at the mouth of the Ems.

Dutch Negotiations with the Belligerents

The treaty which ensured Holland receiving 350,000 tons of German coal each month was about to expire on the 30th of July 1917. It was a serious matter for the Government of the

THE NETHERLANDS

Netherlands, which was already deprived of British coal.

The Germans took advantage of its plight to raise their demands, and insisted upon being granted large credits in florins and increased deliveries of cattle. So severe were the conditions imposed by Germany that negotiations were broken off on the 10th of September.

In the meantime stocks in general in the Netherlands were falling very low and those of corn in particular. The Dutch consumption of corn amounted to 3 million tons, 2 millions of which were imported. There could be no question that shortage of food would prevent the country holding out after the first few months of 1918.

All this while forty-two Dutch ships laden with 194,000 tons of corn and cake were lying in the ports of the United States awaiting orders to sail.

In August 1917 the Government of the Netherlands thought it as well to apply to Great Britain again. An agreement between London and the Hague was drawn up in outline : Great Britain was to supply Holland with 180,000 tons of coal monthly in return for a given amount of tonnage which was to be placed at the disposal of the Allies.

As soon as Germany got wind of these proposals she decided to resume the negotiations which had been broken off with Holland, and a German-Dutch agreement was signed on the 6th of October by which the Netherlands were guaranteed monthly deliveries of 250,000 tons of coal and 20,000 tons of iron ore.

Great Britain in disgust brought increased pressure to bear upon Holland, and on the 12th of October succeeded in inducing the United States to refuse bunker coal to vessels proceeding to neutral ports in Europe : by this means practically all intercourse was severed between Holland and her colonies.

A very lively exchange of notes took place on the subject of the law of angary which had been put into force by the British Government in June 1917 with regard to eight Dutch ships which had refused to put to sea, Holland declaring that by an article of the Queen's Regulations of 1899 Great Britain had given up her claim to exercise the rights of angary.

Further and still sharper notes were exchanged on the subject of the transport of German sand and gravel by the Dutch canals to the Belgian front. During the whole of the previous year Great Britain had been protesting against this traffic, which she held to be incompatible with neutrality, seeing that the gravel was meant to be used for military purposes. Three million tons of gravel had thus reached Belgium from Germany during the first seven months of 1917. Holland replied that the gravel was not meant to be used in the trenches but solely for the upkeep of the Belgian roads.

In the middle of October Great Britain, by way

THE NETHERLANDS

of protest, stopped all telegraphic communication by cable between Holland and countries overseas.

While these diplomatic storms were raging a fresh attempt was made to come to an agreement with the United States. The latter declared its willingness to supply Holland with food provided she agreed not to further German interests directly or indirectly. Furthermore, the Dutch Government undertook to hand over to the Allies a portion of its tonnage that was standing idle, which was to be employed outside the danger zone to carry corn from the Argentine and sugar from Java.

An agreement seemed likely upon this basis. Dutch delegates were sent to London in November 1917, but being unprovided with full powers could only take back a draft agreement to the Hague on the 24th of December, for ratification by their Government. The Government decided to submit the draft to Germany for her approval. The latter naturally declined to approve of an agreement which reduced the export of agricultural produce from Holland in a manner detrimental to herself and placed a portion of the Dutch merchant fleet at the disposal of her enemies.

Holland wavered again : her stocks of wheat, however, were getting so low that famine was impending in the near future. She therefore requested the Allied Powers on the 22nd of February 1918 to advance her 100,000 tons of her wheat quota for 1918.

NEUTRALS AND THE NAVAL WAR

Exercise of the Right of Angary with Regard to the Dutch Merchant Fleet

Upon the 6th of March the Allies agreed to comply with this request, provided that the Dutch tonnage which they had been demanding for some months was placed immediately at their disposal, but as they were getting tired of Dutch vacillation they insisted upon receiving a definite answer by the 18th of March.

Holland replied on the 17th of March to the effect that she would allow her ships to be employed in the service of the Allies provided that none of them were armed nor were used for the transport of troops or war material—a reservation which deprived the Dutch offer of any value from the point of view of the Allies.

The Hague was becoming very nervous: the press began to talk about 'leonine conventions' and 'the knife at our throat'; allied shipping in Dutch ports made ready to put to sea; and Dutch exports to Great Britain, which had slightly increased, were again suspended.

On the 20th of March President Wilson at last issued orders for the requisition of the whole of the Dutch shipping in American ports by right of angary.

The Dutch press became so furious that it actually compared this feat with the Austrian ultimatum to Serbia. As a matter of fact, however, President Wilson's action came as a great

THE NETHERLANDS

relief to the Dutch shipowners. Holland and her colonies retained 450,000 tons of shipping for their own requirements, 100,000 tons of which were allotted to Dutch trade with Allied countries in European waters, and the balance to the export trade of the Dutch East Indies with countries other than Holland. The remaining 500,000 tons were employed in the service of the Allies on terms which were peculiarly favourable for the Netherlands. The latter were authorised to send ships at once to the United States to fetch the corn they needed: the ships that had been subjected to the law of angary were chartered at very generous rates and were to be replaced for their owners in the event of loss. The owners would doubtless have preferred to retain their ships for the period immediately following the war, which they looked forward to as being less dangerous and still more lucrative; but they had to admit that their interests had not suffered.

Hostility to the Allies only persisted in official circles, which had still to consider German susceptibilities.

Discussions between Germany and Holland in 1918

The German-Dutch coal agreement, indeed, was about to expire on the 31st of March 1918. Germany had just signed peace with Russia and, being thus relieved of any further anxiety with regard to the Eastern front, displayed all her old arrogance towards the neutrals. She gave a foretaste of this by making the resumption of negotiations conditional upon the transfer to her of a million tons of Dutch barges, which she seemed likely to need for the importation of wheat from the Ukraine.

The Dutch Government, with a view to supervising the transfer, gave orders for all Dutch barges in the German canals to return to Holland : Germany in reply imposed an embargo upon any Dutch barges she could lay hands on.

Germany then demanded the immediate resumption of the transport of sand and gravel from Germany to Belgium viâ Holland at the rate of 200,000 tons a month, and the unfettered transport of goods over the Dutch line from Roermond. She also simultaneously stopped her coal deliveries, which in any case had become very difficult owing to the congested state of the railways.

The Dutch Government put up a show of resistance : the British raid upon Ostend and Zeebrugge had just made Germany's interest in getting possession of the mouths of the Scheldt still more apparent. All leave in the Dutch army was stopped, measures of defence were undertaken in Limburg, and the Dutch Minister at Berlin came home. But the Dutch resistance did not last long and the questions of gravel and of the Roermond line were settled by a compromise on the 6th of May. The question of coal remained

THE NETHERLANDS

unsolved, as it was Germany's interest to leave it so.

The Netherlands were forced to intensify the production of lignite, which increased threefold between January and July, and of the inferior Limburg coal. They were forced also to restrict the consumption of gas and electricity, and unemployment occurred in several industries.

All this while the food position was getting worse; violent demonstrations by the unemployed took place in Amsterdam and Rotterdam; the Queen was hissed on several occasions by hungry workmen; the daily ration of bread was reduced to 200 grammes per diem and the weekly sugar ration to 250 grammes; certain productions such as fats used in industry became so scarce that in July 1918 a ship with a cargo of soap on board, which had been brought up a canal to the Hague, was at once plundered by the mob.

Germany, knowing that Holland had not much left to offer, became more and more pressing in her demands; in July 1918 she actually demanded the delivery of 60,000 cows and 3,000 tons of poultry. So great was the anger in Holland that the German negotiators became apprehensive of having gone too far, and arranged on the 1st of August, independently of any agreement, to deliver 120,000 tons of coal monthly to Holland at a price of 90 florins the ton.

In spite of these difficulties with Germany Holland's relations with the Allies had not improved since the previous April. The Government of the Netherlands still refused to allow that portion of its merchant fleet which the Allies had left at its disposal to leave port, and sought to justify its inaction on the grounds of the addition to Article 55 C which Germany had embodied on the 17th of April in her Ordinance as to Prizes of 1909.

The Dutch merchant fleet during the summer of 1918 was distributed as follows : 696,000 tons were being employed by the Allies ; 595,000 tons were trading in complete liberty in far distant seas; 519,000 tons were standing idle in European waters.

The greater part of the Dutch merchant fleet could accordingly be taken as being operated on behalf of the Allies, and it would therefore have been open to the German submarines under article 55 C to sink every Dutch ship at sea.

The Affair of the Dutch Convoy

Holland saw fit to vindicate her rights as a neutral by organising a convoy, which was to be escorted by Dutch ships of war, from Rotterdam to the Dutch East Indies. Nothing could be less to the liking of Great Britain, who had no intention of jeopardising the right of search from which merchant ships are exempted when under

THE NETHERLANDS

escort. Article 61 of the Declaration of London stated indeed that "neutral vessels under national convoy" are exempt from search.

Owing to the non-ratification and subsequent abandonment by Great Britain of the Declaration of London she was able to fall back upon her own maritime law, which had always refused to recognise the right of neutral ships under convoy to exemption from search, a right, moreover, which would have rendered any naval action on the part of the Allies absolutely futile if the neutral Powers had demanded its enforcement.

We have seen that as early as 1915 Germany had suggested this plan to the Scandinavian countries as a means of escaping control by the Allied cruisers. The suggestion was not followed up at the time but was revived in the Dutch Parliament in April 1918. On the 29th of that month the chargé d'affaires of the Netherlands in London handed Mr. Balfour a letter informing the British Government of the intention of the Hague " to send a convoy to the East Indies to relieve military men and to send out Government officials with their families and some urgently needed military and other stores." The letter gave a description of the composition of the convoy and added : " The loading of all goods and the embarcation of all passengers will be effected under strict supervision of Netherland Government officials. No private correspondence may be carried. The ships will carry neither ordinary nor parcel mail. Of the Government goods the usual manifesto will be produced with certificates of origin issued by the Inspector of Import Duties."

While arrangements were being made for the convoy the attitude of the Government had become the subject of criticism by the Dutch press, and certain papers emphasised the danger of armed conflict to which the Netherlands were exposing themselves if the British cruisers were to insist upon searching the ships in spite of the opposition of the convoy. In order to allay these fears an official Dutch communiqué was published on the 31st of May which stated : " Warships will only carry naval personnel and war supplies and the merchant ships only Government passengers with their families and Government goods. It is not intended to institute under protection of warships commercial intercourse which without such protection would not be permitted by the belligerents according to their views of the commercial liberty of neutrals. It is obvious that the convoy commandant would not tolerate any examination of the convoyed ships."

As soon as this communiqué reached London Mr. Balfour handed the Dutch Government a note, the concluding passage of which was worded as follows :

" His Majesty's Government feel compelled to reiterate in the most formal manner that the right of visit and search which Great Britain,

THE NETHERLANDS

whether she was a neutral or belligerent, has, in conformity with the rules of international law, consistently upheld for centuries, is not one she can abandon.

" As the Netherlands Government is well aware, the claim that immunity from search is conferred on neutral merchant vessels by the fact of their sailing under the convoy of a man-of-war flying the national flag has never been conceded by this country. By the course they are now pursuing they do in fact demand that Great Britain shall abdicate her belligerent right to stop contraband trade by the regulated exercise of naval force and, in the middle of a great war, abandon the Allied blockade. This is a demand to which Great Britain could not possibly accede."

Nevertheless the British Government accepted a compromise in a memorandum sent by Lord Robert Cecil to the Netherlands chargé d'affaires on the 7th of June. The memorandum opened with the following observation : " It would appear from communications made by the Dutch Government that the latter proposes to afford the belligerents the same guarantees and means of control as the latter would themselves obtain by exercising their right of search. This point of view is hardly to be reconciled with the organisation of the convoy. . . . Clearly if the belligerents are completely satisfied as to the innocence of particular ships' persons and cargoes there can be no need for giving to vessels thus admitted to be innocent the special protection of convoy. In fact the sending of the convoy at all is hardly capable of explanation except on the assumption that the convoyed vessels are to be protected in some transaction which the belligerents do not recognise as legitimate."

The real object of the last sentence was to compel the Dutch Government to declare that it was only anxious to protect its convoy from German submarines.

While regretting, the memorandum continued, that the Dutch authorities had adopted a method which appeared to the British Government " to be lacking in courtesy and wisdom," the latter suggested nevertheless that the matter could be settled amicably if an exceptional procedure was adopted. The convoy would be allowed to make the voyage if the Dutch Government furnished a detailed list of the passengers, full information as to the cargo and, in particular, gave a formal guarantee that none of the goods were of enemy origin.

The Dutch Government accepted these demands on the 15th of June: the lists required were sent to London, and the departure of the convoy was fixed for the 19th June. On the 18th of June, however, the British Government protested against the embarcation of German dyes on board the *Noordam* : a discussion ensued between Great Britain and Holland which led to the resignation of the Netherlands Minister of Marine as a protest against the delay in dispatching the convoy.

On the 29th of June, the Dutch Government decided to land the dyestuffs, and the convoy left on the 5th of July. On the same day Reuter's agency published the following note: " The Dutch authorities must not forget that this mark of benevolence will under no circumstances be repeated."

Resumption of Discussions with the Allies (October 1918)

The N.O.T. in the meantime had become worried at the loss of its imports and was endeavouring on the quiet to renew its semi-official relations with Great Britain. Its intentions were facilitated by a note of the United States Government of the end of September 1918 in which the hope was expressed that the Netherlands Government would follow the example of other neutral countries and pave the way for a general resumption of commercial relations; the United States, however, affirmed its intention of not allowing food to enter Holland until the Dutch merchant fleet went to sea.

By this time the Allied armies had achieved such successes that the issue could no longer be in doubt.

The Netherlands Government let it be known in London that it would be very happy to resume economic negotiations with the Allied and Associated Powers.

France and Great Britain received the announcement with great satisfaction, as both groups of belligerents had been casting greedy eyes upon the financial resources of Amsterdam, and the Entente was hoping, in October 1918, to float a loan of 200 million florins upon the Dutch market.

The official delegation of the Queen's Government left for London on the 25th of October, having just received a proposal from the United States to allow Holland 100,000 tons of coal a month if the latter stopped its agricultural exports to the Central Empires. The friendly dispositions of the Dutch, however, were all in vain; the Armistice intervened, and the Dutch delegation arrived too late to negotiate to any purpose.

The food position in the Netherlands had, incidentally, become less critical since October: Germany, seeing her defeat was impending, had granted safe conducts to 30,000 tons of Dutch shipping to enable them to fetch the 100,000 tons of corn which had been on offer from the United States for some months.

A few days before the Armistice, Germany had ceased to enforce the so-called condition of 'exchange,' which meant that whenever a Dutch ship left for the United States in possession of a safe conduct a ship of equal tonnage had to proceed from the United States to the Netherlands to take its place, so as to keep the whole of the Dutch tonnage immobilised.

THE NETHERLANDS

Holland was thus enabled, after the 11th of November, to increase the bread ration from 200 to 280 grammes and to get the upper hand of the disturbances in the principal towns of the kingdom which had been caused by the economic naval war.

CHAPTER III

SWITZERLAND

Economic Situation in Switzerland Prior to the War

THE Swiss flag was never flown by merchant ships during the war except as a safeguard ; in any case it had always to be flown alongside that of a maritime power, as it was not recognised at sea. The non-existence of her merchant fleet, far from simplifying the problem of the relations between Switzerland and the belligerents, may actually be said to have complicated it.

The problem would have been simple enough if the Helvetic Confederation had been self-supporting and had continued to lead an independent and peaceful existence amid the warring nations. On the one hand, however, Switzerland was incapable of supplying her own requirements in regard to food, and on the other the Allies had need of Switzerland not only as a market for their traders but for the services she could render their manufacturers. Indeed, out of a total area of 2,283,000 hectares of agricultural land only 204,000 hectares (exclusive of forest land) were devoted to the cultivation of corn ; the remainder consisted of natural or artificial grazing land.

SWITZERLAND

Now grazing land only yields one-tenth of the amount of human food that can be produced from an equivalent area of arable land. Switzerland only produced two-fifths of the corn she consumed and had to import 220,000 tons of wheat. Furthermore, she lacked fertilisers, of which she had to purchase 60,000 tons abroad, and also, notwithstanding the extent of her pastureland, had not enough fodder for her large herds of cattle and had to import 117,000 tons of maize and 100,000 tons of cake annually.

The balance of trade was distinctly unfavourable to her: her imports were valued at £56,000,000 and her exports at £40,000,000, the difference being made up by the money spent in Switzerland by tourists from all parts of the world.

The Franco-Swiss Agreement of March 1914

The Swiss Government, doubtless foreseeing that the storm was about to break, had concluded an Agreement with France early in 1914 by which the latter had consented in the event of war to allow American corn for Switzerland to pass through her territory. By the terms of the Agreement the French Government undertook after the twenty-first day of mobilisation not to requisition any corn which might be unloaded at St. Nazaire or Marseilles and dispatched to Geneva.

The Agreement allowed for traffic at the rate of 150 trucks a day. It came into force on the appointed day and, in spite of terrible congestion of the railways on more than one occasion, the French Government managed to carry out its undertaking.

Moreover, in order to avert any suspicion with regard to these consignments the Federal Government reserved to itself, in January 1915, the sole right of importing corn and fodder, and some weeks later took a similar step with regard to mineral oils, imports of which were restricted to 7,800 tons a month. The actual arrangements for these Government imports were made by the Swiss General War Commissariat.

Ever since October 1914 the Entente had been trying to find a means of preventing the Central Empires receiving supplies through Switzerland: it was unwilling to lose its Swiss customers and therefore opened negotiations with the Confederation in the hope of inducing the Swiss Government to forbid the export of metals which might be used for war purposes, and of india-rubber and mineral oils, "irrespective of the stage reached in manufacture or however compounded."

The Swiss Government prohibited the export of india-rubber and mineral oils, but with regard to the other imports from France and Great Britain no agreement was reached.

The situation was all the more difficult for the Allies as Italy, which had not yet entered the war, could afford Swiss trade excellent facilities for receiving her supplies by way of Genoa, and

SWITZERLAND

goods which reached Switzerland by this route were generally passed on to Germany.

The Entente then hit upon the idea of exercising an unobtrusive control by dividing Switzerland into French and German speaking cantons; and as soon as it was in possession of information as to the sympathies of the Swiss importers it arranged to grant permits to those it could trust and refuse them to the remainder. This system, however, was both unreliable and complicated owing to the difficulty of tracing the imports through the various changes they underwent in the course of manufacture and of making sure that they did not reach the Central Empires; to make matters worse the French and British agents who were entrusted with the task of supervision did not always see eye to eye in the matter.

In May 1915 Great Britain sent her delegate on the Board of the Netherlands Overseas Trust, Sir Francis Oppenheimer, on a mission to Berne, and the idea occurred to him of introducing into Switzerland a system similar to the one he was administering in the Netherlands.

Formation of the S.S.S.

Sir Francis Oppenheimer took advantage of being in Paris on the 2nd of June to explain to the R. Committee the advantages of his system, and after emphasising the difficulty of exercising control in a country like Switzerland where the

Government was so jealous of its sovereign rights, he suggested the formation of a Swiss Society of Economic Supervision (the S.S.S.), with an advisory board of sixteen well-known Swiss citizens whose appointment would be subject to the approval of the Federal Government and of the French and British Ministers at Berne. A managing committee would exercise its functions subject to the directions of the Board, and would control syndicates of importers representative of the various industries.

" It is impossible to conceive a better arrangement," said Sir Francis, " as, in my opinion, it is much better for a Swiss to be controlled by a fellow countryman than by a Frenchman or an Englishman."

The R. Committee was not enthusiastic about the plan, as it had no great belief in allowing neutrals to supervise themselves; nevertheless it accepted the Oppenheimer plan, but with some important modifications. The S.S.S. was to be granted the entire monopoly of imports into Switzerland and the War Commissariat was to be abolished. The S.S.S. was also to apply the principle of rationing with the utmost strictness.

The French Ambassador at Berne, for his part, approved of the Oppenheimer plan, as he was assailed with applications and complaints owing to preferential treatment having been given to certain Swiss merchants and denied to others, and thought it high time that a proper

SWITZERLAND

organisation was set on foot and the confusion put an end to.

Accordingly negotiations about the S.S.S. were opened. An Allied mission upon which France was represented by M. Crozier was sent to Berne, and the S.S.S. was formed on the 4th of October 1915, and held its first general meeting on the 25th of October.

The following notices were published in the French *Journal Officiel* of the 15th of November :

" A Society entitled the Swiss Society of Economic Supervision has just been formed at Berne which will undertake to supervise and guarantee the fulfilment of the conditions attached to the importation into Switzerland of the hereinafter mentioned goods.

" The company will commence operations on the 10th of November. Goods contained in the following list may be sent to the Society, the written assent of the latter having been previously obtained.

" No exports or transit permits therefore will be issued in respect of such goods unless the application is accompanied by documentary evidence of the approval of the Society."

The Society had offices in Paris, London and Rome. It differed from the N.O.T. in two most important respects. In the first place it acted in close and official collaboration with the Federal Government, whereas the N.O.T. was independent of the Dutch Government, and in the second, thanks to the insistence of the R. Committee, it was above all a rationing organisation, whereas the N.O.T. more or less retained its original character of a consignee. The second difference was due to the manner in which goods were imported into the two countries, as Swiss imports arrived uniformly by rail and could be checked truck by truck, whereas Dutch imports were effected almost entirely by sea.

Initial Difficulties of the S.S.S.

The S.S.S., however, the advent of which had been hailed with so much optimism, gave rise at first to the most bitter disappointment. The bankers, manufacturers and traders of Switzerland were loud in their complaints and sarcastic remarks. " Before we had the S.S.S. we used to get something from France ; but since it has been formed we get nothing and have to apply to Germany." As a matter of fact the commencement of operations by the S.S.S. coincided with a period of appalling congestion on the French railways.

The unfavourable reception of the S.S.S. by the Swiss public was due, moreover, to the hostile attitude naturally assumed by German Switzerland, and also to the fact that the interests of French Switzerland were very injuriously affected by its existence. Prior to the constitution of the S.S.S. the Allies had naturally given French Swiss importers the preference; since that event, however, the latter had merely received

SWITZERLAND

the proportion of the quota to which they were entitled. The system was also very disadvantageous to the small Swiss trader, who was unable to find the security required by the statutes of the S.S.S. Public feeling was so strong that the S.S.S. was forced to publish the following official apology on the 5th of February 1916 :

" The insistence with which the Governments of France, Great Britain and Italy have urged the formation of the S.S.S. in order to put a stop to fraudulent dealings in connection with the importation of goods into Switzerland from or viâ France and Italy, is a matter of common knowledge.

" The Federal Council gave its assent with the utmost goodwill to the introduction of this system in spite of the disadvantage attaching to it from the point of view of Swiss trade and industry, *viz.* of being compelled to reveal the source of their supplies to a third party, pledged to secrecy though the latter might be.

" Public opinion has at the present time gone curiously astray, and newspaper articles and pamphlets are being published in which the S.S.S. is held responsible for the hindrances placed in the way of trade.

" It seems to be forgotten that the S.S.S. is absolutely tied by its international statutes, that it is bound to investigate thoroughly every question with regard to imports, restrict the latter in amount, provide for the deposit of security, and finally undertake the task of forming syndicates, which has proved a matter of the greatest complexity.

"When once this work had been performed under conditions of peculiar difficulty the S.S.S. could have folded its hands and confined itself to supervising the entry of goods into Switzerland, whereas with a view to promoting the interests of trade, industry and agriculture, which were lacking in certain products, it has opened offices in Paris, London and Rome to ensure the applications of Swiss syndicates or private individuals to the French, British or Italian Governments for permission to import receiving due satisfaction.

"The S.S.S. is also giving its best attention to the question of transport. Instructions have been given to its officials at Genoa, Cette and Marseilles to take care that goods are unloaded, entrained, and dispatched to Switzerland as quickly as possible. We may be sure that if goods only trickle into Switzerland at times, the fault does not lie with the S.S.S."

Reforms in the Organisation of the S.S.S.

Efforts were accordingly made to find out why the S.S.S. was working so badly from the Swiss point of view.

The Allies, declared the British Government, have every interest in upholding and strengthening the S.S.S. by every means in their power; there can be no doubt that the opposition at

SWITZERLAND

present encountered by the Society is due in great measure to the efforts of German agents who have focussed their propaganda upon French Switzerland.

Could not France at any rate put an end to all the difficulties which were being placed in the way of through traffic on its railway system to Geneva? Could not she, above all, persuade the authorities, whose duty it was to issue export permits, that there was no longer any necessity for drawing a distinction between the various firms which had enrolled themselves in the S.S.S., some of which in 1915 had been considered favourable to the Entente and others hostile to it? If these authorities were to continue, as thereunto, to inquire into the opinions of Swiss importers the people of Switzerland would not understand why the Allies had pressed for the creation of the S.S.S.

Of course, the French replied, we must give the S.S.S. credit for good intentions. But we cannot altogether agree with the British point of view. Trading with the enemy directly or through a third party is forbidden by French law. It is therefore impossible for French exporters to consign their wares to firms which are notoriously pro-German in their sympathies, without exposing themselves to the penalties provided by the laws of the 27th of September 1914 and the 4th of April 1915[1] even if these firms are affiliated to the S.S.S. There seems

[1] Which forbade and punished trading with the enemy.

to be no apparent reason why the French and British Governments should not agree to exclude German firms from the advantages of the S.S.S.

The Quai d'Orsay replied in these terms to London, but at the same time complained to the French administrative services about their dilatory methods.

" It is the forwarding of goods to Switzerland above all that gives rise to the most serious complaints. We began by confining the landing of goods for Switzerland to the single port of Cette; the selection of this port, lacking as it does equipment and accommodation, has given rise to very great complaints, especially on the part of Great Britain. We then requested Switzerland to fetch the goods in her own rolling-stock, and she accordingly allotted 4,000 trucks, in other words one-quarter of the trucks she has in service, for this traffic. It has happened too often that the export permits have not arrived in time and the trains have had to waste time standing by or even return empty. If Switzerland is to have confidence in us she must feel that the Allies have confidence in her."

The whole of 1916 was taken up with recriminations of this kind; but the organisation of the S.S.S. was improved at any rate in various important particulars, especially so far as the small Swiss trader was concerned.

Great Britain persisted in her endeavour to place the S.S.S. and the N.O.T. on the same footing by increasing the number of articles consigned to the S.S.S. France, however, pointed out to her discreetly that it was much more important to keep Dutch trade, which had amounted in 1913 to £448,000,000, under close supervision, than that of Switzerland, which was four times less and was much easier to control. She enclosed a comparative table of French and British exports to Switzerland since 1913, according to which British exports had continually increased whereas French exports had dropped from £5,920,000 in 1913 to £5,160,000 in 1914, £4,320,000 in 1915 and £3,600,000 in 1916. In the latter year the value of the goods imported from France by the S.S.S. had amounted to £2,200,000.

Difficulties Caused by the Question of Compensation Goods

In spite of these incidents the matter of the Allied control over their exports to Switzerland could easily have been adjusted but for the disturbing influence of the economic relations between the latter country and Germany. The Federal Government had indeed been forced to bargain with Germany at the same time that it was negotiating with the Allies, and had obtained from the former daily deliveries of 10,000 tons of coal and 300 tons of various goods such as iron, steel, sugar and dyes.

Germany demanded no compensation for her coal and confined herself to seeing that it was distributed in such a way as to prevent as far as possible such firms which were working for the Allies from being supplied with German coal. She insisted, however, on the other hand, upon being supplied with goods in compensation for her other exports and naturally selected them from amongst the Entente imports into Switzerland. This accounts for the persistence with which the Federal Government sought to obtain permission to send 3,800 truckloads of various goods to Germany by way of exchange just at the time the S.S.S. was being formed.

By August 1916 the 3,800 truckloads had been exhausted and Switzerland applied to the Allies for permission to renew her compensation stocks. The French and British Governments declined to accede to this and suggested that the Federal Government should publish its Customs returns, which had been kept secret since 1915. Germany, on the other hand, sent the Federal Government a regular ultimatum to the effect that either compensation goods must be delivered within a fortnight or the German coal deliveries would be stopped.

Switzerland sent delegates in haste to Paris, and a Conference was held there on the 9th and 10th of August between them and the Allied delegates, which ended in a complete failure.

The Swiss were more fortunate as regards Germany; the German and Swiss representatives met in conference at Berne between the 17th and 30th of August and there concluded an

SWITZERLAND

Agreement upon the 2nd of September 1916. By the terms of this Agreement Germany was to resume her deliveries of coal, but the Swiss Government undertook to prevent any ammunition manufactured with this coal reaching the Allies. In exchange for goods of various kinds Switzerland for her part agreed to supply Germany with 38,000 head of cattle in the course of 1916.

This systematic delivery of cattle to the Central Empires was especially annoying to the Allies, as the splendid condition of the Swiss livestock was due to the fodder and cake supplied by them.

The Allied ministers at Berne expressed their astonishment and regret to the Federal Government. Great Britain at once proposed to reduce the Swiss quotas. France asked for time for reflection; it seemed to her that any restriction upon the imports of fodder was certain to be followed by an increase in the export of Swiss cattle to Germany.

The R. Committee arrived at the same conclusion as Great Britain :

" Our hands are now tied with regard to this question. We decided to take stern measures when we refused to give the Swiss delegates what they begged us to grant them last August. The strong wine has been drawn, let us drink it and be of good courage."

This vigorous announcement received unanimous approval and the Allies decided to enforce the regulations of the S.S.S. with the utmost rigour, to keep the black lists of Swiss merchants carefully up to date, and, above all, to revise the Swiss quotas.

Revision of the Swiss Quotas

The latter point was of paramount importance. The R. Committee was accordingly instructed to investigate the matter, and its report was presented to the Government on the 3rd of November 1916.

Switzerland had been rationed as regards 205 articles; it was now proposed that her quota should be reduced in respect of 102 of them, and annulled altogether in respect of a further 21. The latter category included steels of various kinds, live and dead meat, and ordinary kinds of fodder. These measures entailed a reduction of the Allied imports into Switzerland by 33%.

Owing unfortunately to the slow progress of inter-Allied negotiations the foregoing proposals had not been put into force when the year 1917 began. Nay more, it was agreed that quotas which had not been reached in 1916 should be allowed to run till the 3rd of April 1917, and that the balances exported during the first four months of 1917 should be charged to the quotas of 1916.

Furthermore, Switzerland had so benefited by the improved state of communications between Cette and Marseilles and Geneva that at the beginning of 1917 she was receiving 40,000

SWITZERLAND

quintals of goods daily as compared with 25,000 a year earlier.

General Lyautey, Minister of War, and Rear Admiral Lacaze, Minister of Marine, expressed their astonishment at this state of affairs to M. Denys Cochin, Under-Secretary of State for the Blockade. The latter informed them on the 1st of February 1917 that he himself had proposed the reduction of the Swiss quotas. "I am anxiously awaiting," he replied, "the concurrence of the Italian and British Governments with the action it is proposed to take. On the other hand we must look facts in the face. Switzerland gets all her coal from Germany. Can we supply her with it? We cannot do so. She must pay for it with something. We can restrict her trade but we cannot suppress it entirely. We are bound, too, to take account of Swiss public opinion and show some consideration for its susceptibilities."

The Minister of War stated in reply that there appeared to him to be no justification for the facilities that had been granted to Swiss trade. "On the 27th of July 1914 the French Government undertook to allow 15,000 tons of corn and 4,000 tons of oats to reach Switzerland every ten days. By June 1915 these amounts had increased from 19,000 to 80,000 tons, and by July 1916 to 119,000 tons. Not a day goes by without the S.S.S. asking for further facilities and assailing us with recriminations."

The President of the Commission of Exemptions drew the attention of M. Denys Cochin to another consideration : rumours were beginning to be circulated of a German offensive against Switzerland and the Federal Government had collected stocks of considerable magnitude, including sufficient wheat and alcohol to last six and eight months respectively. Was it advisable under these conditions to continue to grant export licences to Switzerland ?

" Let us go on," M. Denys Cochin replied, " applying the existing regulations with all possible strictness. It is quite true that since the outbreak of hostilities the Federal Government has endeavoured to achieve economic independence by collecting stocks within its own territory. The quotas have been calculated on too generous a scale. Great Britain, however, has just informed us of her adherence to our proposals for a reduction of the quotas, and negotiations with the Swiss delegates must soon begin."

Negotiations actually began on the 14th and lasted till the 20th of March 1917. The Allies were unable to entertain the original Swiss proposals. The Minister of Marine stated in a letter to M. Denys Cochin that the conditions put forward by the Swiss would be disastrous from the point of view of the blockade. An agreement was only reached on the 12th of May.

" The agreement," M. Denys Cochin stated, " is more advantageous to the Allies than its predecessor, and less so to the Germans. The only sacrifice we have made is to allow a little more fodder to be carried by our railways in Swiss

SWITZERLAND

trucks. We could not disregard the British demand for milk nor the Italian shortage of wood. People are prejudiced with regard to Switzerland. In 1916 she supplied Germany, inclusive of cows, milk, cheese and chocolate, with 72,000 tons of food at the most. Holland supplied Germany with 1,200,000 tons, and Denmark 600,000 tons.

"She is said to be supplying Germany with the whole of her aluminium; she cannot supply aluminium as she has no bauxite. The Austrians send her bauxite of very inferior quality from the Dalmatian Islands, and it is treated in Switzerland by means of water power. Similarly she manufactures ferro-silicon from German iron and calcium carbide from German coke. She only supplies the power, about two-thirds of which is working for the Germans and one-third for us.

"It is by means of these products of her soil, cattle and water power to wit that she pays for the goods we cannot supply her with, namely, coal, iron and potash. I don't think we can ask much more of Switzerland."

The German-Swiss Agreement of 5th May 1917

While the Entente was concluding this Agreement with Switzerland under which quotas were reduced by about 1,300,000 tons, the Federal Government had renewed its agreement with Germany on the 5th of May 1917. By it the latter agreed to authorise the export of 200,000 tons of coal and 19,000 tons of iron per month at prices, incidentally, which were very much superior to those stipulated in the previous Agreement. Switzerland on her part agreed to advance Germany 20,000,000 francs monthly, in return for which the latter was to abandon her claim to receive compensation goods from the Entente countries. Germany was to continue to supply Switzerland with zinc, sugar and potash and to receive dairy produce, cattle and chocolate in exchange.

As a matter of fact this Agreement worked very badly, as Germany was unable to keep up her monthly deliveries of 200,000 tons of coal; in fact by the end of 1917 they had fallen to 130,000 tons.

The Swiss-American Agreement of 5th December 1917

The news of the American embargo upon exports not unnaturally made the Federal Government very anxious about its corn supplies. A mission was accordingly sent to Washington to obtain wheat, rye and fodder. The United States, very fortunately, were well disposed towards Switzerland. An Agreement was therefore signed on the 5th of December 1917 under which Switzerland was to receive 360,000 tons of wheat, 120,000 tons of oats, 46,000 tons of cake and 60,000 tons of sugar during the first nine months of 1918.

SWITZERLAND

Further Franco-Swiss Agreements

As soon as Switzerland received satisfaction on that point, she began negotiations with France with a view to improving the working of the S.S.S. According to the first Agreement, which had been concluded on the 29th of September for a period of three months, France was to be granted a loan of 30 million francs, in return for which she undertook to import fancy goods into Switzerland to the monthly value of 2,500,000 francs.

A fresh Agreement between France and Switzerland was signed on the 29th of December 1917 for a period of ten months. France was represented during the negotiations by M. de Lasteyrie. Under this agreement the Swiss banks were to advance money to France at a fixed rate of 2,500,000 francs per month and an additional sum which was calculated in the following manner: so long as the imports from France by rail did not amount to 20,000 tons monthly no further advance was to be made; thereafter, the amount was to be increased by 20,000 francs per 100 tons up to 45,000 tons, and 35,000 francs per 100 tons in excess of 75,000 tons.

An agreement of this kind, however much it might be called for in the interests of our finances, was bound to lead to friction between the Ministry of Finance, which was naturally inclined to make no difficulties about speeding up the import of the quotas into Switzerland, and the Ministries whose duty it was to apply the blockade regulations. The Minister of Marine, more especially, persisted in his attitude of suspicion and held up goods addressed to Swiss traders whose names were on the black list. The S.S.S. thereupon complained to the Ministry of Blockade, and the latter protested on the 19th of February 1918 most vigorously against the uncompromising manner in which the Ministry of Marine was carrying out its duties. It was obviously in the interest of the Allies to counteract German propaganda, which was on the lookout for any incident which might lead to a cessation of work in the factories working for the Allies. The suspicions entertained by the Ministry of Marine with regard to goods addressed to traders on the black list were quite unnecessary in the case of the S.S.S., as that organisation had undertaken neither to buy from nor sell to traders of doubtful reputation.

The Minister of Marine replied on the 21st of March that while he was entirely of the opinion of the Minister of Blockade with regard to the *bonâ fide* trade with Switzerland, the French Government had to reserve to itself the right of ascertaining the real destination of goods in transit through French territory. Had not the French administration grounds for suspicion?

Some weeks later the Minister of Marine reverted to the matter. M. Schultess, the Head of the Federal Department for Public Economy, was trying to establish an official monopoly of all purchases of raw material made abroad. This

SWITZERLAND

monopoly, which was to be worked in conjunction with the S.S.S., would have given him the entire control of Swiss trade : the Minister of Marine objected to a proposal which would have placed the entire transit trade at Cette in the hands of foreigners and directed our ambassador at Berne to inform the Federal Government that we could not give up any of our guarantees.

Final Negotiations between Switzerland and the Belligerents

The Federal Government would not have toyed with these proposals for a monopoly of imports but for the gravity of the situation with regard to food in the spring of 1918. The United States had indeed promised to supply Switzerland with corn, as we have already stated ; but the corn had not arrived owing to a disagreement between Germany and Switzerland as to the issue of safe conducts to ships carrying supplies to the latter. The German coal deliveries were falling off and the Entente quotas had been so reduced that any re-export of goods to the Central Empires was almost out of the question.

In addition, the German-Swiss Agreement was again about to expire (on the 15th of May), and Germany was trying to make the renewal thereof conditional upon the acceptance of terms that were quite unbearable. Not only was she actually asking 180 francs a ton for her coal, but she further claimed to exercise so strict a control over the use of the same that the Swiss industries which were working for the Allies would probably be forced to shut down.

France intervened at this point in order to save the Swiss manufacturers who were executing her orders, and offered to deliver to Switzerland 85,000 tons of coal per month at the rate of 150 francs a ton.

The effect of this offer was to render the conclusion of the German-Swiss Agreement very doubtful; the Federal Government sent two delegates to Paris to find out what conditions France was seeking to impose in return for the delivery of her coal.

By the 22nd of May the Federal Government was in possession of full information as to the intentions of both belligerents, and she accordingly signed the final Agreement with the German Government, which was to remain in force for nine months. Under this agreement an organisation similar to the S.S.S. was to be set up to control any Swiss factories which were working with German coal.[1] The Schweizerische Treuhandstelle, or S.T.S. as it was called, only functioned, however, from August to November 1918.

France for her part supplied the factories working for the Entente with 30,000 tons of coal a month, thus enabling them to evade German control of any kind.

---

[1] The price of German coal varied, according to the use it was put to between 120 and 200 francs a ton.

SWITZERLAND

Effect of the Blockade upon the Economic Life of Switzerland

An examination of the balance sheet of Swiss trade as published by the Federal Government for the first six months of the years 1914–18 will afford us a very good idea of the state of industry and agriculture throughout the Confederation.

The wheat imports for each of these half-yearly periods amounted to 210,000, 336,000, 240,000, 158,000 and 23,000 tons respectively.

The trend of cake imports (6,900, 9,900, 10,330, 7,400 and 9,400 tons) was much more regular.

Coffee imports (5,600, 8,100, 16,500, 5,200 and 4,800 tons) fluctuated considerably.

Speaking generally, imports of food may be said to have reached their maxima in 1915 or 1916, and to have fallen in 1918 to or below the level of 1914.

Exports of foodstuffs, on the other hand, remained more or less at peace time level throughout 1915 and 1916, and then declined suddenly in 1917 and 1918.

I will content myself with quoting the figures of the exports of milk, cheese and chocolate for the five years in question.

	1914 tons	1915 tons	1916 tons	1917 tons	1918 tons
Milk	21,000	22,000	21,000	12,000	10,000
Cheese	19,000	20,000	11,600	4,300	500
Chocolate	7,476	10,726	9,260	8,719	4,189

Imports of raw materials which were essential to industry show a similar steady decline.

Coal imports, which amounted to 1,600,000 tons for the first half year of 1914, fell to 1,200,000 tons for the corresponding period of 1918.

Mineral oil imports during the same periods showed a steady decline, falling from 28,000 to 6,000 tons.

In the case, however, of finished goods the figures show an opposite tendency, and are a proof of the extent to which Swiss industry came to the help of the belligerents. During the first half of 1914 Swiss exports of manufactured iron goods had amounted to 2,188 tons, but these figures rose during the corresponding period of the next four years to 5,707, 5,731, 14,000 and 7,000 tons respectively. The advance in the case of manufactured copper goods (151, 348, 3,842, 8,702 and 6,525 tons) and of machine tools (678, 1,904, 8,330, 6,363 and 3,489 tons) was still more striking.

The reader would get a very wrong impression if his conclusions as to the economic activity of Switzerland were based upon these figures and no allowance was made for the contraband traffic which the Swiss customs were not always able to repress. The S.S.S. moreover, whose good faith could not be questioned, always stood up for traders who belonged to its syndicates even when they were caught red-handed in the act of smuggling, and sometimes tried to prove in the face of evidence that the goods sent to Germany had not

SWITZERLAND

been introduced into Switzerland under its ægis. The enormous increase in her trade and industry, coupled with this contraband traffic which was unlawful in the eyes of the belligerents only, was a source of undeniable prosperity to Switzerland; and in 1916 the balance of trade, with exports at £97,880,000 and imports at £95,120,000, turned in her favour for the first time in thirty years. This prosperity coincided, however, during the last two years of the war, with a shortage of food which affected the working classes especially.

I have related the difficulties encountered by the United States in carrying out the Agreement of the 5th of December 1917 concerning the supply of corn to Switzerland; grain vessels only began to arrive regularly in July 1918, and accordingly the imports of wheat, which during the first six months of 1914 had amounted to 210,000 tons, fell to the low figure of 22,000 tons for the corresponding period of 1918.

The daily bread ration had to be reduced to 225 grammes and the normal ration of milk was fixed at half a litre; the Federal Government even went so far as to contemplate the introduction of meat cards at the end of October 1918, a fact which at first sight appears surprising, as Switzerland continued to export cattle up to the Armistice; the shortage of meat was not, however, felt till the spring of 1919, when the price of meat which had been 174 francs per quintal in 1914 increased to 360 francs.

The potato crop of 1918 was below the usual standard.

For these reasons disturbances occurred in several manufacturing towns in the summer of 1918. As a matter of fact the responsibility for the shortage of food in Switzerland during the last year of the war was due to the particularism of the agricultural cantons, which succeeded in isolating themselves, economically speaking, from the rest of the Confederation; workmen in Basle for instance were starving owing to the unwillingness on the part of the neighbouring cantons to allow food to leave their territory. A Swiss family of five persons was paying 2,197 francs in December 1918 for food which it had been able to purchase in 1913 for 944 francs, and was likewise paying 422 francs for fuel which cost only 98 francs in the earlier year.

The working classes, who had become exasperated by the increased cost of living, turned a willing ear to Bolshevist agitators, who had taken advantage of the Swiss right of sanctuary to enter the country; on the 11th of November 1918 they rose and tried to proclaim a general strike. The attempt failed, but during the ensuing months disturbances occurred on several occasions in Switzerland. The Armistice had only relieved the gravity of the situation with regard to food to a very small extent, and the Swiss industries were suffering not only from the complete suspension of orders by the belligerents but from the almost complete

SWITZERLAND

cessation of deliveries of coal and steel by Germany.

It was the Entente which enabled Switzerland to overcome the crisis by affording her facilities for procuring supplies on a large scale.

CHAPTER IV

SPAIN

The Economic Situation in Spain Prior to the War

THE position of Spain as compared with that of the other European neutral states was a peculiar one owing to the distance which separated her from Germany; it was only in 1917 that the effects of the economic measures of the belligerents began to react upon her.

Although agriculture was the main source of the wealth of Spain, half of her territory was uncultivated. The remaining half was only very imperfectly cultivated but sufficiently so to satisfy the needs of a population which only amounted to 64 inhabitants per square mile.

Prior to the war Spain imported a small amount of wheat, but exported both wine and fruit; (400,000 tons of oranges, 28,000 tons of grapes and 3,000 tons of lemons).

Notwithstanding the abundance of her coal deposits she only produced 5 million tons of coal and had to import a further 3 million tons from Great Britain. She also produced 9 million tons of iron ore, 3 million tons of copper ore,

SPAIN

300,000 tons of lead ore, as well as arsenic, zinc, and sulphur. Her converting industries were, however, so little developed that only 500,000 tons of ore were treated in Spain; the remainder being exported to France, Germany, and Great Britain.

With the exception of the weaving industry, which imported all the cotton it needed from the United States, the other Spanish industries may be disregarded. The flocks of the Peninsula, on the other hand, supplied the spinners with 7/10ths of their requirements in wool.

In a word, Spanish industry was dependent for its existence upon British coal, American cotton, and mineral oils which were imported by French firms from the United States.

The extent to which Spanish trade was carried on by sea is very clearly shown by the following table:

	Imports £	Exports £
In Spanish ships	14,720,000	16,000,000
In foreign ships	16,360,000	19,160,000
By land	11,720,000	8,880,000

The Spanish mercantile marine amounted in all to about 877,000 tons.

65 German and 23 Austrian ships, with a total tonnage of 300,000 tons, had taken refuge in the ports of the Peninsula and of the Canary and Balearic Islands at the very outbreak of the war, where their presence had caused considerable congestion.

This tonnage was to become the occasion, as we shall presently see, of very difficult negotiations between Spain and the belligerents.

The Economic Situation in Spain During the War

The economic history of Spain during the war may be divided into three fairly distinct periods : (*a*) August–December, 1914 ; (*b*) January 1915–August 1917 ; (*c*) September 1917–November 1918.

The first period was one of crisis, the second of great prosperity, and the third a period of renewed crisis : the changes of circumstance are very well illustrated by the trend of Spain's commerce from 1914–1918 :

	1913	1914	1915	1916	1917	1918
(In millions of pesetas)						
Imports ..	1,308	1,110	1,252	1,281	1,326	609
Exports ..	1,079	943	1,235	1,383	1,324	947

The crisis at the outbreak of war was due to the confusion into which trade was thrown all over the world.

The second crisis by which the golden age of profitable exports was succeeded was due no doubt to the submarine war, but also to the fact that the Allied countries had adapted themselves to war conditions. During the first two years of the war Spanish co-operation was almost indispensable to

SPAIN

them, but after the middle of 1917 they could do without it.

The crisis was aggravated by another circumstance : in order to protect the exchanges, the Allies imposed restrictions upon consumption and closed their frontiers to Spanish products, and on the other hand the Spanish Government, which was threatened with isolation on account of the submarine war, was forced to forbid the export of a large number of articles in order to safeguard the food supplies of the Peninsula.

The most curious phenomenon, however, in the economic evolution of Spain, was the change that took place with regard both to her customers and her sources of supply. If the figures of her imports are examined we shall see that German imports, as might be expected, suddenly fell off and practically ceased altogether in 1915 : French and British imports, however, also decreased by over 50%, whereas the United States succeeded in increasing their imports for 1917 as compared with those of 1913 to the extent of nearly 400% as will be apparent from the following table :

	Germany	Great Britain	France	United States
		(In millions of pesetas)		
1913	185	244	204	167
1914	108	219	134	147
1915	21	363	93	297
1916	3	326	110	453
1917	0	100	144	779

The increase in the imports from America did not, however, correspond in any way with an increase in Spanish exports to the United States; the latter in fact only increased from 72 million pesetas in 1913 to 95 million pesetas in 1916, whereas Spanish exports to France for the same period increased from 327 to 547 million pesetas, and in the case of Great Britain from 231 to 285 million pesetas.

The war naturally brought about a considerable extension of Spanish industry, an extension which would have taken place on a much larger scale but for the shortage of coal and the inadequacy of the plant. The value of her manufactured woollen textiles increased from 4 to 70 million pesetas, and that of her cotton textiles from 53 to 105 million pesetas. The value of the products of her extractive industries also increased from 270 million pesetas in 1913 to 382 million pesetas in 1916, but this is due rather to the rise in the price of ore than to any increase in the volume of production. The production of coal alone was developed under the pressure of necessity; the figures of 1918 showed an increase of 1,700,000 tons as compared with those of 1914.

The shortage of coal had the further result of forcing the Spaniards to increase the number of their factories which were worked by hydro-electricity; indeed, one-tenth of her hydro-electric plant, which at the present time is estimated to develop 5,000,000 h.p., was laid down in 1917.

SPAIN

Economic Negotiations between Spain and the Allies

We must not, however, lose sight of the fact that the whole of this economic activity was at the mercy of Allied policy: a fact which became evident at the very outset of the economic crisis in August 1917. America ceased to supply cotton to the spinning mills: the non-arrival of British coal on account of the submarine war gave rise to very serious transport difficulties, and the harvest turned out badly owing to the shortage of fertilisers, imports of which had been gradually diminishing.

Threatened as it was with serious difficulties in Catalonia the Government applied to the Allies and began by negotiating with Great Britain.

Spain was still in a good position to bargain; indeed, quite apart from the food products sent by her to France (and in the orange season of 1915 and 1916 traffic on the Midi was held up on more than one occasion by her consignments) she supplied the Allies with products which they could not very well do without: 50% of the Allied requirements in lead, for instance, in the shape of 200,000 tons of that metal, 5 million tons of iron ore and 3 million tons of pyrites, the latter being essential to the manufacture of sulphuric acid.

An agreement between Spain and Great Britain was therefore reached without great difficulty: Spain gave permission for the export of any pyrites and iron ore that Great Britain might require, and the latter supplied her with coal, ferro-manganese and tinplates. Spain then addressed herself to the United States and France.

The United States was in a better position for bargaining than France since it supplied Spain with cotton and petroleum, whereas none of the French exports to Spain were really indispensable to the latter.

Although France was clever enough to try to negotiate conjointly with the United States, two separate agreements were signed in March 1918 between Spain and America in the first instance, and Spain and France in the second.

The United States undertook to allow 35,000 bales of cotton and 4,000 tons of mineral oils and fats to be sent every month to Spain. Spain in return agreed to allow the export of leather, hides, olive oil, fruit, vegetables and rice, so far as was compatible with the exigencies of the food situation at home.

Under the Franco-Spanish agreement Spain consented to place no restrictions upon the export of ore and, subject to the satisfaction of her own requirements, not to restrict that of textiles, footwear, oil and dried fruit. France was to send Spain oleaginous grains, phosphates, electrical plant and chemical products, and further undertook to allow a certain quantity of oranges and fruits and 250,000 hectolitres of wine to be imported monthly. Spain further credited

SPAIN

France with 350 million pesetas with a view to facilitating purchases by the latter, upon the security of French treasury bonds.

It must be admitted that the German offensive of 1918, difficulties in the way of transport and congestion in the French ports, prevented the Allies on several occasions from carrying out their agreements to the letter; the intervention of the King of Spain was needed to bring about the conclusion of a *modus vivendi* at the price of concessions on both sides.

Negotiations with regard to the Utilisation of Spanish Tonnage by the Allies

The negotiations between Spain and the Allies with regard to the exchange of goods were, on the whole, fairly simple, as they did not involve any questions of rationing and contraband. On the other hand the negotiations with regard to Spanish shipping were beset with difficulties.

The Spanish mercantile marine at the outbreak of war amounted to 877,000 tons. A great many Spanish shipowners were unable to resist the rise in the price of ships and sold their ships in 1914 and 1915. In this way 60,000 tons of shipping were transferred to foreign ownership. The Government eventually got anxious and issued a decree on the 7th of January 1916 forbidding any further sale of ships to foreigners. In addition the Spanish mercantile marine was about to suffer further losses in submarine warfare; 60,000 tons had been sunk by the 1st of January 1917.

Shipowners had made considerable profits up to that time, dividends having fluctuated between 70% and 300%; and this prosperity acted as an inducement to the shipbuilding yards to extend their operations. Only 90,000 tons of shipping, however, were completed between the 1st of August 1914 and the 1st of January 1919, owing to the dilatory methods of Spanish yards, which, in view of the shortage of steel plates and machinery, confined themselves to the construction of wooden sailing-ships with auxiliary motor equipment.

Requisition of the Spanish Merchant Fleet

The unrestricted submarine war gave rise to trouble between Spain and the Central Empires in 1917. The Spanish Government was at first inclined to introduce the convoy system, but met with the customary opposition from Great Britain. The idea then occurred to it of selling a portion of its merchant fleet to Great Britain, which would have continued to carry food for the Peninsula but would have carried a defensive armament under the British flag. As soon, however, as Germany became aware of what was contemplated she declared that any such transfer of flag would be considered by her as incompatible

SPAIN

with Spanish neutrality, and there the matter ended.

The idea of a mass transfer having been given up, the Spanish Government then proposed that its ships should sail under their own flag and without any defensive armament but should be insured by Great Britain; Germany thereupon let it be known that she would regard any such system of insurance as a sale in disguise.

It was at the beginning of 1918 that the German submarines were most active in their operations against Spanish merchant shipping. The extension of the blockade zone by a German proclamation on the 8th of January 1918 to the region of the Azores and the Cape Verde Islands interfered very much with the Spanish trade with America.

Germany had become very uneasy at the economic agreements which were, as we have said, on the point of being concluded between Spain and the Allies, and accused the ships of the Peninsula of making use of false papers in order to conceal the destination of their cargoes. She refused to consider the transport of cargoes ' to order ' from one Spanish port to another in closer proximity to the French frontier as a *bonâ fide* voyage, and maintained that the coal which was being carried to Spain from Great Britain was destined for the most part to war industries which were working for the Allies. These various arguments furnished her with as many pretexts for the issue of strict orders to her submarines to destroy Spanish tonnage.

On the 25th of January 1918 the steamer *Giralda*, which was carrying manganese ore, a Spanish product, from Huelva to Pasajes, was destroyed by a submarine solely on the grounds, as alleged by the latter, that the *Giralda's* cargo was consigned to order.

On the 22nd of January another Spanish steamer was torpedoed by a submarine without warning while proceeding from England to Spain with a cargo of coal to order. In reply to Spanish complaints Germany pointed out that " the presumption of contraband applied by Great Britain to goods ' to order ' had gradually acquired the force of a fundamental law, in the course of the present war at sea."

When four more Spanish ships had been torpedoed in the course of the following week the Spanish Government issued a decree on the 14th of February making insurance against war risks compulsory for the crews of merchant ships.

By this time the Spanish mercantile marine had been so intimidated by the campaign carried on at home by the pro-German press and by the number of ships which had fallen victims to the submarines at the beginning of 1918, that it became disinclined to go to sea, and thereby brought about a serious crisis in the economic system of the country.

By April 1918 the Government in Madrid was

SPAIN

considering whether to requisition the entire mercantile marine. On the 30th of April the King said to the German naval attaché: " I wish to tell you frankly that I am forced to have contraband carried in order to obtain what is necessary for our existence. I wish the war would soon come to an end and enable us to avoid any further complications."

On the 14th of May the German naval attaché submitted proposals for the conclusion of a compromise with Spain upon the following conditions : " Germany would extend the list of free goods as regards the Spanish-American trade, and in return Spain would undertake not to treat the sinking of Spanish ships under requisition within the forbidden zone as an incident which must necessarily give rise to political complications."

The German Admiralty replied on the 16th of May that " this proposal was in contradiction of the instructions it had itself suggested being given to the ambassador at Madrid, which were as follows: to make it abundantly clear to the Spanish Government that any co-operation on the part of Spain with the Entente as regards tonnage would compel Germany to retaliate with corresponding measures. To demand a full and categorical explanation from the Spanish Government of the manner in which it intended to settle the question of tonnage, in view of the wishes expressed by the Entente."

The naval attaché replied that the Spanish

mercantile marine would not be requisitioned in the interests of the Entente but only in those of Spain.

The Agreement concluded between the Government and its shipowners was made public by the decree of the 2nd of June. The gist of it is as follows : (1) The whole of the mercantile marine was to be placed under Government control ; (2) Lower rates were to be charged for the carriage of goods which were essential to the needs of the country.

The Question of Safe Conducts

The requisition of the Spanish mercantile marine threw a severe strain upon the relations between Spain and Germany, as we shall presently see. In the meantime, however, troubles arose between the Allies and Spain on the question of safe conducts which were being issued by Germany to neutral shipping on the receipt of an undertaking by the latter not to carry for the Allies. The safe conducts in question were issued under conditions which came to press with peculiar hardship upon Spanish vessels in 1918, as the latter, in order to obtain them, had to agree antecedently to carry goods for traders whose names were on the Allied black lists. Furthermore any ship sailing let us say from Las Palmas to Cadiz had to undertake not to put in at any port in Morocco and to consent to be searched by a German agent on its arrival.

SPAIN

Two policies were open to the Allies, either to deal drastically with any ship in possession of a German safe conduct, or to treat each case on its merits.

The adoption of the second alternative implied the division of Spanish shipping into three categories :

(1) Ships carrying cargo wholly or partly for the Allies which were therefore disqualified from receiving a German safe conduct ;

(2) Ships carrying goods for traders on the black list, which obviously would have to be severely dealt with by the Allies ;

(3) Ships engaged solely in carrying supplies to Spain. The issue of German safe conducts to this category of shipping might prove in the long run to be to the advantage of the Allies.

The apparent vacillation of the Allies was due to the time taken by them to debate these various aspects of the case. They began by drawing up a note to the neutral Powers in which the Allied and Associated Powers stated that the control established by these safe conducts " might entail the forfeiture of their neutral status upon ships accepting such control." The Allied Powers then changed their minds and decided not to dispatch the note. A second note was drafted which left the question of safe conducts untouched but took objection to the conditions under which they were issued.

We have explained in Part I the reasons

which impelled the French Government on the 27th of August 1918 to ordain by Decree that any neutral ship placing itself under enemy control by the acceptance of a safe conduct " which was not recognised by the Allies and was incompatible with the exercise by them of their rights as belligerents would be considered, failing proof to the contrary, to be operating in the interests of an enemy state and therefore liable to capture."

The Decree was not very favourably received by the Spanish public, which was inclined to confound the question of German safe conducts with that of its own food supplies. The Spanish Ambassador at Paris actually went so far as to protest in writing on the 23rd of September 1918 against the French Decree of the 27th of August, and to point out that to confer upon the Prize Court the right of deciding whether the issue of safe conducts was or was not in contradiction with French rights was tantamount to immobilising any ships in possession of safe conducts pending the completion of any inquiry which the Court might direct to be held.

At the beginning of October 1918, however, the system of safe conducts, which was yet undecided at the conclusion of the Armistice, had ceased to be a main issue, and the fate of the German ships which had taken refuge in Spanish ports now claimed the undivided attention of the Allies.

SPAIN

Spain Takes Possession of German Shipping in order to Make Good her Losses at Sea

From the beginning of the unrestricted submarine war up to August 1918 the Spanish losses in shipping had amounted to about 140,000 tons. No distinction had been made in the case of ships which were requisitioned by the Spanish Government, as was proved by the sinking of the *Roberto* and the *Ramon de Larrinaga*.

On the 11th of August 1918 the Government at Madrid sent the following instructions to its ambassador at Berlin: the Government had maturely considered the state of affairs which had been brought about by submarine warfare and had been at the greatest trouble to find out the extent of the damage that had been inflicted upon the national production and the mercantile marine by the torpedoing of ships, which was enormous. Not only had this warfare cost them 20% of their tonnage but had been the cause of numerous fatalities and was rendering navigation daily more difficult, if not impossible.

" The reduction of our tonnage to a point which is hardly compatible with our most pressing needs, and the failure of our expectation, in view of the fact that the Government had taken over the entire control of maritime trade, that our flag would afford sufficient protection to our ships, have left us, much to our regret, no alternative but to safeguard our rights to the uttermost in every case.

"Your Excellency will therefore inform the German Government without delay that if any further cases occur of vessels being torpedoed, subsequently to the receipt of this notification, we shall replace the tonnage that has been sunk by German ships now at anchor in our ports and use them as and when they are required, till the end of the war."

The German Admiralty immediately telegraphed orders to its naval attaché at Madrid "to make preparations for rendering the German ships in Spanish harbours as useless as possible," but to await the receipt of orders from Berlin before putting them into effect.

The Spanish ambassador at Berlin informed his Government that "the replacement of Spanish ships that had been sunk by German ships would establish a precedent of which other neutrals might take advantage, and would amount to placing at the disposal of the Entente the entire available German tonnage, and result in the prolongation of the war." As he considered "this change in the policy of his country to be particularly disastrous," he respectfully tendered his resignation to the King.

Germany, however, did not take the Spanish note too seriously; she let it be known that although Spanish ships which were encountered in the forbidden zone could not be spared, her submarines had received the strictest orders to spare ships outside it, and added that goods consigned 'to order' would not be considered

SPAIN

a priori as being destined to an enemy, and expressed her willingness to pay compensation for any ship which might prove upon inquiry to have been wrongly sunk.

On the 29th and the 31st of August two steamers were sunk while engaged in carrying coal from Great Britain to Spain. Madrid got very anxious and cabinet councils were held by Señor Dato daily. The German Government saw that it would have to make concessions and directed Prince Ratibor, its ambassador at Madrid, to present the Spanish Government with a memorandum which stated at the outset that no concession could be made to Spain within the prohibited zone, but went on to give the latter satisfaction on the following points.

(1) In the event of any ship being sunk outside the prohibited zone the loss would at once be made good by the transfer of a German ship to Spanish ownership prior to any investigation and without any formalities whatever.

(2) No limitation in the future would be placed upon the scale of Spanish exports, even as regards forbidden goods, the list of which was to undergo revision.

(3) Germany stated expressly that she excepted Spain from the application of the 'to order' clause.

She also advised Spain to introduce the system of safe conducts, which had worked very well in Holland and the Scandinavian countries.

Prince Ratibor was also forewarned very confidentially by his Government that " if Spain were to take forcible possession of German vessels in the event of other ships being torpedoed, Germany would make the sharpest of protests but would not regard it as a *casus belli aut rupturæ.*"

Spain became more insistent when she saw that Germany was inclined to give way; Señor Dato was anxious to take over the whole of the interned German shipping on behalf of Spain, whose needs were becoming urgent.

Germany then went a step further in the way of concessions, and on the 27th of September issued the following instructions to Prince Ratibor :

" In spite of the many objections which may be urged against this course of action, H.M. the Emperor has deigned to order that in recognition of the services rendered by Spain throughout the war as a neutral, and more especially as an act of courtesy towards H.M. the King of Spain, Your Serene Highness is to be given full powers to offer to cede to Spain by contract five German steamers now anchored in Spanish ports for the duration of the war whenever you think fit to do so."

Prince Ratibor however had just heard of the seizure by the Chilian Government of all the German vessels interned in Chili, and being apprehensive of the Spaniards following this example begged his Government to allow him to cede a greater amount of tonnage.

Herr Solf, the new German Minister of Foreign

SPAIN

Affairs, telegraphed to him on the 10th of October to offer Spain five ships immediately, and stated further that he was doing his best to have five additional ships placed at the ambassador's disposal, the first five ships to be handed over to make good the ships which had been sunk outside the prohibited zone, and the other five to be transferred upon lease.

On the 15th of October the Spanish authorities took possession of seven interned German ships of a total tonnage of 26,000 tons.

On the 17th of October the German Government increased the offer to be made by five ships " in the event of the Spanish Government carrying out its intention of requisitioning German ships to replace vessels sunk within the prohibited zone." Spain, however, came into collision at this point with the Allied doctrine which forbade any such transfer of flag. The seven ships seized by her had been assigned to the Ministry of Food for use only by that department, the question of ownership remaining unaffected. This was done in order to protect the rights of third parties, in other words, to safeguard any claims the Allies might put forward when the treaty of peace was signed. Nevertheless the Allied Powers informed the Spanish Government on the 1st of November that they did not recognise the transfer of flag which had just been carried out, and that the ships which had been transferred would be seized by their cruisers if they emerged from Spanish territorial waters.

NEUTRALS AND THE NAVAL WAR

The ships had not left port by the time the Armistice took place, and the 246,000 tons of interned shipping which had been a source of anxiety to the chancelleries of the world during the four years they had stood idle were to become the spoil of the victors.

PART III

GERMANY

INTRODUCTION

ALTHOUGH ten years have now elapsed since the end of the war, any examination of the effects of the blockade upon Germany is still a matter of peculiar difficulty owing to the fact that a great many statistical details which alone could give us the information we require either cannot be compiled or are being deliberately withheld. Several neutral powers, it may be mentioned, have either refused to publish their customs returns for the years of the war or have only published them in part. Statistics relative to invisible stocks are almost impossible to obtain.

We shall find Germany on more than one occasion when faced with a shortage of indispensable materials compelling private individuals to surrender every article manufactured wholly or partly of the material of which there was a deficiency. Kitchen utensils, for instance, were bought by the state when there was a scarcity of copper, and organ pipes were requisitioned to make good the shortage of tin. All these kitchen utensils and organ pipes formed invisible stocks which on several occasions got Germany out of her difficulties. No estimate, however, with any pretensions to accuracy has ever been made with regard to them: we know, or rather the German administrative services know, how much copper and tin was used by Germany in the course of any particular year of the war; we cannot tell how many months or years it would have taken to exhaust her invisible stocks.

The time has therefore apparently not yet arrived for giving an exhaustive description of the economic activities of the Central Empires between 1914 and 1918. It seems possible, however, that by confining our examination solely to Germany we can simplify our task and form even now a very fair idea of the effects of the measures taken by the Allies : (*a*) upon Germany's balance of trade, (*b*) upon certain branches of her industries, (*c*) upon her agricultural industry and the food supplies of her inhabitants.

As a matter of fact it is only in the third of these fields of research that the effects of economic encirclement really become apparent ; in the sphere of industry the difficulties and discomfort entailed upon the German Empire by the complete cessation of imports of raw materials have been concealed from us to a great extent by the inventive skill of its chemists and the activity of its manufacturers. I must therefore confine myself to explaining the methods employed by Germany, costly at times though they were, to obtain substitutes for copper, india-rubber, fats, &c. in which she was deficient. Nor shall I deal at any great length with the question of her balance of trade, which is merely the expression in figures of the ideas discussed by me in previous chapters.

CHAPTER I

VARIATIONS IN THE BALANCE OF TRADE

An examination of the German commercial balance sheet for 1913 at the beginning of this book showed that, as regards food, imports exceeded exports by £100,000,000, that similarly imports of raw material exceeded exports by £172,000,000, and that exports of finished goods, on the other hand, exceeded imports by £248,000,000. The following tabular statement gives the figures of her trade in 1913 with seven of the principal countries of the world:

	Imports into Germany £	Exports from Germany £
Russia	78,400,000	30,200,000
Great Britain	40,440,000	57,000,000
France	45,000,000	50,000,000
U.S.A.	67,120,000	32,000,000
British India	22,440,000	5,000,000
Argentina	18,440,000	12,800,000
Australia	12,320,000	4,000,000

The most striking feature of these figures is the number of instances in which the balance was adverse to her; equilibrium was only realised by her exports of finished goods, chiefly to Central Europe. The balance of trade, moreover, on the whole was slightly unfavourable to her.

Germany was able to trade with countries overseas by means of her mercantile marine, which amounted to 5,200,000 tons. Ships of a total tonnage of 29,763,000 tons entered her ports in 1912 with cargoes on board, but of this total only 17,600,000 tons were of German nationality, the remainder being foreign owned. Half of this foreign shipping approximately was of British nationality, the remainder being distributed between the three Scandinavian States.

The period between the 2nd of August 1914 and the 11th of March 1915, that is to say up to the issue of the Order in Council which put a stop to any direct maritime intercourse between Germany and countries overseas, deserves a particularly careful study, as all direct relations between Germany and the United States subsequently thereto were interrupted until the Armistice. Direct imports, indeed, from the United States to Germany were very inconsiderable during that period owing to the preventive measures that had been taken by the Allies. After falling to practically nothing during the first three months of the war, they rose in December 1914 to 2,200,000 dollars as against 32,000,000 dollars in December 1913, and in January 1915 to 6,500,000 dollars, as against 34,300,000 dollars in January 1914.

It was, of course, a very different matter as regards imports from America under cover of the

THE BALANCE OF TRADE

neutrals. Although imports from the United States to Germany in December 1914 and January 1915 had decreased by 58 million dollars, American imports to Holland and the three Scandinavian countries had shown an increase of 39 million dollars during the corresponding period, thus making good the deficiency in direct imports to the extent of some 60%. Direct exports from Germany to the United States, which had amounted to 81,700,000 dollars in the last five months of 1913, sank to 40,000,000 dollars in the corresponding period of 1914.

The export trade of Germany may, therefore, be said to have suffered much less injury during the first period of the war than her import trade. This is accounted for by the fact that under the Declaration of Paris, which was observed by the Allies, the latter were compelled to respect enemy goods under a neutral flag, and were, moreover, precluded from taking exception to contraband goods which were in transit *from* Germany *to* America.

The Order in Council of the 11th of March 1915 put a complete stop to any direct trade between Germany and countries overseas.

No information is available subsequently save that which is contained in the statistics of her trade with her neutral neighbours. The following comparative statement of the trade of Germany with Holland and the three Scandinavian countries for the years 1913 and 1915 has been compiled from official sources.

GERMANY

			1913 £	1915 £
German exports	to	Sweden	16 million	14 million
Swedish	,,	,, Germany	10 ,,	33 ,,
German	,,	,, Norway	8 ,,	8 ,,
Norwegian	,,	,, Germany	5 ,,	11 ,,
German	,,	,, Denmark	18 ,,	11 ,,
Danish	,,	,, Germany	10 ,,	27 ,,
German	,,	,, Holland	87 ,,	50 ,,
Dutch	,,	,, Germany	113 ,,	70 ,,

If the imports from Switzerland (£18,280,000) into Germany, together with those from Roumania (£8,000,000) and Italy (£10,000,000), are added to the above figures we shall obtain a total of £177,000,000 (as compared with £600,000,000 in 1913), a figure which may be said to represent approximately the total amount of German imports in 1915, although of course accurate statistics are not available.

Her exports by an analogous process may be estimated at £112,000,000 for 1915 as compared with £580,000,000 in 1913.

According to the statistics of neutral countries for 1916 the total value of the imports from the latter into Germany amounted, as in 1915, to £180,000,000, whereas the German exports to the same countries fell suddenly to £80,000,000.

In 1917 the imports from neutral countries into Germany also fell suddenly from the figures of the previous year to £109,080,000, whereas the German exports to neutral countries remained more or less constant, at £74,160,000.

In 1918 the imports from neutral countries into

THE BALANCE OF TRADE

Germany only amounted to £66,520,000 and were considerably lower than the German exports to those countries, which amounted to £93,600,000.

These figures are obviously only approximate, and even if complete accuracy were claimed for them we should have to take into account certain exchanges of goods as to which statistics are non-existent. I refer principally to the exchanges with Roumania, several provinces of which came under the control of Germany at the beginning of 1917 who was then enabled to derive a large proportion of her supplies of mineral oils from the invaded area of that country, and also to exchanges which took place with Russia after the break up of the Russian army.

Taking one thing with another however, German foreign trade probably fell from £1,180,000,000 in 1913 to £160,000,000 in 1918. These figures are more or less borne out by the receipts from the German customs, which amounted to 850 million marks in 1913, but only to 133 millions in 1918.

German foreign trade having thus been reduced to one-seventh of its former proportions, it remains to be seen how the Empire managed to solve in the first place certain problems in connection with industry, and subsequently the food problem.

CHAPTER II

INDUSTRY

1. THE COTTON PROBLEM

In peace time Germany consumed annually 430,000 tons of cotton, which came almost entirely from the United States. She was about to use more than 300,000 tons annually solely in the manufacture of explosives.

In August 1914 the French Ambassador at Berne had called the attention of his Government to the importance attached by Germany to the possession of a large stock of cotton. She had just placed big orders in the United States for consignment to her viâ Rotterdam, and in the meantime was appropriating any stocks of cotton in Belgium and the North of France that her armies could lay hands on.

While the Allies were in doubt as to whether to add cotton to their list of contraband, and as we know their doubts persisted till the 22nd of August 1915, the neutral countries adjacent to Germany were not wasting precious time. Holland and the Scandinavian countries, which had only imported 21,000 tons of cotton in 1913, imported 330,000 tons during the first year of the war. Owing, however, firstly to the addition of cotton to the lists of contraband and in the second

THE COTTON PROBLEM

place to the conclusion of quota agreements with Norway and Denmark, the imports of cotton from neutral countries into Germany were reduced to 40,000 tons during the second half of 1915, and the latter, who up to that time had received all the cotton she needed, began to grow uneasy. She began by restricting the activities of her textile industries in order to reserve all the available cotton for the manufacture of propellents. So drastically was her action carried out that by December 1915 the industrial output had been reduced by 70%.

It was obvious, however, that the stocks accumulated in 1915 were running out : since the outbreak of war Germany, besides receiving 200,000 tons from the United States and seizing an equivalent amount in the invaded area, had imported nearly 300,000 tons from neutral countries, or 700,000 tons in all. Allowing for a reduced consumption of only 150,000 tons by her textile industry and of 300,000 tons by her powder factories, the stocks in hand would last till the autumn of 1916 ; but with the exception of the cotton crop of Asia Minor, which amounted at the very utmost to 30,000 tons, no further assistance was to be looked for from any quarter whatever.

Germany appealed to her chemists. The first problem to be solved was that of supplying the powder factories with the necessary raw material. After numerous unsuccessful experiments the chemists succeeded in 1915 in obtaining nitro-cellulose derived not from cotton but from wood pulp. The wood pulp which was used had to be of the purest quality, and was obtained chiefly from the pine forests of Sweden. By 1916 the powder problem had been practically solved; Germany consumed from 120,000 to 160,000 tons of pulp, and the nitro-cellulose obtained from it gave a figure of 1.34% of nitrogen as compared with that of 1.46% given by nitro-cotton.

Notwithstanding the success of these measures stocks continued to diminish, and only 30,000 tons remained in hand at the beginning of 1917, when the activity of the textile industry had to be reduced by 90%, although the clothing problem was still unsolved.

Wool would have been invaluable to Germany in this connection, but the Empire had allowed its flocks to decrease year by year till at length it only produced 22,000 tons of wool against a consumption of 200,000 tons. In 1918 Germany hoped to make use of Roumanian and Russian wool; Roumania alone possessed 5,600,000 head of sheep, and Russia with her 45 million sheep could have provided more than 100,000 tons of wool; but as will be seen subsequently, the Central Empires could only supplement their resources to a very small extent from these two countries in 1918. All the available wool was reserved for the needs of the army, and the civilian population had to look elsewhere.

Very considerable resources were produced by unravelling worn out clothes, a process which

THE COTTON PROBLEM

yielded a kind of flock which could be respun. Substitutes had also to be resorted to.

The area under cultivation of flax was extended from 20,000 hectares in 1915 to 35,000 in 1917, and that of hemp from 1,500 hectares in 1916 to 8,000 in 1917. The yield derived from these experimental cultures, undertaken as they were in war time, was however but a drop in the ocean, as were the 10,000 tons of fibre which were produced from nettles in 1917. From the beginning of the third year of the war paper became the regular substitute.

The results obtained from woven paper were so satisfactory that 250,000 tons were produced in 1917. The strongest paper fabrics were obtained from soda pulp which was imported from Sweden, sulphite pulp being used in the manufacture of inferior qualities. Paper fabric proved on the whole to be a very good substitute in the manufacture of sandbags, aprons, awnings, uppers of shoes and driving belts, but the Germans never obtained a fabric which really afforded protection from the weather by this means.

Pure silk was smuggled in from Switzerland and was found very useful as a substitute for cotton in the manufacture of sewing thread; Switzerland was unrationed in this respect prior to the conclusion of the Agreement of the 4th of September 1917.

The Central Empires at one time thought of overcoming their shortage of textile goods by extending the manufacture of artificial silk, but

GERMANY

the General Staff on being consulted considered that the raw material required for the purpose could be much more usefully employed in supplying the needs of national defence.

Under these circumstances the shortage of clothing attained such serious proportions in Germany in 1918 that the Chancellor stated at one of the conferences held prior to the Armistice, that he considered it to be a more serious matter than the scarcity of food. It was only thanks to dishonest practices at the frontier that the well-to-do classes were enabled to dress decently. Germany for instance imported an unusually large quantity of embroidery from the Swiss canton of St. Gall, until one day in May 1918 the Custom-house officers noticed that shirts, 12 metres in length and containing scarcely any embroidery, were being described as embroidered goods for export.

Thanks to practices of this kind suits for men of real wool could still be bought in Berlin in October 1918 for 1,200 marks; a price which to the average German in his ignorance of the inflation that had taken place must have seemed enormous.

2. THE COPPER PROBLEM

Copper, like cotton, is another raw material which illustrates very strikingly the manner in which the blockade gradually took effect upon Germany. This is due to the fact that her home production before the war only amounted to

THE COPPER PROBLEM

40,000 tons as compared with a consumption of 220,000 tons, the balance being imported from the United States. Her imports in this respect, however, unlike those of cotton, were controlled by the Allies from the very outbreak of the war. Copper was added to the lists of contraband in October 1914, and its export from Allied countries was forbidden in December. In January 1915 Great Britain concluded an agreement with the copper producing corporations in America, and not a single cargo could be exported thereafter without her consent.

Although Germany had not collected any considerable stocks of cotton she was not taken by surprise with regard to copper; she had formed a stock of 150,000 tons at the beginning of 1914 and was accordingly relieved of any immediate anxiety on that account.

Her first care during the first few months of the war was to import copper through neutral states; Switzerland supplied her in 1915 with 6,000 tons, Holland with 1,000 tons and Sweden with 8,000 tons. There was yet another neutral state which could supply the Central Empires with copper ore from its own resources. I refer to Norway, which was capable of delivering 8,000 tons annually.

The sum total of her copper imports from various countries, together with her home production, amounted in 1915 to only 65,000 tons, and her stocks of copper, which had obviously been collected in anticipation of a short war, must have been heavily encroached upon by the middle of 1915.

This assumption becomes a certainty when we find the German Government issuing a decree on the 1st of May 1915 under which manufacturers were compelled to declare their stocks of copper.

The obligatory declaration of stocks was merely the prelude to the requisitioning of articles of copper, which was enforced on the 20th of July in the factories, and was extended on the 8th of December of the same year to private households, and to Belgium and Northern France in October 1916.

The situation had become serious by the beginning of 1916. Pre-war stocks had been reduced to 30,000 tons, and imports from neutrals in the course of the year were not to exceed 12,000 tons. To this total may be added the Serbian output — 7,000 tons perhaps at the most.

Strenuous efforts were made by Germany to increase her home production; work was resumed upon deposits of pyrites and copper schists in the Palatinate and the Black Forest which had been abandoned on account of their small percentage of copper, and her home production rose in consequence from 46,000 tons in 1914 to 59,000 tons in 1915, 79,000 tons in 1917, and 74,000 tons in 1918. Nevertheless, the aggregate yield of her imports and home production in 1916 still fell short of her requirements by 40%.

THE COPPER PROBLEM

Norway was the only country left in 1917 that could still export large quantities of copper to Germany, but the Allies had been buying up the greater part of the copper produced by her since the 31st of August 1915; Germany was therefore only able to obtain from 2,000 to 3,000 tons annually from this source, and her deficiency increased to 50%. She more or less got over her difficulties, however, by reserving her copper entirely for the use of the army, and by requisitioning her invisible stocks upon the one hand and by the ever increasing use of other metals as substitutes on the other.

In the latter respect she displayed extraordinary ingenuity. In peace time 50% of her copper was used in electrical plants, 38% in other machinery, and 12% was absorbed by household requirements. In electrical plants the windings were now made of aluminium instead of copper, and certain electric overhead cables were manufactured of iron wire which had been made weatherproof by means of zinc or aluminium. In the household aluminium was universally substituted for copper and brass.

The greatest difficulties were encountered in discovering a substitute for copper as regards ordinary machinery. Iron and cast iron were used in lieu of bronze, but, not infrequently, with disappointing results.

The two most valuable substitutes used in other branches of industry were zinc, of which Germany never ran short thanks to her own

GERMANY

deposits and to those at Vieille Montagne in Belgium, and aluminium, which was obtained from deposits of bauxite in Hungary and converted by means of hydro-electricity in Switzerland.

3. THE PROBLEM OF METALS IN GENERAL

The investigation of the question of copper has shown how important it was for Germany to find metal substitutes, and how difficult it is to discover how Germany supplied her needs in respect of each metal unless we have a general idea of the resources available to her during the war. I will put the facts as succinctly as possible.

The whole of the industry of Germany is dependent upon the production of coal. The latter varied between 1913 and 1918 as follows (in thousands of tons):

1913	1914	1915	1916	1917	1918
190,000	161,000	147,000	159,000	167,000	158,000

Manganese was the only metal a shortage of which would have been fatal to the German metallurgical industry, as it was essential for the conversion of iron into steel. The annual consumption of this metal in Germany amounted to 671,000 tons, very little of which was produced at home. Of this metal, however, as of copper, Germany had collected prior to the war sufficient supplies to last her for two years.

THE PROBLEM OF METALS

Again, as with copper, she endeavoured to increase her output of manganese (*a*) by treating certain iron ores in the Siegerland, (*b*) by reducing consumption either by substituting calcium carbide containing manganese in making basic steel, or by means of various technical improvements in the furnace, which allowed of a reduction of the consumption of manganese by 66%.

The results achieved were satisfactory: the production of steel in Germany during the war amounted (in thousands of tons) to

1913	1914	1915	1916	1917	1918
19,312	14,408	11,745	13,293	13,156	11,864

We must not, however, lose sight of the fact that from 1917 onwards the importation of Swedish iron ore, from which steel of good quality could alone be manufactured, was of vital importance to Germany. According to statistics the following amounts of Swedish ore were treated by the German industries in the course of the war (in thousands of tons):

1913	1914	1915	1916	1917	1918
7,400	6,600	6,800	6,900	6,200	6,600

The Agreement concluded on the 29th of May 1918 between Sweden and the Allies with regard to the limitation of Swedish exports to the Central Empires was signed much too late to have any results. Moreover if, owing to the prolongation of the war, the Agreement had become effective, Germany would probably have got over her difficulties by importing manganese from Russia; her requirements, indeed, could have been more than supplied by the output of the mines in the Caucasus.

Germany never ran short of zinc any more than of iron, and if there was a greater scarcity of lead than of the other two metals we have just dealt with the industrial economy of the country was never endangered thereby; Belgium, moreover, was forced to supply her invaders with a large amount of lead, as well as of zinc.

Aluminium was another metal of which there was never a shortage. Before the war the annual consumption of aluminium by Germany amounted to 14,000 tons. This aluminium was produced from French bauxite, which was converted into metal in Switzerland or in Germany. Exports of bauxite from France stopped in 1914, and supplies were getting very low in Germany when work was begun upon certain deposits in the provinces of Hesse and Nassau which up till then had been neglected. These deposits, however, were very inconsiderable in comparison with those of Hungary and Dalmatia, which provided the Swiss factories with abundant quantities of bauxite throughout the war, thanks to which the latter were able to supply Germany with 20,000 tons of aluminium yearly.

On the other hand there was an entire lack of tin and nickel and of the so called 'special'

THE PROBLEM OF METALS

metals with the exception of chromium, a satisfactory amount of which was procured from the deposits in Asia Minor.

Tin is one of the rare metals with regard to which the blockade was completely effective. Before the war Germany used 15,000 tons of tin, the greater part of which came from Bolivia and the Dutch East Indies. Supplies ran out by the end of 1915; tin was recovered from solder, empty cans were collected, and bells and organ pipes requisitioned. Aluminium was substituted for tinfoil, and the use of tin solder was eliminated by means of various mechanical processes such as studding and riveting.

When the submarine merchantman *Deutschland* made her celebrated voyage from Germany to the United States, her homeward cargo was chiefly composed of tin. She also carried 300 tons of nickel. Germany had used 2,000 tons of this metal in 1913, but had only produced 300 tons, the balance being imported from Canada and New Caledonia. Norway alone, subsequently to 1914, was able to supply her with about 400 tons of nickel per annum, and indeed did so. By the end of 1915 nevertheless, in spite of work having been resumed upon a few old deposits of nickel bearing pyrites, the shortage of nickel in the manufacture of special steels and of nickel silver became so acute that the nickel coinage had to be withdrawn from circulation and one of zinc substituted for it. In February 1918 the Government actually had to forbid surgical instruments

GERMANY

being coated with nickel, and to allow them only to be bronzed or polished.

Coming to the various kinds of special steel, attempts were made to manufacture tools from steel with a high percentage of manganese and silicon instead of from nickel steel : tungsten steel likewise, which was very scarce in spite of the imports from Sweden of ferro-tungsten, was replaced by chrome steel.

As for platinum, two tons of which had been imported annually into Germany from Russia previously to the war, every article in the possession of private individuals which was made of that metal had to be requisitioned. Here again the effects of the blockade would have been nullified if Germany could have taken due advantage of the peace of Brest Litovsk.

4. THE PROBLEM OF OILS AND FATS

The German industries, as has been pointed out, could get all the solid fuel they needed ; but they also required liquid fuel for their internal combustion engines and, of course, lubricants for their machinery.

The shortage of mineral oils (petrol, petroleum for lamps, and lubricants) was never felt very acutely in spite of the fact that Germany's output only amounted to 120,000 tons against a consumption of 1,440,000 tons. Austria-Hungary, the annual output of whose wells in Galicia amounted

THE PROBLEM OF OILS AND FATS

to 1,200,000 tons, and Roumania, with an annual output of 1,800,000 tons, were able to supply the German motors with all the petroleum they required. Moreover, if the war had lasted beyond the year 1918 the Central Empires could have drawn upon the entire Russian output of mineral oils.

The only critical period, as regards the petrol supply, occurred in 1915, when Galicia was invaded by the Russians, who destroyed the machinery in some of the wells. Thanks, however, to the exports from Roumania (380,000 tons in 1915) Germany was able that year to meet her peace-time requirements, which had moreover been considerably reduced by strict rationing, to the extent of 47%. From 1916 onwards she was able to import a sufficient quantity of mineral oils to cover 70% of her normal requirements.

Her position with regard to mineral oil lubricants was quite satisfactory also; for although her consumption had amounted to 300,000 tons in 1913 she distilled sufficient quantities from coal tar to more than cover her requirements. It was quite a different matter with regard to animal and vegetable oils and fats. When we come to examine the food question we shall see how seriously the German population was affected from the physiological point of view by the shortage of fats; and the lack of industrial oils was almost equally unfortunate from the point of view of German industry. As, however, animal

GERMANY

fats were chiefly required for purposes of food I will deal only with vegetable fats and oils at this point.

Prior to the war Germany imported 1,730,000 tons of oleaginous grain in the shape of rape seed from India, linseed from the Argentine, cotton seed from Egypt, castor seed from China and palm kernels from West Africa. 600,000 tons of oil in all were produced from this amount of grain, the waste products being fed to her cattle in the form of cake; only 25,000 tons of oil were produced from home grown oleaginous grain.

By the end of 1914 all imports of oleaginous grain had ceased. In February 1915 a 'War Committee of Oils and Fats' was appointed with a view to imposing the severest restrictions and increasing the home production of oleaginous grain. The committee did very good work in both respects: 60,000 tons of oil were obtained from home grown crops, and the consumption of fats in industry was reduced by means of restrictive measures from 430,000 to 40,000 tons. This latter result was only obtained, however, at the cost of curtailing the output of the leather and soap industries, both of which were large consumers of fats, to the extent of 90%. Soap was rationed at the rate of 50 grammes of solid soap and 125 grammes of powder monthly; but the soap, such as it was, was devoid of fats and chiefly composed of clay and resin.

As a matter of fact the whole of the fats that

THE PROBLEM OF OILS AND FATS

were produced in Germany had to be reserved entirely for the manufacture of glycerine for propellents and explosives. As the shortage got more and more pronounced the Germans were compelled to use an increasingly large proportion of nitro-cellulose in the place of nitro-glycerine in the manufacture of propellents, and of ammonium nitrate in that of explosives.

But although the problem of explosives was solved, the problem of fats became more and more acute; no product has ever been the object of so much research work; bones were treated by steaming, grease was extracted from rags and household slops, and attempts were made to extract oil from schist and graphite. Germany seems to have left no stone unturned in this respect.

5. THE RUBBER PROBLEM

Germany imported 16,000 tons of rubber annually in peace time for her own consumption. By dint of imposing severe restrictions the Empire was able to meet the requirements of the army from the stocks that were available in German factories and those that were seized at the occupation of Antwerp as well as from the imports from neutral countries although the latter, according to the R. Committee, never exceeded 3,000 tons. A kilogram of rubber from having been worth 4 marks at the beginning of 1914 had risen in value to 45 marks by December of the same

GERMANY

year, to 60 marks in the middle of 1916, and to 150 marks at the beginning of 1917.

Germany tried to get over this scarcity, of which the rise in price was the surest indication, in three different ways : by the manufacture of reconstituted and synthetic rubber, and by the use of substitutes.

Reconstituted rubber was not unheard of prior to the war, and the German manufacturers by improved methods of manufacture managed to produce a ' war rubber ' which was five times more expensive than in peace time and of rather inferior quality. It served its purpose, however, inasmuch as it enabled raw rubber to be reserved for the manufacture of tyres.

The Germans improved on the existing methods of manufacturing synthetic rubber, but did not achieve any practical results from the point of view of industry : the product derived from acetone had such an affinity for oxygen that it deteriorated very rapidly in air and was incapable of being vulcanised ; they were able, however, to obtain ebonite from it for the accumulators of their submarines. Free rein was given to the imagination in the pursuit of substitutes ; leather, steel springs, wood, paper and cork were experimented with in turn. Certain firms made a speciality of manufacturing tyres of woven steel wire or even of layers of very thin paper soaked in tar oils.

6. THE LEATHER PROBLEM

The fact that 1,100 boot factories out of 1,600 were closed in February 1917 is eloquent of the shortage of leather in Germany. Nevertheless, the tanning industry in Germany prior to the war had been of considerable importance. 315,000 tons of hides, of which 180,000 tons were imported, were treated by it, and 360,000 tons of tanning substances were used in order to produce 135,000 tons of leather.

The problem of the shortage of footwear did not become at all acute till December 1915, when a maximum price was fixed for leather. It got rapidly worse owing to the lack of tanning substances, especially of quebracho wood, and to the inferiority of Bulgarian sumac, bark or pine needles, which were used as substitutes.

Only 12 million pairs of boots instead of 120 millions were manufactured in 1917 and of this number a large proportion were so called ' National ' shoes, with vamps of leather, legs of paper fabric or old cloth, and soles of wood. A trial was also made of felt material impregnated with silicates or resin.

Driving belts were manufactured from hemp, nettles, jute, paper fabrics and steel ribbon, but the results were not very satisfactory.

Although the needs of the army were always met the blockade proved very effective with regard to leather; but here again the results already achieved might have been compromised when Russia, who was prepared to supply leather in large quantities, appeared upon the scene. The German tanning industry, indeed, was foremost in demanding during the war that Germany should turn her attention, in the economic sense, to the East, where inexhaustible supplies of the necessary raw material lay awaiting her in Russia, China and Afghanistan.

CHAPTER III

FOOD

No other European country is so absolutely dependent upon fertilisers for the success of its agriculture as Germany; fertilisers in peace time were used there much more extensively than elsewhere. Potash, nitrogenous and phosphatic fertilisers were all essential to her agricultural industry, but of these three in 1914 she possessed unlimited quantities of the first alone.

The deposits of Stassfurth, which employed 42,000 workmen before the war, together with those in the Saar district not only provided German agriculture with all the potash it needed but supplied the German shipping companies with one-third of their outward cargoes. Moreover, whenever Germany was engaged in negotiations with neutrals she always offered them raw materials of two kinds in exchange for their food products, namely coal, and potash which was second only in importance to coal itself.

Her position with regard to nitrogenous fertilisers, on the other hand, was much less favourable; before the war one-half of the total amount consumed by her was produced from Chilean nitrates and the other from ammonium sulphate which was manufactured within the Empire. Now, the Allies had put a stop to any imports of Chilean nitrates at the beginning of the war, and the whole of the artificially produced nitrogen would have been used in the powder factories had not the German Government, with praiseworthy tenacity of purpose, done its very best to develop the manufacture of synthetic ammonia and built the factories of Leuna near Merseburg and Oppau near Ludwigshafen while the war was in progress.

Thanks to her chemists Germany was able to supply the needs of her agriculturists in respect of nitrogenous fertilisers to the extent of 50% as long as the war lasted. Her soil instead of receiving 210,000 tons of pure nitrogenous matter as in 1913 only received 73,000 tons in 1915, 80,000 tons in 1916, and 100,000 tons in 1917; the increase, however, in 1918–19 would no doubt have been much more considerable.

Production in general would therefore have taken place on a much larger scale in 1919, and that is one of the reasons which have led economists to believe that the effects of the blockade, had the war been protracted, would not have increased mathematically as time elapsed, and that the latter, from 1918 onwards, in this respect at least would have worked against the Allies in favour of Germany. The shortage of phosphatic fertilisers detracts of course from the force of this argument.

FOOD

Prior to 1914 Germany imported from the United States and Algeria two-fifths of the phosphoric acid required by her agriculturists, the remaining three-fifths being derived from dross from dephosphoring provided by her factories. At the beginning of the war imports of phosphates ceased altogether : the manufacture of super-phosphates had to be stopped entirely in Germany by 1915 in order to avoid a shortage of sulphuric acid, which was urgently needed for military purposes. The soil of Germany instead of receiving 630,000 tons of phosphoric acid as in 1913 only received 425,000 tons in 1915, 368,000 tons in 1916, 325,000 tons in 1917, and this decline, instead of being arrested as was the case with nitrogenous fertilisers, was continuous.

Germany endeavoured to replace the fertilisers in which she was lacking by those which she possessed in abundance ; she supersaturated her soil with potash to the extent of actually using 834,000 tons in 1918 instead of 356,000 tons in 1913. These measures, however, only achieved very inadequate results ; the poor yield of German agricultural land during the war can be easily accounted for by the shortage of manure, aggravated as it was by labour difficulties similar to those encountered in France. I will confine my investigations in this respect to wheat, rye, barley and potatoes.

In 1913 the Empire was more or less self-supporting in bread-stuffs, but it had fostered

GERMANY

the production of rye at the expense of its wheat, as the former was better suited to the nature of its soil. Although it was continually increasing its exports of rye it was becoming more and more fastidious about the quality of the flour that was used in bread-making and had therefore imported 1,600,000 tons of wheat in 1911. There can be no doubt in any case that the country usually produced enough corn to supply the 70 millions of Germans with the 180 kilogrammes that a man is said to require annually.

On the other hand Germany barely produced 50% of the requirements of her inhabitants and of her distilleries with regard to barley—the balance being imported almost entirely from Russia.

The production of potatoes in Germany was equal to the consumption, enormous though the latter was; she devoted 3,300,000 hectares, or about one-fifth of her cultivated area, to the production of potatoes and was ahead of every other European country in that respect. So considerable indeed was her potato crop that it was used partly as fodder for her cattle and partly for industrial purposes; in fact it was upon potatoes that the German chemists counted to make good the shortage of food in the event of a blockade; unfortunately, as they observed, potatoes contained very little albumen and even less fats.

The results of the harvests for the years 1913 to 1918 inclusive were as follow :

FOOD

	Wheat Tons	Rye Tons	Barley Tons	Potatoes Tons
1913	4,400,000	12,000,000	3,500,000	52,000,000
1914	3,700,000	9,000,000	2,415,000	45,569,000
1915	2,999,000	8,900,000	2,000,000	24,699,000
1916	3,086,000	8,936,000	2,796,000	25,740,000
1917	2,226,000	6,900,000	1,957,000	34,410,000
1918	2,458,000	8,000,000	2,258,000	29,469,000

The manner in which Germany was compelled to solve her bread problem can be easily inferred from these figures: her population was very severely rationed from the first year of the war, an increasingly large proportion of rye and potato flour was used in the manufacture of bread until the weekly bread ration of the notorious K K bread was fixed at 1,900 grammes per head. Yet in 1917, even this result, poor as it was, could only be attained by the importation of corn from Roumania, with the consent of the latter in 1915 but independently thereof in 1916. The amount thus obtained, however, was not apparently very large if the German figures are to be trusted.

Not a single neutral country could be counted upon to improve matters; Denmark alone was able to export a very small quantity of wheat, and the other neutral countries were so short of corn that their Governments had reserved to themselves the sole right of importing flour and grain as early as 1915 or 1916.

Equally little reliance could be placed upon the potato crop, which had turned out very badly

GERMANY

in 1916; indeed on the eve of the horrible 'turnip' winter of 1916–17, the weekly potato ration had at one time been reduced to 3 lbs. per head. It was raised to 5 lbs. in the following July and to 7 lbs. a few weeks later. The Socialist papers nevertheless were loud in their demands for an increase in the ration to 10 lbs. But the farmers, who were very influential in the Reichstag, maintained that an increase of this kind would endanger the crop of the following year and so deprive them of the means of feeding their live stock and bring about the complete ruin of German agriculture. They carried their point and the potato harvest of 1917, which amounted to 35 million tons, was distributed as follows:

	Million tons
As seed potatoes	5.3
As food for the agricultural classes	6.6
As food for the rest of the civilian population	10.7
As food for the army	3.2
For the distilleries	2.5
To be fed to cattle	6.7

Germany, in consequence, was unable to relax the severity of her bread card system in any way: her bread, as it was, consisted in December 1917 of 55% of rye flour, 35% of wheat flour and 10% of substitutes. It may therefore well be imagined what sanguine expectations were entertained by the German people when at the

FOOD

beginning of 1918 the treaty of Brest Litovsk was signed (upon the 9th of February) which gave them access as they believed to the granaries of the Ukraine, and the Chancellor mounted the tribune and declared : " Gentleman, peace is at hand with regard to bread."

An economic agreement with the Ukraine was hastily signed upon the 9th of April ; a trade bureau was established at Kieff to buy up all the available stocks of corn, which were estimated, by the most pessimistically inclined, to amount to not less than 1,600,000 tons ; the railway lines were to be reconditioned immediately and, in case they should be unable to deal with the traffic, an Office of Black Sea Transport was established at Braila to undertake the transport of corn by way of the Danube.

The permanent way, however, turned out to be in such a plight that no trains could make use of it till the following summer ; the train from Petrograd–Kieff, which did the journey in thirty-seven hours before the war, took six days to do it—on the rare occasions when it started at all.

400,000 tons of shipping were still available in theory in the Black Sea, but only 75,000 tons were in a fit state to be chartered ; the remainder were rotting in harbour.

Anyhow, the tonnage available turned out to be more than sufficient to convey the stocks of grain in the Ukraine—for they were non-existent.

GERMANY

A great deal had been sent into the other Russian provinces by the Bolsheviks, and the peasants, who were under no sort of control whatever, had turned what was left into brandy and drunk it.

The Germans were so angry that they occupied the country : they made the Ukrainian Government responsible for the disorder, dissolved the Rada and set up the hetman Skoropaski who was in sympathy with them as dictator in its place. But it was all to no purpose ; nothing was to be got from the Ukraine that year. By the 1st of June the German press had changed its tone. " We shall do well," it said, " not to count upon the Ukraine as a reliable factor for the present in making any political or economic forecast."

Roumania, too, notwithstanding the condition of economic servitude to which she had been reduced by the Treaty of Bucharest upon the 7th of May, was to prove almost equally unreliable, as the land upon which fighting had been going on since 1916 could hardly be brought under cultivation for another twelve months.

There was nothing left to the Imperial food office but to reduce the bread ration in June 1918 from 1,500 to 1,250 grammes if the country was to hold out till the following harvest.

But there were other countries in the world besides Germany. On the 17th of June riots broke out in Vienna upon the announcement by Dr. Paul, the Minister of Food, that the bread ration, which had already been reduced to 1,102 grammes per week for workmen and to 600 grammes per week in the case of adult non-manual labourers, was to undergo a further reduction. The Austrian stocks of corn had actually been exhausted two months previously, since when the Government had only lived from hand to mouth; it had, moreover, concluded an agreement with Germany under which it had renounced all claim to the stock in Bessarabia and the Ukraine on condition that Germany supplied her with enough food to carry her till the 15th of August. But owing to the non-existence of the stocks in Bessarabia and the Ukraine Germany had not only been unable to keep her promise but had actually failed to the extent of 2,000 truckloads, and for the week ending upon the 22nd of June the Austrian food office had only 420 truckloads available.

These precarious conditions lasted until the advent of harvest in July which, luckily for the Central Empires, turned out, as we have seen, to be much better than that of 1917. Upon the 1st of August the bread ration was again raised to 1,850 grammes and underwent a further increase of 100 grammes upon the 1st of October.

Can it be assumed that the Germans would have been able to get whatever corn they needed from the Ukraine and Roumania if the war had been prolonged? It is an eventuality which might well have materialised. They might perhaps equally well have obtained from Russia the barley of which they had such an inadequate supply that brewing had to be reduced by 80%, and the civilian population from 1917 onwards was compelled to drink as beer a liquid which had nothing in common, save the name, with the beverage the Germans are so fond of; the German breweries, which had used 1,700,000 tons of barley in 1913, were only allowed 131,000 tons in 1917 and 133,000 tons in 1918.

No question in Germany gave rise to more heated discussions between producers and consumers than that of meat, which was as intimately connected with the question of fodder as the problem of corn production with that of fertilisers; for the producer was anxious to preserve his livestock, and the consumer, not unnaturally, had no inclination to die of hunger. The fate of the Government actually depended at one moment upon the solution of the question, and the Chancellor Michaelis, under pressure from the agrarians, had to get rid of Herr von Batocki, his Minister of Food, for having allowed the stock of pigs to melt away in order to help the consumer. He was succeeded, for the last half year of the war, by Herr von Waldow, an outstanding agrarian, who defended the interests of the landed proprietors with a tenacity that had earned for him the sobriquet of "old ramrod," when he was provincial governor at Posen.

The question of livestock was a difficult one to solve as the Empire before the war had been unable to satisfy even approximately its own

FOOD

requirements in the way of fodder; the hay crop in the years 1914–18 varied between 28 and 21 million tons; but prior to 1914 Germany had been compelled to import a further 7 million tons of fodder, by far the greater part of which came from Russia.

Furthermore, not only had she to import, either directly or in the shape of oleaginous grain, nearly the whole of the 1,740,000 tons of cake which were consumed by her livestock, but of the 1,730,000 tons of oleaginous grain imported by her in 1913, 400,000 tons came from British India, 450,000 tons from the Argentine Republic, and 200,000 tons from Egypt. Her actual imports in the form of cake, moreover, came either from Russia or one or other of the Allied countries.

Germany, therefore, was unable in peace time to supply her livestock, which consisted of approximately 22 million oxen, 11 million cows and 29 million pigs, with food from her own resources.

According to statistics the annual consumption of meat of the German adult had increased from 40 kilogrammes prior to 1900 to 50 kilogrammes in 1914. Nine-tenths of this demand was supplied by the German livestock, and the remaining tenth by imports from Holland and Denmark and frozen meat from the United States.

In 1915 the German Government very wisely decided to save its livestock at all costs; it therefore introduced meat cards and meatless days, and imposed severe restrictions upon slaughtering.

GERMANY

I will not take up the time of my readers with a detailed account of these regulations, which were the subject of many and various decrees; generally speaking, when the harvest was impending and the bread ration had been cut down the Government increased the meat ration and again reduced it at the beginning of winter; sometimes also with the advent of spring it gave permission for slaughtering on a large scale owing to the shortage of fodder and the consequent inducement to the peasants to get rid of their livestock.

As might have been expected, the neutral countries adjacent to Germany furnished her with considerable supplies of meat. The assistance derived by her from this quarter may be taken as amounting to one-sixth of the total consumption in 1916, and one-twelfth in 1917. According to German statistics, 356,000 head of live cattle were imported into the Empire in 1916, 236,000 in 1917, and 125,000 in 1918. Imports of dead meat fell from 120,000 tons in 1916 to 45,000 tons in 1917, and 8,000 tons in 1918.

It was owing to these imports and the adoption of severe measures of control that the German horned livestock was preserved. Her oxen and cows, which in 1914 amounted in numbers to 22 and 11 millions, had only fallen by 1918 to 18 and 9 millions respectively. Her pigs on the other hand had suffered severely, the stock being reduced from 26 millions in 1914 to 6 millions in 1918. This hecatomb was effected in order to

FOOD

preserve for human consumption potatoes which would normally have been used as fodder.

Although the German livestock had been saved it was none the less extremely ill fed, so much so indeed that during the four years of the war her cattle on an average produced only 150 kilogrammes of meat and her pigs only 45. Her meat ration had in consequence to be reduced in 1918 to 250 grammes per week; and what was more serious still, milk, butter and fat became very scarce. Berlin, instead of receiving 864,000 litres of milk a day as it had done in 1914, received only 302,000 litres in 1918. The effect as regards fatty substances was even more alarming. Germany before the war produced 1,600,000 tons of animal fats and imported 268,000 tons. 430,000 of these 1,868,000 tons were absorbed by industry and the remainder was utilised for human consumption, at an average weekly rate of 190 grammes per head. By 1917 however the production of animal fats had been reduced in Germany by nearly 50%; in 1918, for instance, she was producing only 280,000 tons of butter as against 450,000 tons in 1913. Fats were imported by her in the following quantities: 175,000 tons in 1916, 95,000 tons in 1917, and 27,000 tons in 1918.

The average weekly ration of fats, which had been originally fixed at 120 grammes per head, was decreased in the first instance to 75 grammes at the end of 1917, and finally to 62 grammes in 1918.

GERMANY

However serious the situation might be just then with regard to animal fats, it was much more so as regards vegetable fats, which of course were mainly reserved for industrial purposes.

To say that Germany was really emaciated in 1918 is no figure of speech but an actual statement of fact, as there was hardly anything left to take the place of bread, meat and fats.

Sugar was chiefly used to take the place of other foods, for whereas France had to fall back upon saccharin Germany always had abundance of sugar. It was nevertheless as strictly rationed as any other article of consumption. The sugar ration at the end of the war amounted to 187 grammes per week. The beet crop was allowed to decrease from 17 million tons in 1913 to 10 million tons in 1918 without the supplies of sugar ever being endangered.

Fish might have proved a very useful adjunct to the food supplies of Germany. Her fisheries could have provided her with 6,600 tons of fish a week (or the equivalent of a weekly ration of 100 grammes per head) but for the requisitions and restrictions upon the right of fishing, which disorganised the industry. She had therefore to fall back upon imports from abroad, and 420,000 tons of fresh, salted or canned fish were imported in 1916, 150,000 tons in 1917 and 80,000 tons in 1918.

Although the foregoing figures with regard to the decrease in neutral imports have been supplied by German writers who were naturally anxious after the war to enlist the sympathies of foreigners on behalf of Germany in her distress, they are none the less a striking proof of the efficacy of the measures adopted by the Allies subsequently to 1916.

The consumption of cocoa amounted to 51,000 tons in 1913, but fell to 43,600 tons in 1915, 11,000 tons in 1916, 1,200 tons in 1917, and to practically nothing in 1918, when it was replaced by substitutes of one kind or another of which Germany made such an extensive use at the end of the war, sometimes with very harmful results.

Of all the various foods of which a scarcity existed none were the object of so much research from the point of view of *ersatz* as fats. Bones and knackers' carcasses were treated, and even slops were put under contribution: oil was extracted from every kind of seed (beechmast and lime seeds) and from the stones and pips of fruit.

The Situation on 11th November 1918

I have already remarked that Germany would appear to have left no stone unturned to get the fats she needed. She succeeded in doing so only very imperfectly, to judge by the unprejudiced statements contained in the report of the Committee which was appointed in November 1918 by the Allies to inquire into the food situation in Germany. The terms of the Armistice had of course provided that the blockade was to be

GERMANY

maintained with the utmost strictness, but the Allied and Associated Powers had declared that they would allow Germany to obtain supplies of food "so far as might be considered necessary."

A standard had accordingly to be fixed, and the Allies set to work on the rather theoretical basis of the number of calories needed to sustain human life. Their task was by no means an easy one. The Reich was in the throes of a revolution, and demobilisation had taken it by surprise although a very careful scheme of demobilisation had been drawn up upon the theory that the war at the worst would end indecisively.

The 'Council of the Representatives of the People' nevertheless set up an 'Office of Economic Demobilisation' on the 13th of November with none other than Colonel Koeth, the former 'Chief of the Imperial Department of War Supplies of Raw Materials' and a nominee of Herr Ebert, at the head of it.

The Allies proceeded to draw up Germany's diet sheet on the basis of a daily average ration for the country of 2,100 calories per head. This figure was obtained upon the assumption that children below fourteen years of age, amounting to 29% of the population, needed only 1,200 calories, that adults, amounting to 51% of the population, consumed 2,700 calories, and that the elderly people, amounting to 20% of the population, required only 1,800 calories. Sugar,

FOOD

which was available in large quantities, and fish, which the German fishermen would soon provide, were not taken into account, and the investigation was confined to the problems of corn, potatoes, meat and fats.

The potato crop had amounted to 28,000,000 tons. On the assumption that 6 million tons had been consumed by the 15th of November and that Germany would have to last till the beginning of the following June, 5,300,000 tons were reserved for seed, 2,500,000 tons for fodder, an allowance of 5 million tons was made for offal, and the weekly ration was fixed at 7 lbs. a head.

As regards meat it was reckoned that if 112,000 beasts were slaughtered weekly, and that 156 kilogrammes of meat were obtained per head of cattle slaughtered, Germany could provide each of her inhabitants with 246 grammes weekly, and that, if the 1,630 tons of mutton and 3,670 tons of pork were taken into account, this ration could be increased to 322 grammes. This amount was obviously very inferior to the average pre-war ration in France, which was estimated at 600 grammes. On the other hand in view of the bad condition of the cattle it would have been unwise to increase the weekly ration beyond 250 grammes.

These figures showed that Germany was short to the extent of 50% of the amount of ordinary meat that was necessary if her population was to exist without privation; and that 16,140 tons of meat would have to be imported into Germany weekly.

The Allies, however, observed that the shortage of meat was equivalent to one of 30,000 million calories, and that Germany could procure an additional 46,000 million calories and make up for the shortage of meat merely by doubling the sugar ration; and moreover that as 2,500,000 tons of potatoes had been set aside for the needs of her livestock the latter was bound to gain considerably in weight during the winter of 1918–19.

The question of fats alone remained to be dealt with. The annual production of milk in Germany was estimated at 280,000 cubic metres, 139,000 of which were absorbed in the manufacture of butter, the weekly ration of which amounted to 88 grammes per head, the remainder being reserved for that section of the population which needed milk foods.

As the butter ration of 88 grammes required supplementing by at least 40 grammes of fats or margarine, 2,640 tons of fatty or oleaginous substances had to be found weekly. Germany, however, was unable to contribute more than 1,000 tons towards this total amount and it was therefore found imperatively necessary to import 1,700 tons of fats into Germany weekly.

Such in its main outlines was the position in Germany with regard to food upon the 15th of November 1918.

FOOD

The figures we have adduced prove that the action taken by the Allies with a view to achieving the economic encirclement of Germany had undoubtedly affected the food supplies of her people. It would be very unwise, however, to form any conclusion as to the condition of the Empire at the time of the Armistice upon the strength of these figures alone, which only apply to an imaginary individual called 'the average man.' No such person really existed in Germany.

First of all came the fighting men, to whose needs everything was sacrificed. At no time did they suffer hunger, and beyond having to eat bread of a dark grey hue, being rationed with regard to meat and experiencing at times a shortage of coffee, tobacco and alcohol, they were never more than very indirectly affected by the blockade.

In the second place the producer, the peasant that is to say, in spite of innumerable inspections and requisitions, succeeded in retaining for himself and his family a very large proportion of the harvest; and all the efforts of the Imperial Food Office to discover the hiding places where the peasants had hidden their sacks of potatoes were unsuccessful.

Last of all came the middle class citizens and the working class inhabitants of the industrial centres. It was these two classes exclusively which felt the whole weight of the measures of restriction. The blockade indeed may be said to have borne with scandalous severity upon the town dweller and the inhabitant of the industrial West as compared with the country dweller and the inhabitant of the agricultural East.

The death rate of the workmen in the Krupp factories rose from 4.12 per thousand in 1914 to 5.84 in 1915, 6.5 in 1916, and 8.7 in 1917. This of course is attributable to a variety of causes which are almost of too complex a nature to allow of analysis but certainly in some measure to the blockade.

According to the statistics the death rate of the civilian population alone increased, as compared with peace time, by 9.5% in 1915, 14.3% in 1916, 32.2% in 1917, and by 37% in 1918. Deaths from tuberculosis are also said to have increased by 20%. It must be remembered, however, that the health average of the civilian population had been very much lowered by the departure of its most vigorous members for the front.

This inequality of conditions as between the various classes in the Empire was not due solely to purely geographical causes but was very notably aggravated by transport difficulties, which from 1917 onwards affected adversely the whole of the German economic system. The other belligerents were similarly affected, but only at certain times in the year, in the autumn for instance when harvest was in progress, whereas in Germany the difficulties increased as the years went by.

FOOD

One of the indirect results of the blockade was to throw an enormous burden upon the German rolling-stock from 1915 onwards. Owing to the cessation of any activity in the ports traffic was diverted from the waterways, which hitherto had relieved the railways to the extent of 50%. Moreover, the process of concentration which industry was undergoing in Germany entailed the building of a great many new factories and the transport on a large scale of building materials, coke and ore. Lastly, by reason of her occupation of foreign territory Germany was forced to use her rolling-stock outside the country on an increasingly large scale. In 1917 4,300 of her 25,176 engines were being used in the invaded area. So great was the strain thrown upon them by the traffic with which they had to deal that 23% of this number were usually undergoing repairs simultaneously as compared with a percentage of 8% in peace time.

Such was the shortage of lubricants, that German trucks were actually sent into Switzerland on their outward journey with their grease boxes empty in order to compel the neutrals to fill them.

The most curious result of these transport difficulties was to bring about a severe coal crisis in 1917 in a country which before the war exported 30 million tons yearly, and thereby increase the miseries of the underfed townsfolk, especially in Bavaria and East Prussia. Railway

GERMANY

and tramway services had to be cut down and fuel and lighting restricted. At Königsberg shops were actually closed by order at 1 p.m. in December 1917, while stocks of coal were accumulating at the pit heads.

CHAPTER IV

LESSONS OF THE BLOCKADE

THOSE who confine their study of the effects of the blockade, so far as Germany was concerned, upon the townsman on the one hand and the countryman on the other, are bound to come to widely different conclusions.

I am unwilling to conclude this study without paying my tribute to the German people, which they certainly deserve. Germany no doubt had her *Schieber* as we had our profiteers. No doubt also the Imperial Government availed itself of every possible device to delude a peculiarly credulous people as to the prospects of victory. Whereas for instance the Allied Governments kept on telling their people when the war seemed to be going badly that time was bound to tell in their favour as the blockade took effect, the representatives of the German Admiralty one after the other kept on repeating that the submarine war was bound to give the Central Empires the victory with mathematical certainty.

Undertaken as it was with a purely military object this war certainly helped to allay the feeling of obsession by which any country, threatened with strangulation, is bound to be affected. I am nevertheless convinced that very few nations

THE NAVAL BLOCKADE

would have borne almost uncomplainingly, especially during the last two years of the war, the privations which the German people suffered in consequence of the blockade. The remembrance of her protracted economic siege during which she withstood a host of enemies is still a source of patriotic pride to the Germans with which we cannot but sympathise.

It was indeed upon the civilian population that the action of the Allies bore with the greatest weight, since Germany was able, thanks to her energy and ingenuity, to keep her armies supplied with food and material up to the Armistice. Nevertheless the Central Empires would do well not to protest against the action of the Allied navies on the grounds of morality. It was Germany herself, as we have seen, who tightened the bonds by which she was being suffocated by her declaration of submarine war, the main object of which from February 1915 onwards was to prevent Great Britain receiving supplies and in which no attempt was made to discriminate between the military and civilian population of that country.

Moreover, the sufferings entailed upon the civilian population by the action of the Allies would not have been so intensified but for the restrictions which the German Government, which controlled the food supplies of the whole Empire, imposed upon civilians for the sake of the army.

This particular effect of the blockade is due

LESSONS OF THE BLOCKADE

unfortunately to the conditions of modern warfare, under which the whole of the vital forces of a nation are brought into play and non-combatants are directly affected.

Another inference has also been drawn by the Germans from the blockade which is of the greatest importance to us; namely that the countries which are complementary to Germany, those that is to say which are geographically continuous with her and together form an economic agglomeration capable of withstanding victoriously the longest of sieges, lie not to the West of her but to the East.

"It is a mistake," say the principal German economists, "to try to develop our trade with the Western countries and the United States. We must look Eastwards; Russia will supply us with the corn we need, the fodder which is essential to our cattle, and the fats which are indispensable to us as food and from the point of view of industry. The metals of the Urals, the mineral oils of the Caucasus and the cotton of Asia Minor await us. The ancient dream of the *Drang nach Osten*, the thrust Eastwards even towards the route to India, has received definite encouragement from the events of 1914–18."

The Allies on the other hand will find it very difficult to learn any very definite lesson either from the manner in which the blockade was conducted or from the results achieved thereby. If the latter are examined it will be found that victory would never have been secured solely and exclusively by the economic encirclement of the Central Empires. The effect of the blockade would not have been felt so severely had not Germany devoted the best part of her resources to the army, and it was by the action of the Allied armies upon the different fronts that Germany incurred her most serious loss of substance. It is none the less certain that Germany was shaken and enfeebled by the steady pressure of the Allies; in 1917, however, when the encirclement was about to become effective, such a breach was made in the East by the defection of Russia that none but a bold man would affirm that in the event of hostilities having been prolonged any more definite results would have been achieved by the economic war.

If the methods of the blockade are examined they will be found to bear the stamp of empiricism. The economic blockade itself was one long process of adaptation to the end in view. Its conduct was marked for two years by infirmity of purpose born of the fear of offending the neutrals, and it was only increased in severity at the request of a newcomer among the belligerents, when the United States entered the struggle. Not until the armies of the Central Empires had been defeated did it bring about the total demoralisation of an underfed nation which, after setting a wonderful example of endurance for four years, gave way for a short time to despair.

In view, however, of the impossibility of determining with any degree of certainty the extent to

LESSONS OF THE BLOCKADE

which the economic blockade was responsible for victory, certain authors have assumed that, upon the whole, the naval economic war was not a profitable operation for the Allies. " By the exercise of the right of capture," they wrote,[1] " the Allies succeeded in partially drying up the sources of Germany's supplies, but were unable to obtain a decisive result. On the other hand they supplied Germany with a pretext for waging war by means of her submarines upon commerce, a war which proved ineffective, as the Allied ports were never so busy as in the years 1917–18.

" This war led to the waste of private property, destroyed 15 million tons of shipping, was responsible for the crisis in freights, and is the cause of all the economic and financial difficulties from which Europe is suffering."

There can be no doubt whatever that the economic war was not in itself a profitable operation; but to demonstrate its ineffectiveness we should have to prove that the result of the war would have been the same if Germany had not had her hands tied in any way with regard to trade overseas, a purely hypothetical assumption. We can only go by the facts, in the light of which it seems impossible to deny that the enfeeblement of Germany by reason of her economic encirclement was one of the main factors of victory. Economic encirclement after all was only an

[1] See *Les aspects économiques du droit de prise avant et depuis la guerre mondiale,* by Jacques Dumas, Chap. VI.

THE NAVAL BLOCKADE

achievement incidental to the successful accomplishment by the Allied navies of their main task of acquiring and maintaining the mastery of the seas without which victory would have been impossible.

BIBLIOGRAPHY

BASDEVANT.—*Droit maritime international. Conférences de l'Ecole de guerre navale.*
A. LAURENS.—*Le blocus et la guerre sous-marine.*
FAUCHILLE ET BASDEVANT.—*Jurisprudence britannique en matière de prises maritimes.*
FAUCHILLE.—*La guerre de 1914* (Vols. I., II., III.).
FAUCHILLE.—*Jurisprudence allemande en matière de prises maritimes.*
A GROUP OF COLLABORATORS OF DENYS COCHIN.—*Les organisations de blocus en France pendant la guerre 1914–1918.*
MINISTÈRE DU TRAVAIL.—*Statistiques générales de la France.*
CONSETT.—*The Triumph of Unarmed Forces.*
JACQUES DUMAS.—*Les aspects économiques du droit de prise avant et depuis la guerre mondiale.*
MÉRIGNAC ET LÉMONON.—*Le droit des gens et la guerre de 1914–1918.*
CH. DUPUIS.—*Le droit de la guerre maritime.*
The Statesman's Year Book (1912–1920).
HENRI CANGARDEL.—*La Marine marchande française et la guerre.*
SIR ARTHUR SALTER.—*Allied Shipping Control: an Experiment in International Administration.*
AEREBOE, FRIEDRICH.—*Der Einfluss des Krieges auf die landwirtschaftliche Produktion in Deutschland.*
ALESSANDRI, J.—*Contribution à l'étude des blocus nouveaux.*
LEBON.—*Problèmes économiques nés de la guerre.*
VICTOR BORET.—*La bataille économique de demain.*
ED. VERMEIL.—*L'Allemagne contemporaine.*
ACKERMANN, C. W.—*L'Allemagne de l'arrière.*

BIBLIOGRAPHY

MAURICE BERGER.—*La nouvelle Allemagne (Enquêtes et Témoignages)*.

KARL HELFFERICH.—*Der Weltkrieg*.

BURTON J. HENDRICK (edited by).—*Life and Correspondence of Walter H. Page*.

SIR EDWARD GREY.—*Twenty-five Years*.

ERZBERGER, M.—*Erlebnisse im Weltkrieg*.

MICHELSEN, ANDREAS.—*U-Bootskrieg 1914–1918*.

ARCHIBALD HURD.—*The Merchant Navy*.

THOMAS G. FROTTINGHAM.—*The United States in the War*.

JAUREGUY, FROMENT ET STÉPHEN.—*L'Industrie allemande et la guerre*.

DELBRÜCK, C.—*Die wirtschaftliche Mobilmachung*.

INDEX

A

ADMIRALTY: Notices regarding mines, 30, 31; objects to blockade of entire German coast, 52; Lord Jellicoe's letter to, 66; Transport Department of, 89; this is separated from the Admiralty, 90; sets up Advisory Coal Committee, 96; House of Commons' suggestion that direction of economic war be transferred to, 110; Lord R. Cecil's reply to this, *ib*; Admiralty's opinion, *ib*.
Advisory Coal Committee appointed, 96
Allied Maritime Transport Council (A.M.T.C.) created, 118; its duties, 119; its activities, 129
Allies Blockade Committee, 113; personnel of, 113–14
Allizé, M., 182
American Overseas Corporation, 144
Amery, Mr. L. S., 114
Angary, the law of, 122, 123, 194, 196
Antwerp, ships detained at, in 1914, 10
Argentina, export of oleaginous grain to Germany, 295; value of her trade with Germany, 261
Associated Norwegian Importers of Mineral Oils, 82
Association of Notable Traders of Copenhagen, 164
Australia, value of her trade with Germany, 261
Austria, mercantile marine of, 9

B

Balfour, Lord, 201, 202
Baltic, British submarines in, 52
Barcelona, 'cruising grounds' established off, 29
Bathurst, search station proposed at, 119
Batocki, Herr von, 294

Berlin, the, 31
Bermuda, search station proposed at, 119
Berne, German-Swiss Conference at, 220
Bessarabia, 293
Bismarck, Prince, 28
BLACK LISTS: origin of, 94; application of, 96; published in *London Gazette*, 97; adopted by France, 98
BLOCKADE: essentials for an effective, 13; of entire German coast urged by France, 52; objection of the British Admiralty to this, *ib*.; virtually effected by Order in Council of 11 March 1915, 49; Great Britain's view of the, 73, 74; France's view of the, 74; turning point in the history of, 102
Board of Trade, 89; sets up the Ship Licensing Committee, *ib*.
Braila, office of Black Sea Transport established at, 291
Briand, M. Aristide, 72

C

CECIL, LORD ROBERT (Lord Cecil of Chelwood): becomes Minister of Blockade, 68; good relations with M. Denys Cochin, 73; effect of his appointment, 75; his work, 76–8; confers with M. Métier, 106; defends his policy in House of Commons, 110; urges importance of Order in Council of 11 March 1915, 120, 121; sends Memorandum to Holland, 203
Cette, 128, 216, 218, 222
Chamber of Danish Manufacturers, 164
Charpentier, M., 114
Chili, export of nitrates to Germany by, 285–6; requisitions German ships, 254
Claveille, M., appointed Under-Secretary for Transport, 93
Clemenceau, M., 73

315

INDEX

Clémentel, M., presides over Permanent International Committee of Economic Action, 74
coal supplies of Allies, 94, 95; Advisory Coal Committee set up, 96; supplies allotted to France and Italy in 1918, 130; coal fleet (French) operated by Ministry of Public Works, 92
COCHIN, M. DENYS: appointed head of Committee of Restriction, 68; becomes Under-Secretary for the Blockade, 71; creates the French Committee of Blockade, 72; good relations with Lord R. Cecil, 73; defends his policy, 110; leaves the Ministry, 112; is succeeded by M. Métier, 106; his proposals concerning the Swiss quotas, 223, 224
coffee, increase in Scandinavian exports to Germany of, 110; difficulties in fixing Dutch quotas of, 185
Committee of Blockade: formed, 72; set up in London, 113; fails to adjudicate, 128
Committee of Exemptions from the Prohibition to Export, 40, 59; personnel of, 65
Committee of Maritime Transport appointed, 93
Committee for Preventing Supplies reaching the Enemy (*i.e.* Committee of Restriction, *q.v.*)
COMMITTEE OF RESTRICTION: formed, 39; reformed, 64; its duties, 65; placed under M. Denys Cochin, 68; suggests a new policy, 103; placed under M. Lebrun, 113; in favour of rationing Holland, 182–7; objects to Dutch decree, 188–9; accepts Oppenheimer plan, 212; agrees with England concerning Swiss quotas, 221; revises Swiss quotas, 222
Company of Notable Traders (Copenhagen), 82
Conference at Berne (17 Aug. 1916) 220
Conference at Copenhagen (20 Jan. 1915), 138
Conference at London, 16, 59, 62
Conference at Paris (29 Nov. 1917), 118

Conference at Paris (9 Aug. 1916), 220
Conference at Stockholm, 137
Conference, the first inter-Scandinavian (24 Oct. 1914), 137
Consett, Rear-Admiral, 70
'continuous voyage,' doctrine of, 18, 19
CONTRABAND: definitions of, 14, 17, 18; 'absolute,' 17; 'conditional,' 17–20, 23; destination of, 18, 20, 22–4, 26; extension of lists of, 55, 57; final list of (25 Oct. 1918), 57; German memorandum concerning, 46; Russian decrees as to, 15
Contraband Committee, 64, 114
Controller of Equipment appointed, 91
Controller of Food appointed, 91
Controller of Shipping: appointed, 90; his powers, 91; sits at A.M.T.C., 118
Copenhagen Conference, 138
COPPER: (*see also* under GERMANY (ii), Raw Materials, and the neutral countries). Cargo of consigned to Swedish Telegraphic Bureau, 67; exports from Holland, 271; from Norway, 155, 271, 273; from Serbia, 272; from Sweden, 271; from Switzerland, 271; increase in Scandinavian exports to Germany, 110
Corn Commission appointed, 91
COTTON (*see also* under GERMANY (ii), Raw Materials): vast increase in U.S.A. export to Scandinavia and Holland in 1914–15, 53; Allies' difficulties in stopping this, 55; annual needs of Germany for explosives, 266; omitted from contraband lists in 1914, 26; France proposes to make linters contraband, 56; Order in Council of 26 April 1915 makes Egyptian and Indian cotton contraband, 56; the Allies forced to buy U.S.A. cotton crop by loan floated in New York, 56; all raw cotton and linters declared contraband by Allies (22 Aug. 1915), 57; Germany's imports of, 266; Scandinavian imports of, 266; Dutch imports of, 266

316

INDEX

Crewe, Lord, appointed Chairman of War Trade Advisory Committee, 39
Crowe, Sir Eyre, 59, 60, 114
Crozier, M., 213
'cruising grounds' established by Allies, 29
Customs Service and the blockade, 38 ; commission set up for, *ib.*

D

Dato, Señor, 253, 254
DECLARATION OF LONDON (26 Feb. 1909) : 16–21, 22–6 ; fate of, 21 ; principles of it adopted by France and Germany, 21 ; U.S.A. suggests its adoption in 1914, 22 ; Allies' reply concerning this, 23 ; Germany's reply concerning this, *ib.* ; terms modified by French Decree, 24 ; validity recognised by Order in Council, 26 ; abandonment of, 75 *seq.*
DECLARATION OF PARIS (18 April 1856), 14 ; effect on German trade, 44, 263 ; infringed by German Declaration of 1 Feb. 1917, 122
Decree of 25 Aug. 1914, 23
Decree of 6 Nov. 1914, 25–26, 28 ; inadequate results of, 57
Decree of 13 Mar. 1915, 47 ; inadequate results of, 57
Decree of 27 Aug. 1918, 128 ; its reception in Spain, 250
Delavaud, M., appointed head of submarine department of blockade, 112
DENMARK : Acreage and Produce, 161, 162
    Agreements with Allies, 123, 168, 169, 173
    Agreements with Germany, 169
    Agricultural produce exported, 162, 166, 167
    Company of Notable Traders formed, 82
    Cattle census in 1918, 172
    Exports : Agricultural produce, 162, 166, 167 ; butter, 162 ; corn to Germany, 289 ; corn surplus to Sweden, 150 ; fish to Germany, 168, 169 ; meat, 162, 167–8 ; general to Germany, 58, 132, 166, 174 ; to England, 166, 175 ; food to Germany, 225
    Imports : in 1913 and 1915, 58 ; in 1917–18, 132 ; corn, 162 ; general from England, 175 ; from France, 176 ; from U.S.A., 43, 176 ; lard, 61
    Negotiations with U.S.A., 169–173
    Quotas fixed, 165, 168, 169
    Re-export trade, 137, 165
    Smuggling subterfuges, 165
    Tonnage, 162, 169, 170, 173
    Value of Trade with Germany, 264
Destination of neutral ships and Right of Search, 37–8
Deutschland, the, 277
Deviation of course, 29, 32, 98 ; French Admiralty's opinion on, 37 ; British Government's opinion on, 37–8 ; more rigorously enforced in 1918, 126
Dutch Convoy, affair of the, 200–5

E

Ebert, Herr, 300
Eden, Mr., 147
Egypt, export of oleaginous grain to Germany by, 295
EXPORT COUNCIL : created by U.S.A., 104 ; its duties, 105 ; becomes practically a Ministry of Blockade, 106 ; operates under the War Purchasing Commission, 107

F

fats, increase in Scandinavian exports to Germany, 110
Favereau, Vice-Admiral, 32
fish, increase in Scandinavian exports to Germany, 110
Foreign Office : issues a White Book on the blockade, 66 ; sends a circular Note to neutral shipping companies, 95
France : adopts Order of the Day concerning food-stuffs quotas, 111 ; imports from U.S.A., 133 ; fall in her production of cast-iron, 92 ; value of her trade with Germany, 261
freight charges, 1914–16, 88
Fromageot, M., 21, 59
Frozen Meat Commission appointed, 91

INDEX

G

Galician oil wells, 278, 279
General Embargo Proclamation, 105 ; principles adopted by France and England, 106, 107
Genoa, 'cruising grounds' established off, 29
GERMANY (for her activities in Neutral Countries, *see* under those Countries).

(i.) GENERAL :
Article 55 C. published, 124 ; object of this, 125, 126
Black Sea tonnage, 291
Contraband Memorandum to Allies, 46
Cotton industry controlled, 56
Customs receipts, 133
Death-rate during War, 304
Exports : value of, 261, 264, 265 ; in 1913, 10, 11 ; to U.S.A., 44
Harvest in 1917–18, 84
Imports : in 1913, 10, 11 ; in 1918, 132 ; from U.S.A. in Dec. 1914, 43 ; from U.S.A. during War, 262, 263 ; value of, 261, 264, 265 ; aluminium, 159, 225, 274, 276 ; calcium carbide, 156, 157, 159 ; coal, 150 ; copper, 84, 155, 157, 271, 272 ; fats, 297 ; fish, 157 ; iron ore from Sweden, 149, 150, 275 ; meat, 296 ; nickel, 156, 159 ; zinc, 159
Japanese Proposal concerning alliance against the U.S.A., 102
Maritime Trade, 10–12
Mercantile Marine, 9, 262
Mexican Proposal concerning alliance against the U.S.A., 102
Potato crop fails, 83
Railways and rolling-stock, effect of blockade on, 305
Rationed by Allies after Armistice, 300
Submarine warfare ; begun, 46, 47 ; effect of this on other Powers, 47 ; protest against by U.S.A., 47 ; first reprisals by Allies, 48 ; the

Submarine warfare—*Continued*
Order in Council of 11 March 1915 concerning, 48 ; unrestricted warfare begun, 85 ; reasons for this, *ib.* ; ordered at Pless Conference, 101 ; her calculations of the effect on England, 99, 100 ; fallacy of these calculations, 101
'Turnip Winter,' 83
Ukraine Agreement, 291 ; disappointment thereof, 291, 292

(ii.) RAW MATERIALS :
aluminium, 274, 276
castor seed, 280
chromium, 277
coal, 150, 274, 305–6
copper, 12, 84, 155, 157, 259, 270–4
cotton, 12, 56, 84, 266, 267–70 (*See also* in General index)
cotton seed, 280
fats, 278–81, 297, 299
fertilisers, 11, 285
flax, 269
hemp, 269
iron ore, 148, 149, 150, 275
lead, 276
leather, 12, 280, 283
linseed, 280
manganese, 12, 84, 149, 274–5, 276
metals, 12, 274–8
mineral oils, 12, 278
nickel, 84, 276, 277
nitrates, 285, 286
oils, 278–81, 297, 299
oleaginous grain, 12, 280, 295
phosphates, 287
phosphoric acid, 287
platinum, 278
potash, 11, 285
quebracho wood, 283
rape seed, 280
rubber, 12, 281
silk, 269, 270
steel (*See* METALS)
sumac, 283
textile plants, 12
tin, 12, 84, 259, 276, 277
tungsten, 278
wood pulp, 268
wool, 12, 268
zinc, 159, 273, 276

INDEX

(iii.) MANUFACTURES :
  ammonia, 286
  aprons, 269
  awnings, 269
  beer, 294
  belts (driving), 269, 283
  boots, 269, 283
  clothing, 270
  driving belts, 269, 283
  ebonite, 282
  electric cables, 273
  electrical apparatus, 273
  explosives, 267, 281
  glycerine, 281
  household utensils, 273
  leather, 280, 283
  lubricants, 278, 279, 305
  machinery, 273
  paper, 269
  petrol, 278, 279
  sandbags, 269
  shoes, 269, 283
  soap, 280
  solder, 277
  steel, 275
  sulphuric acid, 286
  surgical instruments, 277
  textiles, 267, 268
  thread, 269
  tinfoil, 277
  tools, 278
  tyres, 282

(iv.) FOOD :
  Austrian stocks, 293
  butter, 297, 302
  cereals, 11, 84, 288–94
  cocoa, 298
  fats, 297–8, 302
  fish, 298
  fodder, 295
  harvests, 289
  hay, 295
  K.K. bread, 289
  livestock, 295–7
  meat, 11, 84, 294, 296, 301–2
  milk, 84, 297
  oil, 299
  oilcake, 295
  potatoes, 11, 83, 288, 290, 301
  sugar, 298

Giannini, Signor, 114
Giralda, case of the, 246
Gout, M., 69
Great Britain : imports of, 133 ; her exports to neutrals in the North Sea, 104 ; value of her trade with Germany, 261
Grey, Sir Edward (Lord Grey of Falloden), 15, 50, 51, 179
Guernier, M., 117

H

Hague Convention (1907), 15, 16, 29
Halifax, search station proposed at, 119
Handelskommission, the, 151
Harris, Mr. Leverton, 113
Harwood, Mr., replies to Lord Jellicoe, 67
HOLLAND : Affair of the Dutch Convoy, 200–5
  Agreements with Allies, 187, 189, 193
  Agreements with Germany, 193–4
  Agricultural produce, 186
  Coal quota, 187, 193
  Exports : copper, 271 ; corn, 22 ; fodder, 185–7 ; food to Germany, 110, 225 ; general to Germany, 58, 132 ; gravel, 194, 198 ; meat, 185–7 ; value of, 177
  Food rations, 199, 207
  Imports : coal, 191, 192, 194, 199 ; copper, 177 ; iron and steel, 177 ; tin, 177 ; general from U.S.A., 43, 58, 83, 132 ; value of, 177
  Negotiations with Germany, 197
  Negotiations with U.S.A., 195
  Netherlands Oversea Trust formed, 82
  Quotas fixed, 180 *seq.* 187, 193
  Ships in U.S.A. ports requisitioned, 123 ; sunk by Germany replaced, 191–2
  Smuggling subterfuges, 182, 183
  Tonnage, 196–7, 200
  Value of Trade with Germany, 264
Hoover, Mr., 105
Hudson's Bay Fleet, 93
Humber, German mines in the, 30
Hurst, Sir Cecil, 21

I

India : export of oleaginous grain to Germany by, 295 ; value of her trade with Germany, 261
International Committee of Economic Action, 74

INDEX

International Quota Commission set up, 62, 65. (*See also* QUOTA SYSTEM)
Inter-Scandinavian Conference, the first, 137
Italy: value of her exports to Germany, 264

J

Jellicoe, Admiral Lord, his letter to the Admiralty criticising blockade methods, 66; his opinion on search at sea, 36–7

K

Kieff, German bureau established at, 291
Kim, case of the, 61
Koeth, Colonel, 300
Kogrund Passage, mines laid in, 141, 146

L

Lacaze, Admiral, 223
lard, cargo of S.S. *Kim*, 61; Danish imports of, 61
Lasteyrie, M., 72, 227
Lebrun, M., appointed Minister of Blockade, 112; his duties, *ib.*
licenses, 116; the system of, 89, 107, 108
Licensing Committee, the Ship, 89
Lindemann, Admiral, 145
London Conference (1908–9), 16; Aug. 1915, 59; Oct. 1915, 62
London, Declaration of, *see* DECLARATION OF LONDON
Lyautey, General, 223

M

MacCormick, Mr. Vance, 106
Mannheim, Convention of (1868), 22
Manouba, case of the, 30
Mediterranean, search ports in, 33
Memorandum of 3 Nov. 1914 by France and Great Britain to Neutrals, 41
MERCANTILE MARINE: Allies' at outbreak of War, 9; Austria's ditto, 9; Germany's ditto, 9; Neutrals' ditto, 9; the world's ditto, 9, 86
Freight charges (1914–16), 88
French tonnage in 1917, 116, 117
German and Austrian ships in neutral ports, 9

Mercantile marine—*Continued*
Government control of, 116, 117
Increase in shipbuilding (1914–17), 87
Neutral tonnage obtained by Allies, 123; permitted by international law to trade with belligerents, 12
Requisition of ships, 86, 90, 94, 115, 117
Tonnage built in 1913–18, 124; in 1916, 115; in 1918, 129
Tonnage required by Allies in 1916, 90; requirements allotted in 1918, 130, 131
Tonnage shortage in 1918, 129, 130
Tonnage sunk in 1915 and 1916, 87; monthly in 1915, 89; in 1917, 115; in 1917–18, 124.
Tonnage used to transport U.S.A. troops, 130
Métin, M., 106; succeeds M. Denys Cochin, 112; is succeeded by M. Lebrun, *ib.*
Michaelis, Herr, 294
mines, Admiralty Notices concerning, 30, 31; laid by British ships, 31; laid by German ships, 30
Ministry of Blockade (English) created, 68; (French) created, 112; Swiss negotiations of, 228
Ministry of Commerce (French), 93
Ministry of Food, 91
Ministry of Food and Maritime Transport (French), 116
Ministry of Marine, 93, 97, 228, 229
Ministry of Merchant Shipping, created, 90
Ministry of Munitions, 91
Ministry of Public Works operates coal fleet, 92
Ministry of War creates port commissions, 92
Monzie, M. de, appointed Under-Secretary for Merchant Shipping, 116
Moreau, Rear-Admiral, 21, 39, 64

N

Nansen, Dr., goes to U.S.A., 158; his success there, 159
Netherlands, the. *See* HOLLAND

INDEX

Netherlands Overseas Trust (N.O.T.), 82, 179–89, 205, 214, 218; forbidden by Dutch Government to accept consignments of cereals, 188

Neutral ships permitted by international law to trade with belligerents, 12

Neutral ships, right of search of, 12, 13

Neutrals' trade with Germany, the Allies' efforts to stop, 81, 82

New Amsterdam, case of the, 29

Nike, case of the, 142

Noordam, case of the, 204

North Sea, proclaimed a war zone, 31, 32; Germany's protest against this, 46

NORWAY: Acreage and Population, 152
 Agreement concerning fish, 158
 Associated Norwegian Importers of Mineral Oils, formation of, 82
 Bombs secreted in her ships, 156
 Copper, annual production of, 155; the Allies secure her output, *ib.*
 Exports: aluminium, 159; calcium carbide 156, 157, 159; copper, 155, 271, 273; general to Germany in 1917 and 1918, 58, 132, 157; nickel, 156, 159, 277; zinc, 159
 Fishing industry, 152
 Food rationed, 158
 Friendliness to the Allies, 123; puts her mercantile marine at their disposal, *ib.*
 Imports: in 1913 and 1915, 58; in 1917 and 1918, 132; from U.S.A., 43, 83; coal, 156
 Quotas fixed by Allies, 154, 155
 Tonnage, 153, 160
 U.S.A., friction with, 159
 Value of Trade with Germany, 264
 War Losses, 153, 156, 158, 161

O

Oppenheimer, Sir Francis, appointed Controller of N.O.T., 180; goes to Berne, 211, 212; visits Paris, 211

ORDERS IN COUNCIL: 20 Aug. 1914, 23; 30 Oct. 1914, 26; 11 Mar. 1915, 48; protested against by U.S.A., 49–52; strengthened drastically in Feb. 1917, 54; the importance of, 54–5; extended, 120; 7 July 1916, 80; 16 Feb. 1917, 121, 127

P

Paris, Conferences at, 118, 220
Paris, Declaration of, 14. (*See under* DECLARATION OF PARIS)
Paul, Dr., 292
Permanent International Committee of Economic Action created, 74
Pless, German Conference at, 101
potato crop, failure of Germany's, 83
privateering, abolition of, 14
PRIZE COURT, THE INTERNATIONAL: instituted, 15, 19; conditions governing French and British decisions, 77
prohibited exports. *See* CONTRABAND

Q

QUOTA SYSTEM: 110, 111; first appearance of, 58, 59 *seq.*; extension of in 1916, 82; International Commission set up, 62; protest against by U.S.A., 62, 63; placed under M. Lebrun, 112

R

Ramon de Larrinaga, case of the, 251
Ratibor, Prince, 253, 254
Ribot, M., 116
rice, quota fixed for Holland, 184
RIGHT OF SEARCH: 12, 13, 28–38; ports at which conducted, 29, 32, 33, 34; U.S.A. protests against, 34, 35; Holland protests against, 29; case of the *New Amsterdam*, 29; precedent of the *Manouba*, 30; difficulties of, 30; British Admiralty shepherds neutral ships into Straits of Dover, 32; France adopts British measures, 33; Anglo-French Conference concerning, 33; protests of neutrals, 34; Great Britain's memorandum to Neutrals concerning, 41, 42

INDEX

Rotterdam, Germany imports corn via, 22
Roberto, case of the, 251
Roumania, exports corn to Germany, 289; petroleum, 279; value of her exports to Germany, 264; wool production, 268
Ruby, case of the, 163
Russia, exports barley to Germany, 288, 293–4; leather, 284; platinum, 278; value of her trade with Germany, 261; wool production, 268

S

S.T.S., 230
SAFE CONDUCTS, 125–9, 160, 248
Salisbury, Lord, 27
Salzig, potash deposits at, 11
Scandinavian Conference, the first, 137
Scandinavian Kings, meeting at Malmo of, 138, 153
Scandinavian exports to Germany, 1913–16, 110; to U.S.A., 1913–14, 44; to Germany, *ib.*
Scavenius, Mr. de, 164
Schultess, Mr., 228
Schwartz, Mr., 147
Schweizerische Treuhandstelle, 230
Search, the Right of. *See* RIGHT OF SEARCH
Search Ports, 29, 32, 33, 34
Search Stations proposed at Halifax, Bermuda and Bathurst, 119
Serbia exports copper to Germany, 272
Sheldon, Mr., 114
Shipbuilding, increase in during 1914–17, 87, 116. (*See* main entry under MERCANTILE MARINE)
Ship Licensing Committee, 89
Shipping and ships. *See* MERCANTILE MARINE
Shipping Board (U.S.A.), 117
Shipping Control Committee, 90
Shipping Controller appointed, 90; his powers, 91; sits at A.M.T.C., 118
Skjolborg, case of the, 163
Slade, Admiral, 21
Society of Economic Supervision (S.S.S.), 82; formed, 212; its functions, 213–16; its work, 216–19, 228–29, 232

Solf, Herr, 254
South American States, licences granted to for trade with U.S.A., 108
SPAIN: Acreage and Population, 236
  Agreement with England, 241, 242
  Agreement with France, 242
  Agreement with U.S.A., 242
  Exports: fruit, 236; metals, 241; value of, 238–240
  Imports: coal, 236; corn, 236; general from U.S.A., 83, 237, 239–40; value of, 238–40
  Her King intervenes, 243, 247
  Metal production, 236–7
  Negotiations with Germany, 244, 247, 251–5
  Requisitions German ships, 251 *seq.*
  Sea-borne Trade, 237
  Shipbuilding, 244
  Textile industry, 237
  Tonnage, 237, 243, 256
  War losses, 244, 246, 251, 253
Statutory Lists, 97
Statistical Department, 114
Stockholm Conference, 137
Submarine warfare. *See* under GERMANY (i) GENERAL
Suez Canal, enemy ships in, 10
sugar, England's imports of, 91
SWEDEN: Acreage and Population, 139
  Agreement with Allies, 123, 147, 275–6
  Agreement with England, 123, 146
  Difficulties in dealing with, 82
  Exports: coal, 150; copper, 142, 271; ferro-tungsten, 278; iron ore, 149, 150, 275; general to Germany, 58, 132
  Federation of Neutrals attempted, 153
  Imports: coal, 140; copper, 67; corn, 140; cotton, 142; fodder, 140; mineral oil, 140, 144; potash, 140; general in 1913–15, 58; ditto in 1917–18, 132; from U.S.A., 43, 83, 132
  Iron ore production, 148
  Shipping Agreement with England, 146
  Ships controlled by German Admiralty, 143

INDEX

Shortage of necessaries in 1917, 146
Tonnage, 145
Value of Trade with Germany, 264
SWITZERLAND : Acreage, 208
　Agreement with France, 209, 224, 227
　Agreement with Germany, 219, 221, 225, 229, 230
　Agreement with U.S.A., 226
　Agriculture, 209
　Aluminium industry, 225, 276
　Compensation goods, 219–21
　Conference at Berne, 220
　Conference at Paris, 220
　Exports : cattle, 221, 233 ; copper, 271; food to Germany in 1916, 225 ; manufactured goods, 232, 233 ; value of, 209 ; ditto French, 219 ; ditto Germany, 132, 264
　Food riots, 234
　Imports : coal, 219–21, 223, 225, 230 ; corn, 209, 223, 226, 229, 231–3 ; daily in 1917, 222–3 fertilisers, 209 ; fodder, 209 ; foodstuffs, 219, 222, 224–6, 231 ; iron, 225–6 ; sugar, 226 ; value of, 209 ; ditto French, 219 ; ditto U.S.A., 132
　Loans, 226, 227
　Quotas revised, 222–5
　Rations her population, 234
　Smuggling subterfuges, 232, 270
　Society of Economic Supervision formed, 82

T

Tardieu, M., 107, 110, 117
Tonnage. *See* MERCANTILE MARINE *and also* the various Countries
Transit Maritime et Affretements Généraux, 92
Transport Department. *See* under ADMIRALTY
Triumph of Unarmed Forces, the, 70
Truck system, 103
Tyne, German mines in the, 30

U

Ukraine, Germany's Agreement with the, 291 ; occupied by Germany, 292
Under-Secretaryship of State for Merchant Shipping, 92, 116
Under-Secretaryship of State for Transport created, 93
UNITED STATES OF AMERICA :
　(i.) GENERAL :
　Championship of neutrals' rights assumed, 52 ; this is welcomed by the Allies, 54
　Cotton : vast increase in export to Scandinavia and Holland in 1914–15, 53 ; Allies' difficulties in stopping this, 55 ; annual needs of Germany for explosives, 266 ; forces Allies to buy crop by loan floated in New York, 56 ; value of, exported to Germany, 266 ; ditto to Scandinavia and Holland, 266
　Declares war on Germany, 102 ; effect of this on the blockade, 102, 103
　Diplomatic relations with Germany broken off, 102
　Enquires concerning attitude of belligerents to international law, 22 ; suggests adoption of Declaration of London, *ib.* ; Germany's reply to this, 25
　Export Council appointed, 104
　General Embargo proclaimed, 105
　Law of Angary exercised over Dutch ships, 123
　Protests against Order in Council of 20 Aug. 1914, 25 ; England's reply to this, 25–6
　Protests against Order in Council of 30 Oct. 1914, 26 ; England's reply, 27
　Protests against Order in Council of 11 March 1915, 49–50 ; the Allies' reply, 50–1
　Protests again against the same Order, 52 ; the Allies' reply, 52–4
　Protests against Quota System, 62 ; England's reply, 62–3
　Protests against Right of Search, 34 ; England's reply, 34–5
　Protests again against the same, 36 ; England's reply, *ib.*

INDEX

(i.) General—*Continued*
  Requests to Allies to allow foodstuffs to pass into Germany, 47
  Requests to Germany to refrain from torpedoing merchant ships, 47; Germany's reply to this, 48
  Troops sent to Europe in 1918, 130
  War Purchasing Commission appointed, 107
(ii.) TRADE:
  Exports: immense increase to European neutrals after 4 Aug. 1914, 27; ditto in 1914–15, 53; to Germany in Dec. 1914, 43, 44; to European neutrals in 1913–14, 43, 44; to Holland ditto, *ib.*; to Sweden, Norway and Denmark ditto, *ib.*; to European neutrals 1913–17, 83; ditto 1916–18, 132; value of exports to France, 133; to Great Britain, *ib.*; to neutrals, 132, 263; value of cotton exports to Germany, 266, 267

(ii.) Trade—*Continued*
  Imports: from Germany in 1913–14, 44; from neutrals, ditto, *ib.*

V

Vienna, food riots in, 292
Vollenhoven, Mr., 183

W

Waldow, Herr von, 294
War Purchasing Commission, 107
War Trade Advisory Committee, 39, 64
War Trade Board, 64, 108
War Trade Department, policy of, defended by Mr. Harwood, 67
White Book on blockade issued by Foreign Office, 66
White Lists, origin of, 95; application of, 96
Wilson, President, appoints Export Council, 104; requisitions Dutch ships, 196; signs General Embargo Proclamation, 105
wool, 268